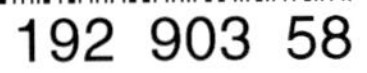

CHINESE BRONZES

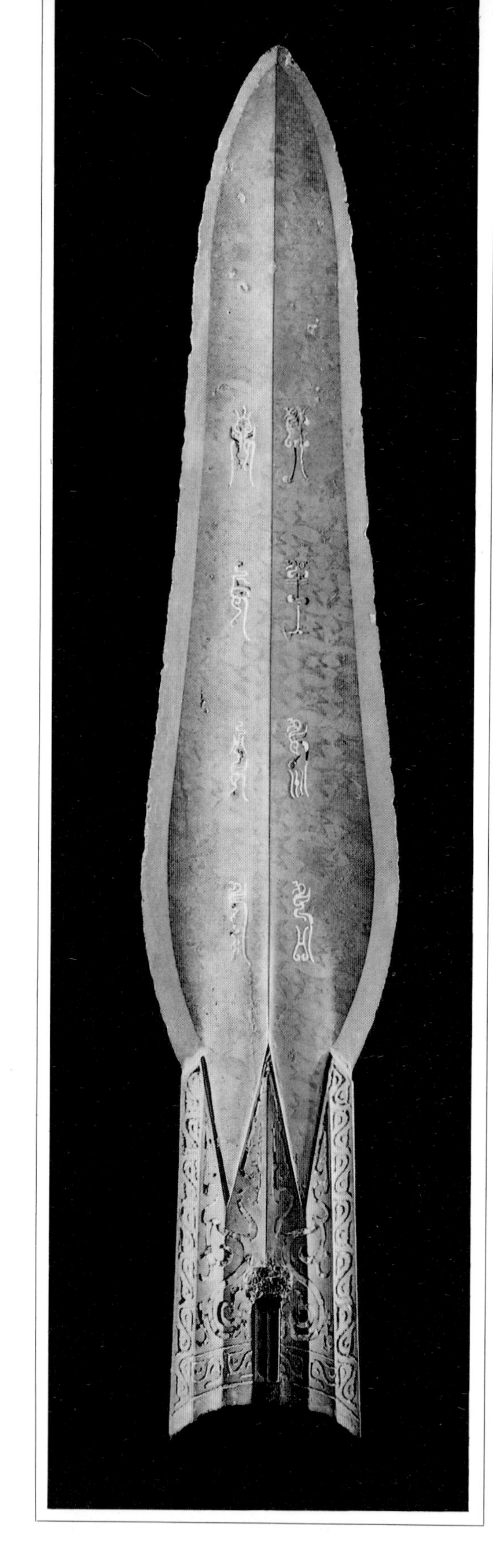

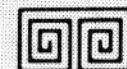

CHINESE BRONZES

Art and Ritual

JESSICA RAWSON

Published for the
Trustees of the British Museum
in association with the
Sainsbury Centre for Visual Arts
University of East Anglia

Published by British Museum Publications Ltd
46 Bloomsbury Street, London WC1B 3QQ

British Library Cataloguing in Publication Data

British Museum
Chinese bronzes: art and ritual.
1. Bronzes, Chinese—To 618—
Exhibitions
I. Title II. Rawson, Jessica
739'.512'0931 NK7983.2

ISBN 0-7141-1439-1

Designed by Harry Green

Set in Palatino by Tradespools Ltd, Somerset
and printed by Jolly & Barber Ltd, Rugby, Warwickshire

COVER
Detail of the *Zhao Meng jie hu* (no. 34).
PAGE 2
Spearhead (no. 36).

The Trustees of The British Museum acknowledge with gratitude the generosity of the Sainsbury Centre for Visual Arts towards the production of this book and of the Arthur M. Sackler Foundation for the grant which made possible the inclusion of colour plates.

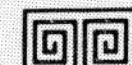

Contents

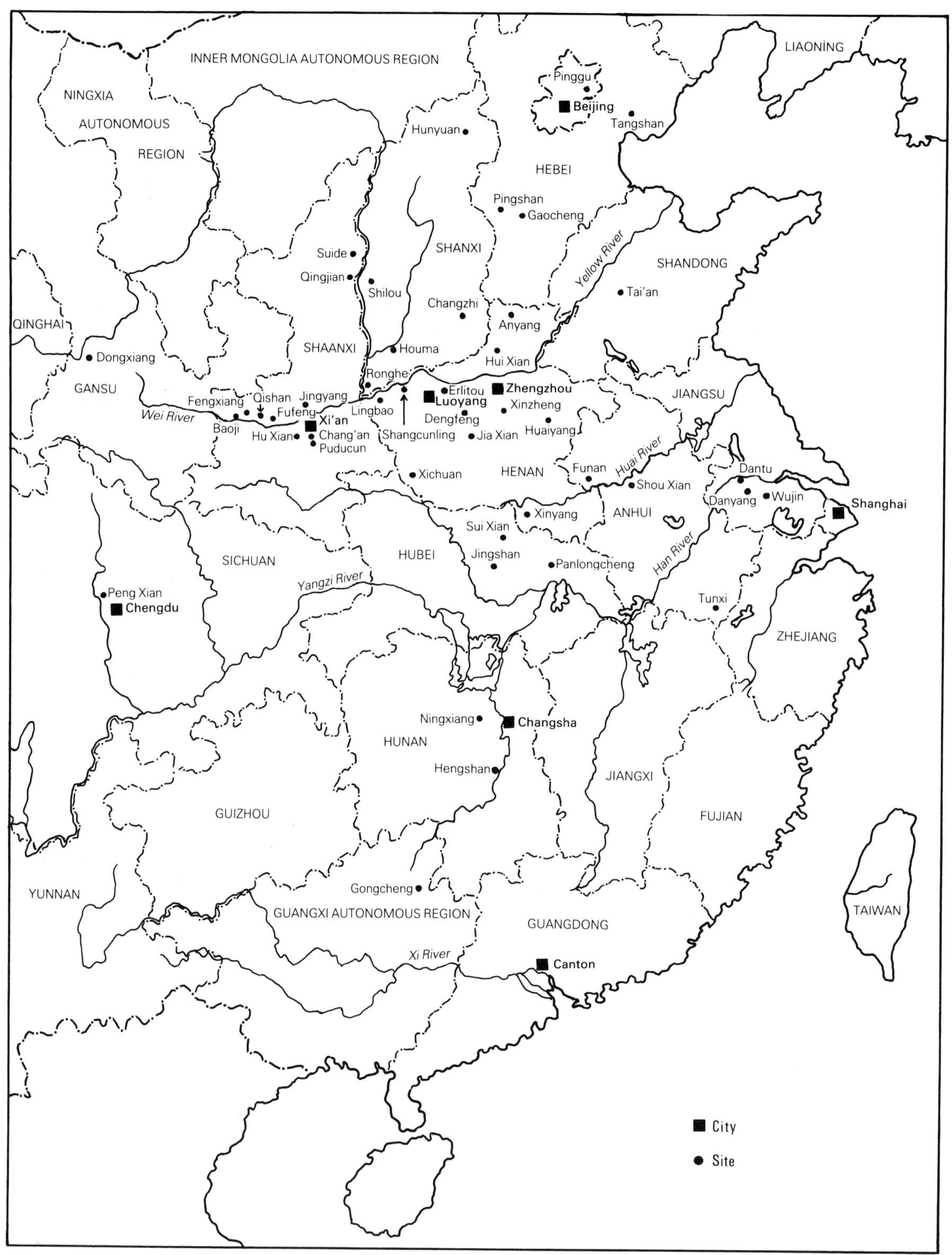
INNER MONGOLIA AUTONOMOUS REGION
LIAONING
NINGXIA
AUTONOMOUS
REGION
Pinggu
Beijing
Tangshan
Hunyuan
HEBEI
Pingshan
Gaocheng
Yellow River
SHANDONG
Tai'an
Suide
Qingjian
Shilou
SHANXI
Changzhi
Anyang
QINGHAI
SHAANXI
Houma
Hui Xian
Dongxiang
GANSU
Ronghe
Erlitou
Zhengzhou
Luoyang
Xinzheng
JIANGSU
Fengxiang
Qishan
Jingyang
Fufeng
Lingbao
Dengfeng
Wei River
Baoji
Xi'an
Hu Xian
Chang'an
Puducun
Shangcunling
Jia Xian
Huaiyang
Xichuan
HENAN
Funan
Huai River
Shou Xian
Dantu
Danyang
Wujin
Shanghai
Xinyang
ANHUI
Sui Xian
SICHUAN
HUBEI
Jingshan
Panlongcheng
Han River
Yangzi River
Peng Xian
Chengdu
Tunxi
ZHEJIANG
Ningxiang
Changsha
HUNAN
Hengshan
JIANGXI
GUIZHOU
FUJIAN
YUNNAN
Gongcheng
GUANGXI AUTONOMOUS REGION
GUANGDONG
TAIWAN
Xi River
Canton
City
Site

PREFACE

This catalogue, published in association with the Sainsbury Centre for Visual Arts, University of East Anglia, accompanies an exhibition of ancient Chinese bronzes from the British Museum displayed at the Burrell Collection, Glasgow, and at the Sainsbury Centre. The bronzes have been chosen to illustrate the artistic and technological achievements of Chinese bronze casting from the Shang dynasty, *c.* 1500 BC, to the end of the Zhou dynasty in the third century BC. The exhibition includes both the Museum's most famous bronzes, which rank among the foremost surviving bronzes anywhere, and many recent acquisitions made to extend the range of types and regions represented. Since many of the Museum's bronzes are extensively published, it has proved impracticable to list all relevant publications. Wherever known, catalogues of collections to which the bronzes formerly belonged have been given and also references to works on inscriptions that themselves contain exhaustive publication information. Rubbings of the inscriptions on the vessels are illustrated at the end of the catalogue.

The study of Chinese bronzes has been greatly advanced in recent years by remarkable excavations in China. I am indebted to the work of archaeologists in China, and am grateful for help that I have received on visits to China from the Bureau of Cultural Relics and the Institute of Archaeology of the Chinese Academy of Social Sciences. My colleagues in the British Museum's Research Laboratory have also contributed important technical work. In working on a catalogue of Western Zhou bronzes in the Arthur M. Sackler Collection, I have gained important insights and wish to acknowledge the help I have had from my collaborators on the project, Robert Bagley and Jenny So; the former kindly read the text in manuscript.

I am grateful for the enthusiastic support of Rosemary Watt of the Burrell Collection and of Derek Gillman of the Sainsbury Centre in selecting and organising this exhibition. We are grateful to the Arthur M. Sackler Foundation for a grant to allow the inclusion of colour photographs. Geoffrey House, Head of Public Services in the British Museum, generously supported the exhibition.

Many members of the Department of Oriental Antiquities have helped in the production of the catalogue, and I am especially grateful for the help of Anne Farrer and Shelagh McPherson. The drawings are by Ann Searight, who has ably translated often inadequately published excavated material into clear comparative figures. I am also grateful to David Gowers of the British Museum Photographic Service for the photographs. Deborah Wakeling, of British Museum's Publications, has given unstinting support throughout the production of this catalogue.

JESSICA RAWSON
May 1987

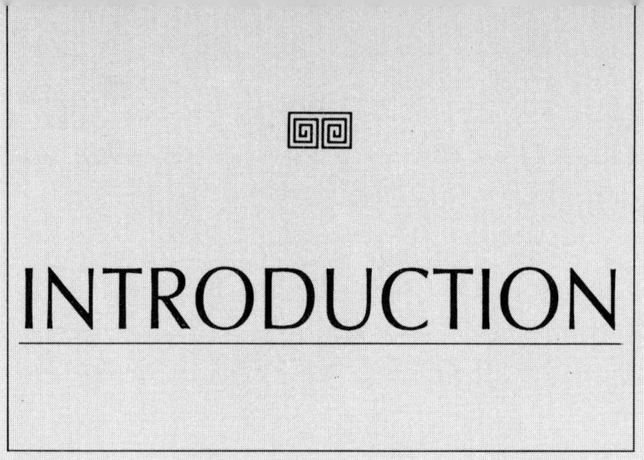

INTRODUCTION

The bronzes described in this book were made for the kings and great families of the early Chinese dynasties – the Shang (*c.*1700–1050 BC) and the Zhou (*c.*1050–221 BC). On the evidence of later texts Chinese scholars have in the past also attributed bronzes to another, earlier dynasty, the Xia. However, although in the last few years some archaeological sites have been tentatively assigned to the Xia, most of the known bronzes are Shang in date.

Bronze-casting conferred power: with bronze weapons the Shang and the Zhou controlled the peoples around them; but although weapons were undoubtedly essential to military success, as much, or more, attention was paid by casters and their patrons to vessels in which food and wine were offered to ancestors. These sacrifices were expected to ensure the survival and success of those who performed them, above all of the kings, their families and their ministers. They were weapons against evil spirits and natural disasters that might beset the state and the family. Care lavished on the vessels was commensurate with their roles. Nowhere else in the ancient world were such sophisticated bronze vessels cast.

Owners of some surviving vessels have been identified by the inscriptions cast on them. At first very brief, but later much longer and circumstantial, the contents of these inscriptions are linked to individuals and events described in much later historical texts. They therefore substantiate the texts and are essential elements of the historical record.

This catalogue illustrates the history of some of the principal types of ancient Chinese bronzes from the collection in the British Museum, relating them to major discoveries of the last few years. The period covered is from the early or middle Shang to the end of the Zhou. Ritual vessels occupy most of the discussion, but some weapons, chariot fittings and other bronze types have also been included.

Over several centuries of study the history of Chinese bronzes has received much attention, and many questions have been resolved. However, part of the fascination of the material lies in the difficulties that still remain. This introduction will pinpoint some of the questions that are still to be answered, throwing light on the role and development of the bronzes, as well as revealing their extraordinary qualities.

The origins of bronze-casting

Cast bronze was fully developed in China during the Erlitou and Erligang periods in Henan province astride the Yellow River. The later stages of Erlitou and the whole of Erligang have been identified as belonging to the Shang dynasty and will be discussed in Chapters 1 and 2. Erlitou bronzes are advanced, and their antecedents have been sought not only in Henan but also in other parts of China. Several candidates have been offered as predecessors, but as yet none is convincing. Some of the evidence for predecessors is reviewed here, although such a review serves only to demonstrate that the early history of metal-working in China is yet to be penetrated.

Scattered neolithic finds of the Yangshao (*c.* 4000 BC) and much later Longshan cultures (*c.* 2500 BC) have stimulated intense discussion. Metal fragments from Yangshao sites at Banpo and Lintong, both in Shaanxi province, contained nickel and zinc respectively. Although some scholars have argued that such metal remains are the earliest evidence of Chinese metal-working, these notions have been discounted by An Zhimin of the Institute of Archaeology in Beijing, who treats both finds as later intrusions.[1]

Other discoveries do not purport to be so ancient. Small copper-alloy tools recovered from the Longshan neolithic site at Dachengshan, Tangshan, in Hebei province have also excited much attention, but these tools too have been discounted by An Zhimin because in his view the stratification has not been properly interpreted. An argues that the tools belong to the lower levels of Xiajiadian culture, known for its painted pottery, which stretched across north-eastern Hebei, south-western Inner

Mongolia and western Liaoning. The lower levels of this culture have now been dated to periods equivalent to Erligang or later, to be discussed in Chapter 2. Nevertheless, it seems likely that metal-working during the Longshan period prior to Shang dominance will be established in due course.

Evidence for early metal-working has been persistently reported from western China. A small curved bronze knife from Majiayao levels at Gansu Dongxiang Linjia, dated to *c.* 3000 BC, is often, though not invariably, recognised as one of the earliest metal artefacts discovered in China. It is as yet a somewhat isolated find. The area may have been an important centre for early metal-working, as copper and bronze tools and weapons dating from before 1600 BC have been found at several Qijia culture sites in Gansu and Qinghai provinces. Some of the copper items were worked cold rather than cast, illustrating a stage prior to the full development of bronze-casting that is well known in many parts of the world but little seen in China.

Gansu lies to the west of the central areas of China, especially Henan province, where the major bronze-casting tradition developed.[2] The question therefore remains how and when, if indeed at all, was contact established between the western metal-working areas and the growing cities of Henan that flowered in the second half of the Erlitou period? At present the direct antecedents of the sophisticated cast vessels from Erlitou-period tombs excavated at Yanshi near Luoyang remain undiscovered. Traces of earlier metal-working at Yanshi are hinted at in remains of crucibles and metal fragments, but much more information is still required. Archaeological work in China reveals surprises daily;[3] it seems likely, therefore, that earlier stages of the Chinese bronze age will be uncovered in due course.

Notes

1. For a survey of early metal-working remains in China see An 1982, where references to archaeological reports are given; see also *Kaogu xuebao* 1981. 3, pp. 287–301.
2. For discussion of ceramics based on wrought-metal vessels in the Qijia culture see Bylin-Althin 1946, pp. 426–7, and in Henan see Bagley 1987, Introduction, Section 1.1.
3. Current interest focuses on the Hongshan culture in Liaoning province. Although there is no suggestion that this culture employed bronze, the very advanced society and techniques evident in the remains of buildings, jades and sculptures indicate a stage of cultural development that was up to that time unknown (*Wenwu* 1984.6, pp. 1–5; *Wenwu* 1984.11, pp. 1–11; *Wenwu* 1986.8, pp. 1–17). Other similarly advanced settlements may well come to light in other areas; among these may yet be found early stages of bronze-working.

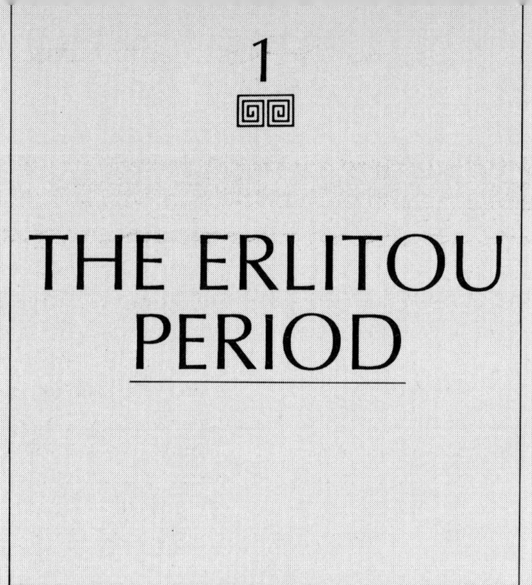

1

THE ERLITOU PERIOD

That bronze was cast in what is now described as the Erlitou period is without doubt. The areas of controversy concern such questions as who were the peoples who created the Erlitou culture, and how were they related to the peoples later settled at Zhengzhou and Anyang identified as the Shang.

Sites designated as belonging to the Erlitou culture have been found in Henan province and also in southern Shanxi and southern Hebei, the most important being the city site at Yanshi Erlitou near Luoyang. Four phases of development have been recognised. Phases I and II are defined by various sizes of bag-shaped jars, flat basins on three wide legs and bowls on three pointed legs. Considerable changes in vessel type characterise phases III and IV. New ceramic forms include a wide-mouthed jar that tapers towards the bottom, tri-lobed *li* vessels and ceramic *jia* (wine cups with a handle and three legs). Most important of all, cast bronze vessels and very sophisticated jade carving of this date have been found. Carbon-14 dating has established that the four phases were spread over about 500 years, from *c.* 2000 to 1500 BC.[1]

The city at Yanshi has revealed the remains of two large palaces or ceremonial buildings whose construction is entirely familiar from later Chinese architecture. They both consisted of large courtyards lined with covered walkways or minor structures. In each courtyard, slightly to the rear, a large building was aligned east–west with its openings on the south side. Stamped earth (*hangtu*) platforms were foundations for buildings of wooden columns supporting horizontal beams.[2]

These impressive structures were accompanied by remains of workshops and by intact tombs. Strangely absent is any trace of a city wall. This feature is also missing at the much later and larger site of Anyang, and at both sites the lack of a defensive wall is a considerable puzzle. The most likely explanation is that the walls crumbled as later inhabitants mined them for materials.

The size and complexity of remains at Yanshi have led inevitably to speculation as to who built the city. Unfortunately, no written evidence survives to secure an identification. Legend and later history describe a Xia dynasty preceding the Shang, and some writers have been tempted to link part, or all, of the Erlitou occupation with the Xia. Xia studies are at present an area of considerable controversy, and in the absence of any contemporary accounts the issues are difficult to resolve. It is impossible to be sure whether any of the sites identified as Xia were ever occupied by such a people. These sites include remains of a walled city on the Song Shan near Dengfeng pre-dating the Erlitou culture.[3]

A definition of the differences between Erlitou phases I, II, III and IV has led to the suggestion that political change overwhelmed Yanshi. Some authorities draw the divide before phase III and some after it, but there is general recognition that the ceramics, bronzes and jades of the second half of the Erlitou occupation differ somewhat from the preceding stages and resemble material from Erligang-period sites at Zhengzhou. The second half of Erlitou is therefore often, though not invariably, treated as belonging to early Shang, while parts of the previous phases are thought by some to be Xia occupation or to be the remains of other peoples as yet unidentified. Many more Erlitou sites are under excavation, however, and until they have all been fully published it will remain difficult to describe the relation of Erlitou to Shang.

Erlitou phases III and IV certainly seem to mark

a divide. Sophisticated cast bronze vessels occur, and there was a preoccupation with jade. However, bronze-casting must have been developed before this date as a foundation for these complex items. The first finds of both bronzes and jades came from pits and from surface deposits, but more recently tombs have been excavated at Yanshi. Here two types of bronze vessel have been found, *jue* and *jia* (Fig. 1). Small bronze bells, *ling*, were also quite common, and some bronze weapons and tools have been retrieved.[4]

Jue and *jia* occur regularly with a ceramic pouring vessel, known as a *he*, which slightly later appears also in bronze. It is possible that even at this date occasional *he* were made in bronze and that those in ceramic were substitutes for burial. Ceramic *jue* and *jia* were also made in large numbers. Indeed, *jue* and the slender beaker, later known as a *gu*, had been made in ceramic from the beginning of Erlitou. Other standard ceramic vessels include a wide-mouthed jar tapering towards the bottom, and tripods, later the model for the bronze *ding*, dishes on a high foot, known as *dou*, and basins on a ring foot, known as *gui*. Vessels recurring in several of the Yanshi tombs suggest that certain types had specific ritual purposes, either in routine daily sacrifices or at burial ceremonies. These assemblages seem to be the ancestors of Shang ritual vessel sets. If it is correct to interpret continuity of form as indicating also a continuity of function, then it can be argued that sacrifices of food and wine to ancestors had already been established.

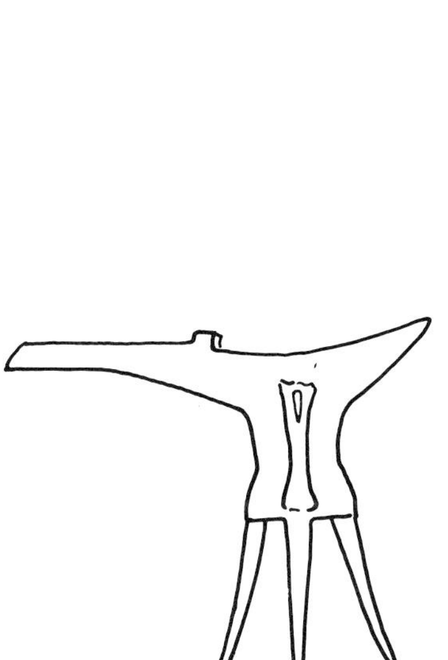
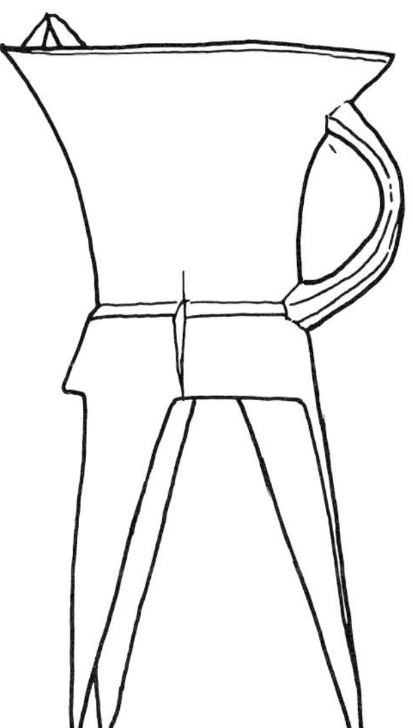
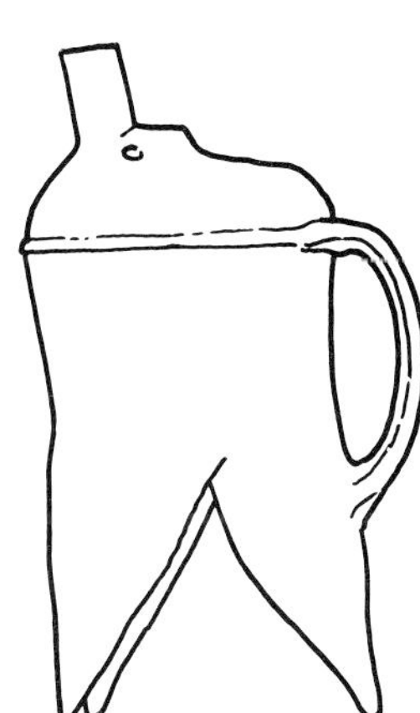

Fig. 1. Drawings of vessels from tomb M9 at Henan Yanshi Erlitou; *from left to right*, bronze *jue*, H. 16.4 cm; bronze *jia*, H. 30.5 cm; ceramic *he*, H. 22.7 cm.

Bronze vessels should not be considered individually but in groups as ritual sets. These sets are defined as the range of vessel types required for the correct performance of ritual at any given time. The composition of these sets can be inferred from two sources – intact tomb groups and vessels that share a common dedication. In the case of vessels interred in tombs it seems likely that the occupant of the tomb was expected to continue to offer sacrifices to his ancestors after his death and that vessels were buried for this purpose. It is also possible that they were used at funeral rites. Vessels with shared inscriptions have usually come from hoards. In such cases it is not always possible to be sure how complete the set is.

It seems almost certain that at all times bronze vessels were supplemented by containers in other materials, such as ceramics, lacquer and bamboo, as suggested in the case of ceramic *he* found at Erlitou (Fig. 1). Over time many of these containers were copied in bronze to make the full ritual sets of the Shang. To ceramic- or lacquer-derived forms were added other shapes developed as part of the evolution of the casting technology. Most of these changes were gradual, but once or twice in the history of ritual vessel casting sudden and substantial changes were effected. Ritual is never a trivial matter, and major changes in vessel shape must have reflected different religious preoccupations. Although it is difficult to establish what these involved, their occurrence should at least be emphasised.

Although the sources of Erlitou bronze-casting are not known, its high level commands respect. The few weapons excavated so far are not particularly remarkable: they were cast in either single or double moulds, such as might have been used in many parts of the world. The vessels, however, are highly unusual. They too were made in moulds of separate pieces, or sections; but because the shapes were highly complicated, moulds with many sections had to be devised to accommodate them.

The moulds were of clay formed around a model of the piece to be cast. To take out the model before casting the clay wrapper had to be cut into sections and removed from the model, just as the peel of an orange is stripped from the fruit. This technique was to influence profoundly the development of the shapes and decoration of Chinese bronze vessels. Indeed, neither the shapes nor the decoration can be appreciated or explained without an understanding of the effects of this technology.[5]

Before the moulds could be used for casting, a core had to be placed at the centre so that the vessel would be hollow (Fig. 2). Small fragments of bronze, often from broken vessels, were inserted between the moulds and the core. These small fragments are known as spacers or chaplets. Large numbers of later Shang moulds have been found at Zhengzhou and Anyang. Rather mysteriously, however, complete vessel models have not come to light. Were they, like the moulds, made of a fine sandy ceramic, which was later pared down to become the cores? A few excavated ceramic handle-terminal models suggest that the principal vessel moulds must, indeed, have been of the same type of ceramic as the moulds.

In recent years the chemical and mineralogical composition of cores and moulds has been analysed. The material resembles quite closely loess, the yellow earth of northern China blown from Central Asia and the Gobi Desert. Only very fine particles could be borne long distances by the wind. These consist almost entirely of minute crystals of quartz, felspar and mica with small quantities of clay. This material is especially suitable for bronze-casting moulds: it can be carved or impressed with detailed ornament and is resistant to heat. Decoration on all ancient Chinese bronzes, but especially those of the Shang, was so intricate that any

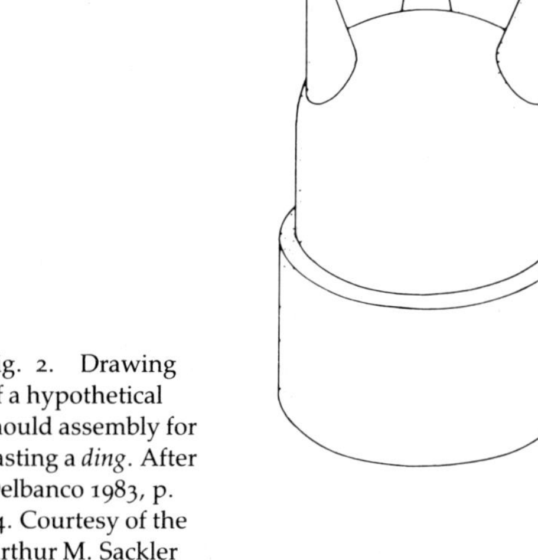

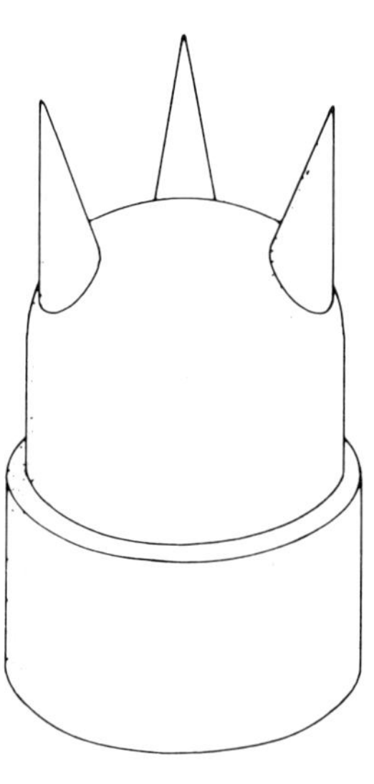

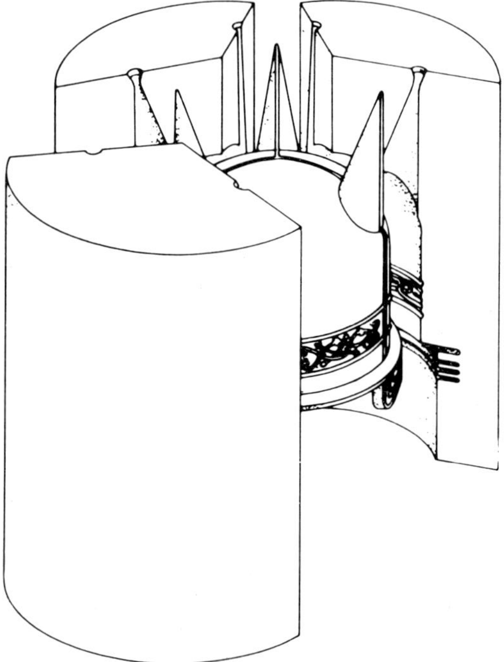

Fig. 2. Drawing of a hypothetical mould assembly for casting a *ding*. After Delbanco 1983, p. 14. Courtesy of the Arthur M. Sackler Foundation.

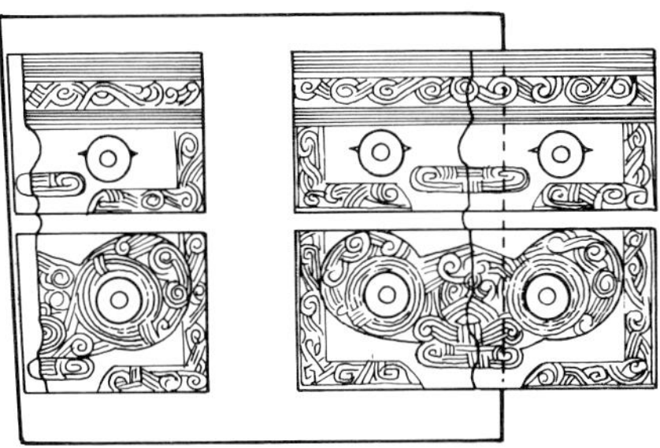

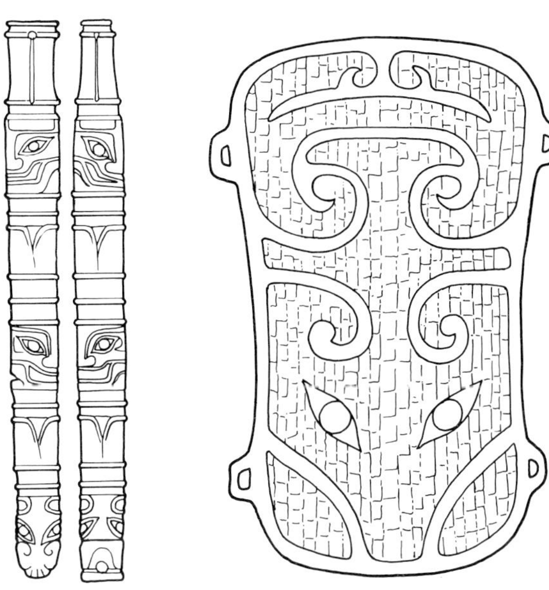

Fig. 3. Drawings of face motifs: *top*, on a jade *cong* from Jiangsu Wujin Sidun tomb M4, neolithic period, H. 4 cm; *left*, on a jade handle from Henan Yanshi Erlitou, H. 17.1 cm; *right*, on a bronze plaque inlaid with turquoise from Henan Yanshi Erlitou, tomb M11, H. 16.5 cm.

shrinkage, either when heating or firing the moulds before use, or when receiving the hot metal, would have been fatal to the design. Much of the success of Chinese bronze-casting may well have been the result of the fortuitous availability of loess and the choice of the casters to use it rather than the clays that were also to hand.[6] The brilliance of Shang and Zhou bronze-casting depended in very large measure on the consummate skills of Chinese potters and mould makers.

In addition jade carving contributed to later bronze art. It is a very specialised skill, and was highly developed in eastern Chinese neolithic cultures. Numerous jades in later Erlitou burials suggest that there had been some contact between Henan and the east coast. Among the jades is a small handle exquisitely carved with faces (Fig. 3). The handle's corners divide the faces at the nose. This arrangement follows a model set by much earlier carvings of the Liangzhu culture in the south-eastern provinces of Jiangsu and Zhejiang (Fig. 3). Here large numbers of ceremonial jades of square section drilled vertically, known in much later terminology as *cong*, were decorated with faces, whose eyes were also arranged either side of the corners (Fig. 3).[7]

Such jade carvings seem to have been at least one of the sources for the preoccupation with face motifs (known today by their later name, *taotie*) on Erligang-period bronzes. Two small bronze plaques from Yanshi (Fig. 3) are intermediaries between such early jades and rather later bronze vessel motifs.[8] Both of them are inlaid with strange monster faces in turquoise, whose features reappear later on the bronze vessels. The later history of this ornament will be discussed in Chapter 4.

Notes

1. For a discussion of the Erlitou culture see Yin 1986 and references supplied there. More recent discussions of the culture appear in *Kaogu xuebao* 1986.1, pp. 1–19, and *Wenwu* 1986.6, pp. 41–7.
2. Excavations of the Erlitou palaces are reported in *Kaogu* 1974.4, pp. 234–48, and *Kaogu* 1983.3, pp. 206–16.
3. The city near Dengfeng is described in *Wenwu* 1983.3, pp. 8–20; a second city is reported in the same issue of *Wenwu*, pp. 21–36.
4. For the more extensive finds of bronzes and jades from pits and tombs at Yanshi see *Kaogu* 1976.4, pp. 259–63; *Kaogu* 1983.3, pp. 199–205, 219; *Kaogu* 1984.1, pp. 37–40; *Kaogu* 1986.4, 318–23; see also *Kaogu* 1978.4, p.270
5. The fullest and most persuasive account of the influence of casting methods on the appearance of the bronzes is given by Robert Bagley in his contributions to New York 1980 and in the introduction to *Shang Ritual Bronzes in the Arthur M. Sackler Collections* (Bagley 1987).
6. The views expressed here are based upon comments made by Ian Freestone on thin sections of bronze-casting moulds prepared in the British Museum's Research Laboratory. Analyses of Shang-dynasty moulds are published in *Kaoguxue jikan* 1, 1981, pp. 244–72, and *Kaogu* 1986.3, pp. 269–77, I am greatly indebted to Nigel Wood for his comments on these results. Western Zhou moulds are discussed in *Kaogu* 1984.7, pp. 656–63, and Eastern Zhou ones in *Kaogu* 1986.4, pp. 355–62, 369.
7. In recent years a number of neolithic sites in the south-east have revealed *cong* carved with faces. The most impressive group came from a burial at the Sidun site at Wujin in Changzhou, Jiangsu province (*Kaogu* 1984.2, pp. 109–29); see also *Wenwu* 1984.2, pp. 1–5, 6–11, 12–16, 17–22, 23–36; *Wenwu ziliao congkan* 3, 1980, pp. 1–14.
8. The plaques are described and illustrated in *Kaogu* 1984.1, pp. 37–40, and *Kaogu* 1986.4, pp. 318–23. A lacquer fragment also decorated with a face ancestral to the *taotie*, as the Shang monster face is described, is reported in *Kaogu* 1983.3, pp. 199–205, 219, fig. 9:9.

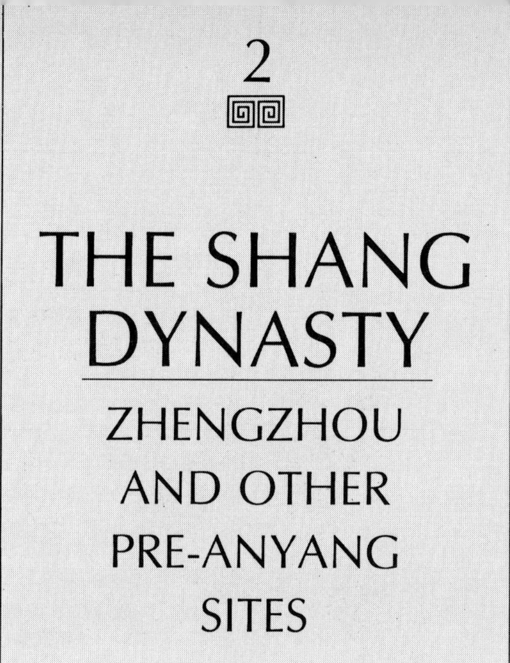

2

THE SHANG DYNASTY

ZHENGZHOU AND OTHER PRE-ANYANG SITES

A brief history of the Shang dynasty is given in the *Yin ben ji* ('The Annals of the Shang'), a chapter in the *Shi ji*, a history of the Han dynasty and its predecessors, composed by the court historian Sima Qian (*c.* 145–86 BC). This short, factual description of the Shang names their kings and describes their various capitals. Anyang, a small town in northern Henan province, has been identified as a late Shang city, known to the Zhou as Yin. Inscribed oracle bones found there confirm that the last Shang kings named by Sima Qian ruled Anyang.[1] Several sites in Henan and other provinces display the Erligang culture, which falls stratigraphically and on the evidence of radio-carbon dating between the Erlitou occupation and the Anyang period to be discussed in Chapter 3. The Erligang period therefore represents the early to middle stages of the Shang period. How much of the early Shang falls within the Erligang phases depends on whether or not part of Erlitou is Shang. If phases III and IV of Erlitou are Shang occupations, then the city at Zhengzhou belongs well into the Shang period; but if the Erlitou culture antedates the whole of the Shang period, then the Erligang period is early Shang.

The largest and most important Erligang site to be investigated is the ancient city discovered at Zhengzhou and under excavation since the 1950s. At the modern city of Zhengzhou, now the provincial capital of Henan, a massive city wall has been uncovered. This huge, obviously defensive structure has stimulated a search for the identity of the city. Sima Qian mentioned several capitals preceding Yin in date, and many authorities have tried to match the site at Zhengzhou to one of these names. The one suggested most often is Ao; but there is no evidence as yet that this is correct.

The Erligang culture identified at Zhengzhou is recognised as much by its distinctive ceramic forms as by its bronzes. These ceramics include large wide-mouthed containers also found at Erlitou sites. However, it is the bronzes that are significant: they have come from pits, unstratified finds and a few tombs. Bronze vessels from a tomb at Zhengzhou Baijiazhuang included *jue, jia, lei* and a *pan*; in other words two wine cups descended from the Erlitou examples, a new wine container shaped like a ceramic jar constricted at the neck – known as a *lei* – and a bronze version of a shallow water vessel very common in ceramic at Erlitou.

The *lei* and *pan* were missing from tomb M2 at Minggonglu at Zhengzhou, but a *ding,* a tripod-shaped food vessel, had been added (Fig. 4). In this tomb a single *ding* was combined with two *jue,* two *jia* and a single *gu.* Additionally this tomb contained a large high-fired shouldered ceramic jar illustrating the role of ceramics in burial and ritual assemblages. Such jars have been found in a number of tombs and probably enjoyed a status higher than ordinary earthenware. High-fired ceramic *zun* seem to have been the ancestors of vessels such as no.3. Apart from the *ding* and the *pan,* all the bronze vessels and the ceramic *zun* were for wine; without doubt the offering of wine must have been one of the main elements of the ritual.[2]

The ritual use of bronze vessels in life as opposed to after death is attested by two large bronze caches

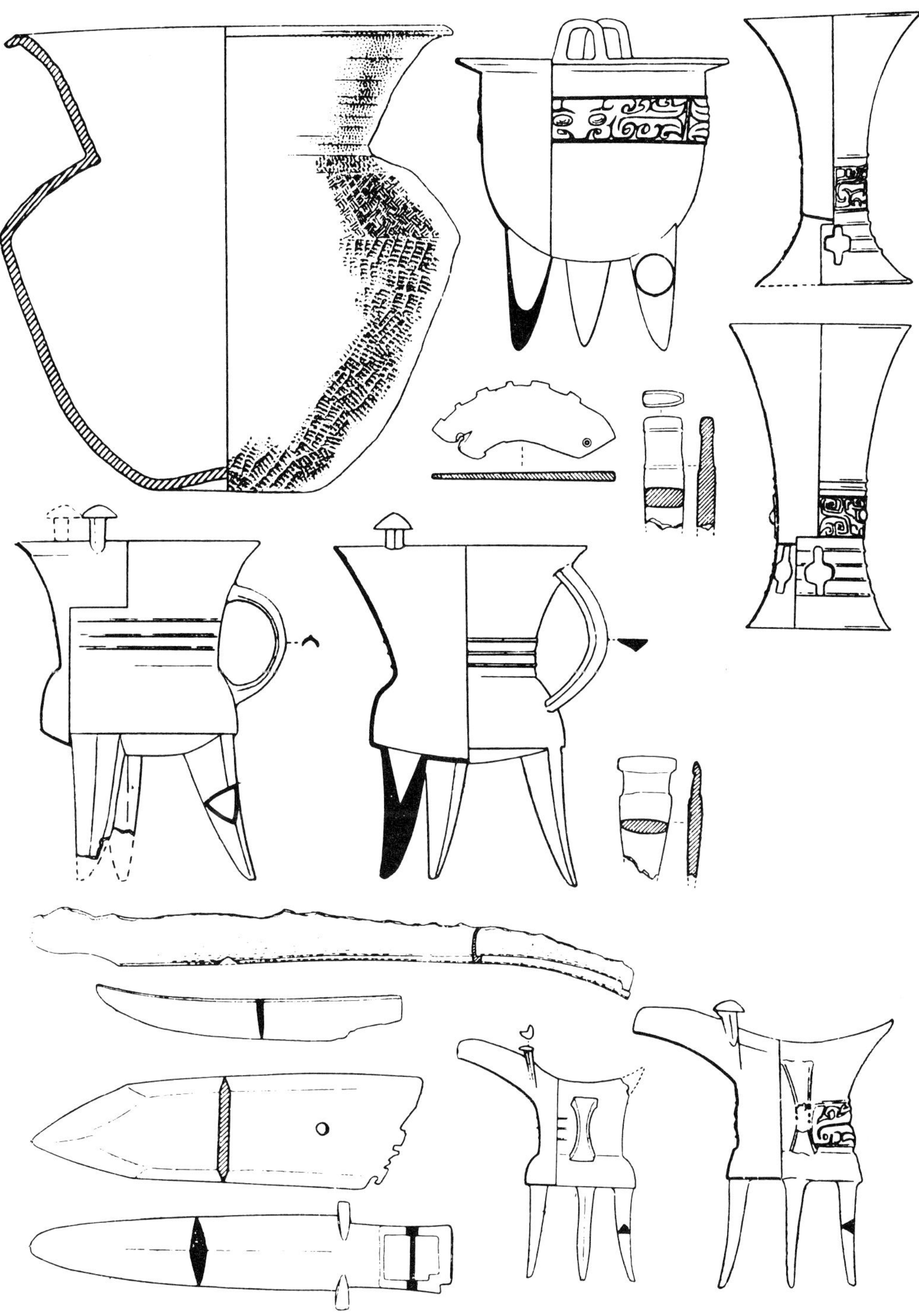

Fig. 4. Bronzes, ceramics and jades from tomb M2 at Henan Zhengzhou Minggonglu. Shang dynasty, Erligang period. H. of high-fired ceramic *zun* (*top left*) 27 cm.

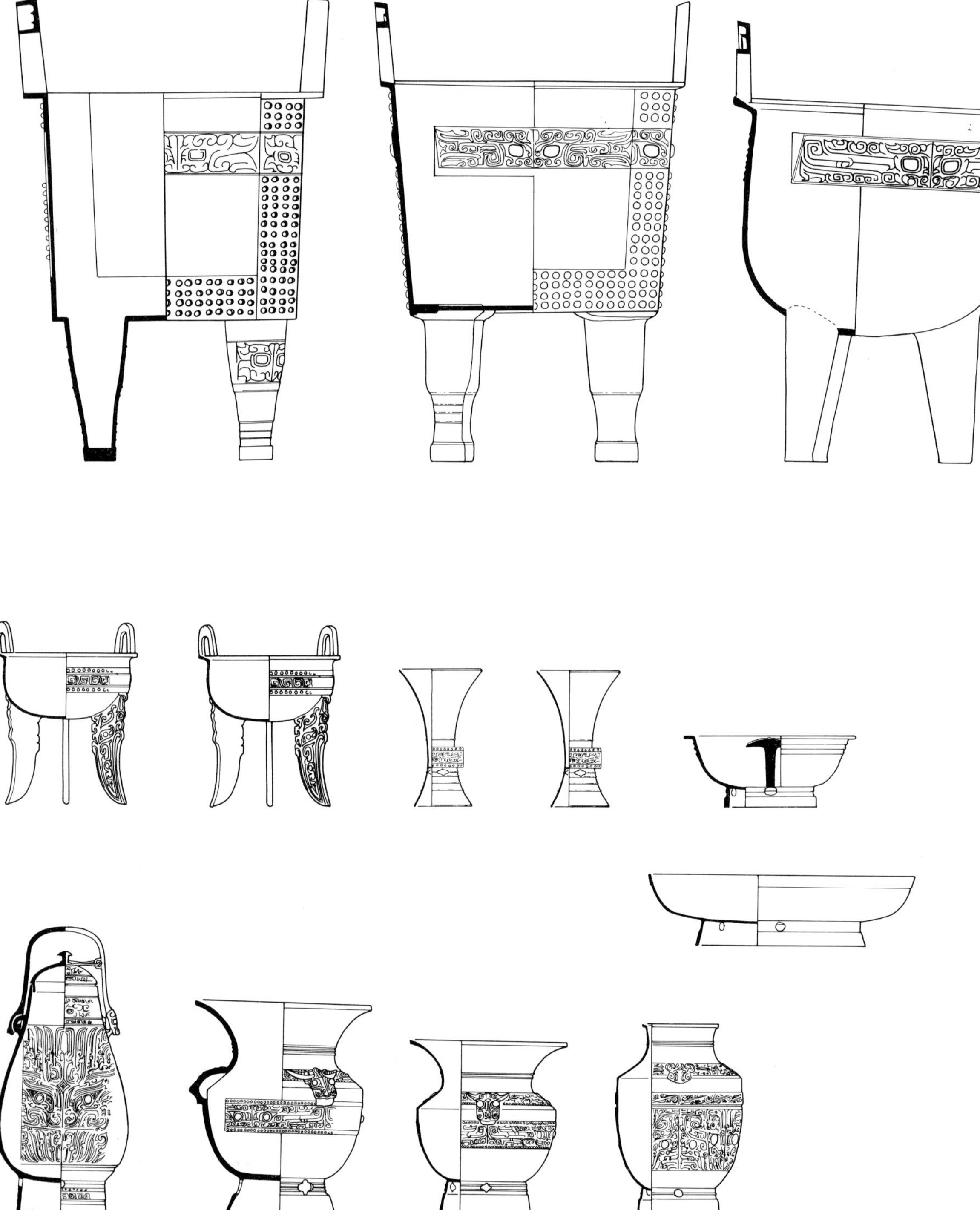

Fig. 5. Drawings of bronze vessels from a hoard from Henan Zhengzhou. Shang dynasty, Erligang period: *fang ding*, H. 81 cm; *fang ding*, H. 81 cm; *ding*, H. 77.3 cm; two *ding* with flat legs, H. 31.7 cm; two *gu*, H. 24 cm; *yu*, H. 12 cm, DIAM. 29.3 cm; *pan*, H. 12.7 cm, DIAM. 49 cm; *you*, H. 50.2 cm; two *zun*, H. 37 and 30 cm; *lei*, H. 33 cm.

found at Zhengzhou. Spectacular examples were recovered from two pits rather than burials, in which the vessels were carefully placed, one inside the other. The most remarkable pieces from these finds are two pairs of rectangular *ding*, or *fang ding*, as they are known. They are very large, ranging in size from 87 to 100 cm in height. In addition to two *fang ding* the second deposit contained three *ding*, two shouldered *zun*, a *lei*, two *gu*, a *you*, a *yu* and a *pan* (Fig. 5).[3]

This assemblage includes vessels more elaborate than the general run of Erligang bronzes and may well be later than the contents of the tombs described. Alternatively the vessels belonged to the higher-ranking individuals than did the bronzes recovered so far from tombs. They illustrate a growing confidence in casting to produce large and dramatic shapes. New features were also developed that showed ingenious command of section-moulding.

The very deep rectangular *ding* obviously posed considerable casting problems; in most cases they had to be made in two or more pourings. One of them consists of four flat cast side sections which were made first and then inserted into a mould assembly for the rest of the vessel. In later Shang times such rectangular vessels were very popular, the pouring of sufficient molten metal presumably having been mastered. Flat-sided containers were in fact particularly easy to cast using section-moulds:[4] this is attested by the large numbers used in the first half of the Anyang period (no. 5). Angular vessels were one of the ways in which a ritual repertory initiated by neolithic ceramics was extended with new types.

Blade-like legs on *ding* were also easy to cast in section-moulds. The legs fell at divisions in the mould and were made by cutting depressions into inner faces of adjoining mould sections. Because the legs were cut into the solid sides of the mould, they could easily be given a jagged edge, a shape inspired by earlier ceramics.[5] A flat leg with an irregular hooked profile, often projecting beyond the line of the rounded body, was, as Robert Bagley has pointed out, the model for flanges on bronze containers. Large curly flanges occur on a few Erligang bronzes.[6] Far from being a way of hiding a defect, as many commentators have supposed, flanges were important artistic devices that had their origins in the casting methods developed for flat legs.

The extent of Erligang-period finds has been greatly enlarged in recent years. Both ceramics and bronzes in impeccable Erligang style have come from far-flung sites in the north, west and south, illustrating the great penetration of this culture.[7] In all these areas some Erligang features of vessel shape or bronze design survived long after the beginning of the Anyang period in Henan. Amongst the most interesting sites is a city at Hubei Huangpi Panlongcheng, which stands on a peninsula, almost an island, in one of the large tributaries of the Yangzi.[8] It is likely that Panlongcheng's political strength and impressive casting were founded on economic power – in later times large copper-mines were exploited not far away at Tonglüshan. This outpost may have controlled valuable trade to central Henan or even the shipment of metal.

Finds from Panlongcheng extend the vessel types known from Zhengzhou by adding to *jia, jue, gu, lei, zun, ding* and *pan*, a *yan* for steaming rice, a *he*, thought to be for water to dilute wine, a *you* of a shape slightly different from the one found at Zhengzhou, and a *gui* with handles, a type that did not become popular in bronze before the end of the Anyang period. These finds illustrate the growing ritual apparatus and also the increasing strength of bronze technology.

Bronzes more advanced in shape and decoration than standard Erligang pieces have come from many sites in northern, central and southern China. Such finds have been labelled transitional and bridge the gap between Erligang and the first stages of casting at Anyang.[9] Dwellings, pits and burials at Taixicun Gaocheng Xian in Hebei province belong to this transitional period. Other sites of a similar stage of development have been found at Pinggu Xian, at Beijing, and Lingbao, further south in Henan province. Vessels from these sites include a new type; the *pou*, a rounded squat jar slightly constricted below the lip (Fig. 6). The British Museum's example may be rather later than many of the vessels from these transitional sites; it displays, however, fine quilled *taotie*, typical of the period. On many of these bronzes Erligang-period *taotie* faces and dragons were greatly elaborated. In addition they were combined with relatively realistic modelled heads, as on the *pou*, and very occasionally with intaglio designs inside the vessels, particularly of turtle and fish (rubbing no. 1). Striking examples occur on a *pan* from Pinggu Xian near Beijing.[10] These creatures were far more obviously representational than the *taotie*. In part, realistic intaglio motifs may have been a sign of an advanc-

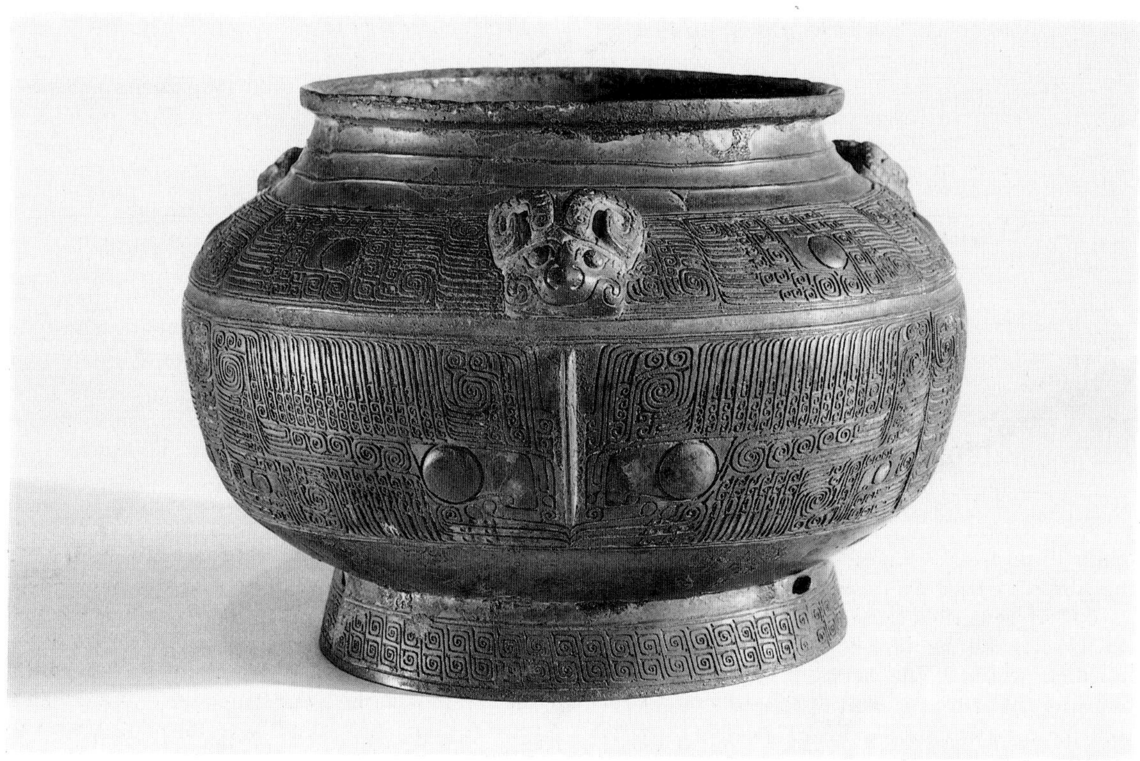

Fig. 6. Bronze ritual vessel *pou*. Shang dynasty, transitional period. H. 20.3 cm. British Museum, Seligman Bequest (1973.7–26.13; see also rubbing no. 1).

ing industry, but they also seem to be features local to a large area on the periphery of the Chinese central region. In due course such motifs were also adopted in Shang centres in Henan. Fu Hao's tomb contains *pan* (ancestral to no. 21) decorated with such representational motifs.[11]

A notion of a distinct culture embracing this northern area and extending westwards through Shanxi into Shaanxi, Sichuan and even south-west to Yunnan is helpful in elucidating some of the variety of the Chinese bronze age.[12] This area inherited many aspects of Erligang culture but was undoubtedly somewhat outside the Anyang sphere of influence. Peoples living in areas within this great arc developed their own culture and were also open to central Chinese and outside influence. They shared several cultural traits, notably weapon types and burial patterns, and displayed an enduring interest in realistic animal motifs, which will be mentioned again in discussion of both Shang and Western Zhou zoomorphic ornament.

NOTES

1. For background on Shang capitals see Chang 1980; contrast Watson 1981. For a discussion of Zhengzhou see An 1986.
2. The tombs are reported in *Wenwu* 1955.10, pp. 24–42, and *Kaogu* 1965.10, pp. 500–6; see also Watson 1973a, no. 70–3; Chang 1980, fig. 71.
3. The two deposits are reported in *Wenwu* 1975.6, pp. 64–8, and *Wenwu* 1983.3, pp. 49–59; see also New York 1980, no.11.
4. Rectangular vessels were made in ceramic in the Erlitou period (*Kaogu* 1965.5, pp. 215–24, pl.2). On present evidence such containers pre-date the casting of flat-sided bronze containers.
5. For Robert Bagley's discussion of both features see New York 1980, no. 11, and Bagley 1987, Introduction, Sections 1.8, 1.9.
6. Beijing 1981a, no. 76.
7. Bagley 1977; Lin 1986, pp. 238–9.
8. For a discussion of Panlongcheng see Bagley 1977.
9. This transitional phase was first described by Robert Bagley (New York 1980, p. 112).
10. *Wenwu* 1977.11, pp. 1–8, fig. 5.
11. Beijing 1980f, figs 21, 22.
12. Several authors have tackled this subject, all from rather different perspectives; see Watson 1971; Lin 1986; Tong Enzheng 1986.

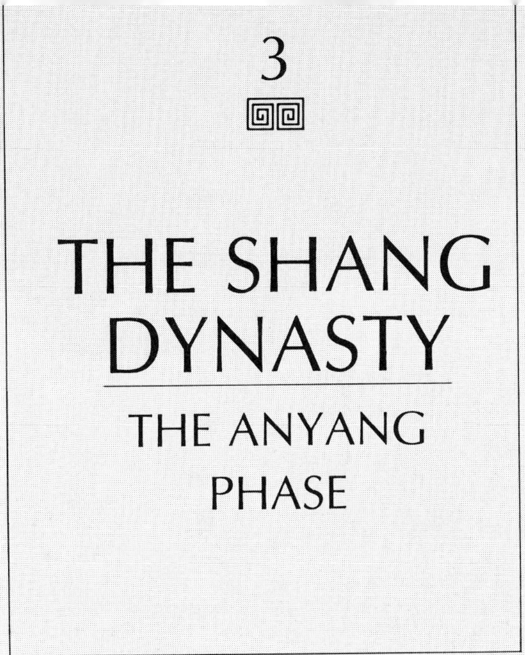

3

THE SHANG DYNASTY

THE ANYANG PHASE

Anyang is a town in northern Henan province. Its name is now used to embrace the archaeological sites excavated on its outskirts, many of which are also designated by the names of small villages surrounding the town: Xiaotun, Xibeigang, Houjiazhuang, Wuguancun and Dasikongcun to name only the most important. In addition sites of the same date in other parts of China are often described as dating to the Anyang period, meaning that they were contemporary with the Shang occupation of Anyang, although their culture may have differed considerably from that of the major centres.

Anyang became famous at the end of the last century when small fragments of bone were noticed by scholars to have a few characters incised upon them. Bought in Beijing, these fragments were traced back to Anyang.[1] From this chance discovery grew the largest of all Chinese excavations. Work started at Anyang in 1928: progress was interrupted by the war that followed the Japanese occupation and once the new government was established, excavation began again and has continued more or less ever since.

As with Zhengzhou, attempts have been made to link Anyang with one of the capitals known from the later history of the Shang given in the *Shi ji*. Over many centuries the area was identified as Yinxu, the 'wastes of Yin', and this identification is still broadly accepted. Many, but not all, scholars regard Anyang as Yin, the city to which the Shang king, Pan Geng, is said to have moved his capital.[2]

Like Zhengzhou, Anyang is the site of a large city. The remains differ, however, from those of the Erligang-period cities of Zhengzhou and Panlongcheng in that there is no trace of a city wall. This striking difference has prompted the suggestion that Anyang was a ritual centre and that the administrative capital lay elsewhere.[3] It is certainly likely that other large cities were contemporary with Anyang, but until they have been located and excavated Anyang's standing relative to these other centres cannot be assessed.

Remains of large structures, palace buildings and lesser dwellings, have been found at Xiaotun outside Anyang. As with all the buildings already mentioned, the foundations were made of stamped earth, *hang tu*, on which the edifices were constructed with wooden columns supporting a roof. Tombs identified as royal lie north-west of Anyang at a site known as Xibeigang, outside the village of Houjiazhuang. Other tombs have been excavated at Wuguancun near by, at Dasikongcun nearer Anyang, at Hougang just outside Anyang, and in an area known as the western sector of Yinxu.

The large tombs at Xibeigang had mostly been robbed before excavation; but many of the smallest tombs were intact. Especially important to present Shang studies is the tomb of Fu Hao, discovered at Xiaotun in 1976. Fu Hao has been identified as the consort of Wu Ding, a major reformer and one of the most influential of the Shang kings in the first part of their rule from Yin.[4] Such identifications depend upon studies of the oracle-bone inscriptions essential to any discussion of the Shang, since they are the earliest contemporary written evidence. Information from the inscribed bones has confirmed some of the accounts given in the *Shi ji* and other later historical works. Anyang has therefore become the pivot of Shang history: it stands as a fixed point between the undocumented early Shang remains and the fuller but varied accounts of Zhou cities.

Oracle bones are shells or bones used by the Shang for divination.[5] Two types were employed, scapulae, the shoulder blades of oxen, and turtle shells. A divination involved drilling holes and applying hot brands to the holes, cracking the bone or shell. The divination depended on reading the crack. This had been practised long before the Shang came to power: bones dating to 3,000 or 4,000 years BC have been retrieved at north-eastern neolithic sites. Later, similar practices were taken up in Henan. However, these early examples carry no writing, and we know nothing of the kinds of divination undertaken.

Only during the Anyang period are the Shang bones regularly inscribed. These bones record both the questions asked by the diviner and the responses given as a result of the interpretation of the crack. The questions are set out in the positive and negative – will it rain, will it not rain, and so on? The subjects covered by the questions are very large: matters of state, such as military campaigns, commands to officers, building of settlements, tribute; the welfare of the monarch and his consort.

In oracle-bone texts kings and their ancestors are given titles such as Wu Ding or Zu Geng. The first character either names the ancestor as in Wu, meaning martial, or calls him Fu or Zu, meaning father or ancestor; the second character, which is one of ten, designates a day within a repeating cycle. Some of these characters were used more frequently than others in posthumous or ritual names. The same type of posthumous title appears in the inscriptions on some bronze vessels, and often refers not to the king's ancestors but to the ancestors of the person who had the vessel cast.

Sacrifices to the ancestors were one of the methods by which benefits to the king or his family were sought and evil averted. The oracle-bone inscriptions mention these sacrifices, asking whether an offering to a particular ancestor will be efficacious. Both the divination and bronze inscriptions illustrate the importance of ritual offerings to ancestors as assisting the royal family and, by extension, noble families. Like the divinations sacrifices of food and wine offered in bronze ritual vessels were part of the apparatus of the Shang state and society, designed to invoke the aid of the ancestors in supporting the life of their descendants and protecting them from harm. This was not a private religion directed towards the salvation of a soul, but one intended to ensure the continuation of life on earth in a satisfactory and orderly manner.

In addition to providing evidence of the role of ritual sacrifices in Shang society oracle-bone inscriptions contribute to a discussion of the chronology of Anyang sites and artefacts found in them. Divination inscriptions are dated by their content, their calligraphy and by the names of the diviners in the inscriptions. Traditonally the bones have been divided into five periods spanning the Anyang occupation. However, it seems likely that Li Xueqin's arguments for reducing the number of periods from five to four are correct.[6]

Anyang occupation is also divided into four periods on the basis of pottery types.[7] These four periods approximately match the evolution of bronze vessels, but although some correlation of oracle-bone inscription periods, ceramic types and bronze vessels is possible, they probably varied independently of each other.[8]

Tombs and vessel types

Early tombs at Anyang reveal vessels that resemble bronzes from the transitional sites at Gaocheng Xian in Hebei province and Pingu Xian at Beijing. Tomb M232 at Anyang Xiaotun can be taken to represent this stage.[9] The tomb contained a *ding*, two *jue*, two *jia*, two *gu*, a *lei*, a *pou* and a *pan*. The *jue* are similar to one another, but the two *jia* and two *gu* are not: one *jia* has a rounded base, the other has a flat underside; one of the *gu* is wide and relatively squat, the other is taller and more fully articulated. The *pou* is a marker of the transitional character of the assemblage. Both the vessel shapes and their decoration of monster faces, *taotie*, in long fine quills and scrolls descend from the Erligang and transitional stages already considered.

Between the construction of this early Anyang tomb and that of Fu Hao, excavated in 1976, a revolution took place. The tomb contained over 200 bronze vessels, many weapons and other bronze fittings, and a rich haul of jade, ivory and marble carving. A large number of the vessels were inscribed with the name Fu Hao. Although the identity of Fu Hao has been much debated, it is generally accepted that she is the lady referred to in many oracle-bone texts of period II as a consort of Wu Ding. Her bronzes are therefore dated to his reign or to the immediately succeeding period.[10]

When first discovered, the contents of the tomb challenged the assumptions about the speed and

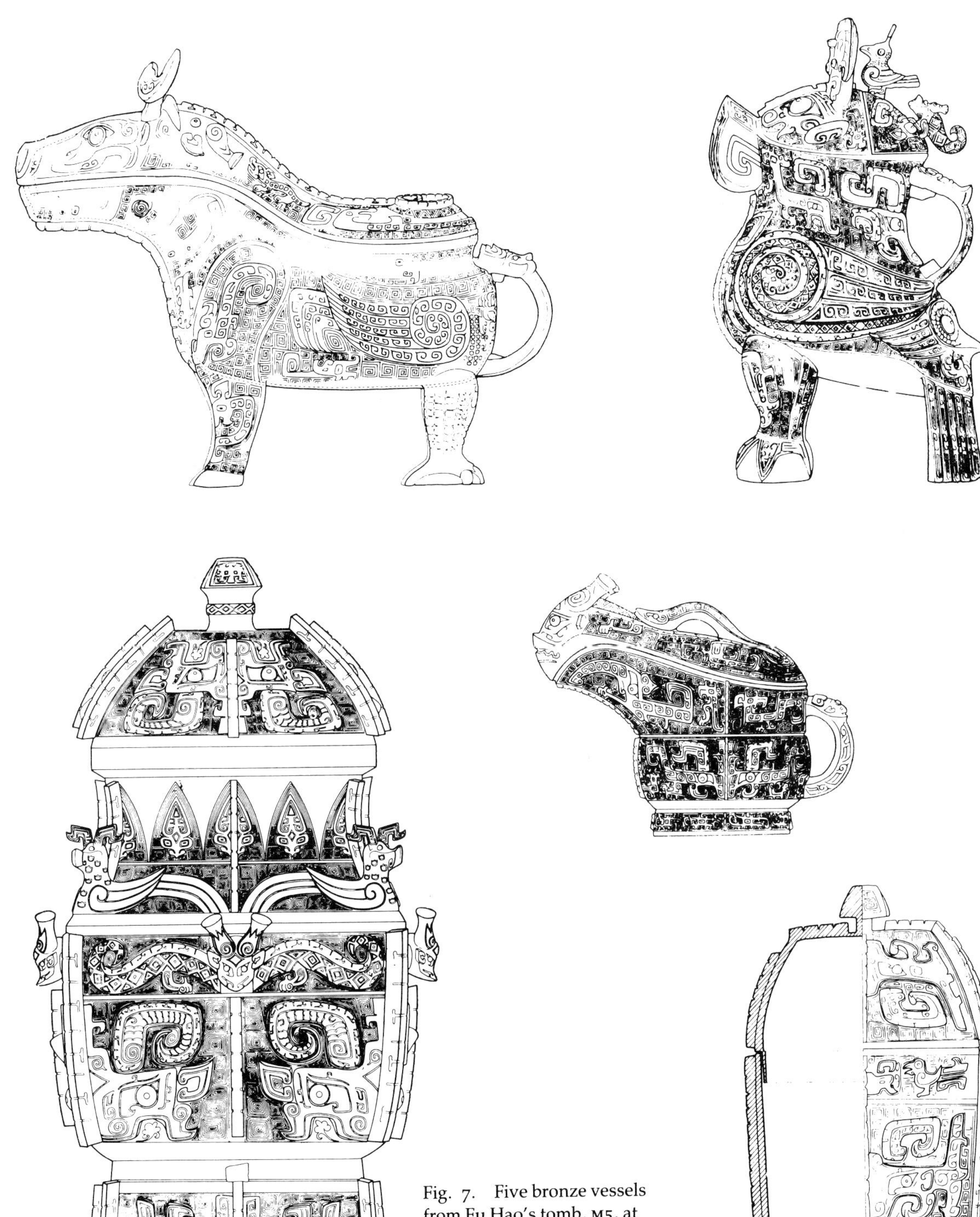

Fig. 7. Five bronze vessels from Fu Hao's tomb, M5, at Henan Anyang Xiaotun. Shang dynasty, Anyang period: animal *zun*, H. 36 cm; bird *zun*, H. 45.9 cm; *gong*, H. 18.2 cm, *fang hu*, H. 64.4 cm; *fang yi*, H. 36.6 cm.

character of the development of Shang bronze art. With the dating now accepted it must be admitted that very early in the Anyang period enormous changes took place in bronze design with an abundance of new vessel types, new shapes, and new ways of treating surfaces.

The new vessels included animal shapes, *gong* – a wine pourer that in part takes the shape of an animal – and a rectangular, box-like container called a *fang yi* (Fig. 7). In addition to the *fang yi* a large number of other already existing vessel types, such as *jia* and *zun*, were cast with square or rectangular cross-sections. As discussed in connection with the Zhengzhou *fang ding*, such square sections were particularly easy to cast with piece-moulds. Many of these new angular forms were decorated with vertical flanges. In the past scholars have suggested that these were intended to cover up failures in the mould assemblies which allowed small amounts of bronze to squeeze through the joints; however, this does not seem to be the case at all. Robert Bagley has demonstrated that the Shang were already accomplished at casting vessels without flanges. They did not need flanges to cover up failures because these were insignificant. Flanges were invented by analogy with flat legs on *ding* (Fig. 5); they were multiplied to articulate angular and square-sectioned containers and to act as frames for ever more complex decoration.[11]

While square-sectioned vessels were formal and regular, animal-shaped containers had a quite different effect. Their shapes were asymmetrical and their surfaces a riot of creatures (Fig. 7). Within the context of highly regulated rectangular vessels and decoration neatly organised in compartments, their shapes and surfaces were almost anarchic. At this time two less dramatic vessels, the *gong* and the owl *you*, were developed. The *gong* (no. 6) seems to be a regularised form of the animal *zun*. The owl *you* looks as though it was invented by putting two bird-shaped containers, such as those in Fu Hao's tomb (Fig. 7), back to back to make a single vessel. Many owl *you*, including the vessel in the British Museum (no. 7), are covered all over with a variety of zoomorphs, just like the animal-shaped containers. Owl features were also added to more conventional *you* with round cross-sections and slender necks.

The growing ritual assemblage also gained bells. In Erlitou and later tombs small single bells were quite common, as were chime stones. Fu Hao's tomb, however, contained two kinds of bell: eighteen small *ling* continued the earlier tradition, while bells with tubular handles were relatively new. Both types were to have a later history in southern China but did not assume importance in the north until the second half of the Western Zhou period.

Several of the royal tombs at Xibeigang are thought to be approximately contemporary with Fu Hao's tomb. However, when excavated, they were already robbed and so cannot be compared with it. Some imposing vessels surviving in museums can be identified as coming from these tombs.[12] Royal bronzes were evidently very splendid. In discussing later Anyang casting, however, we are hampered by not knowing which bronzes, if any, come from later royal tombs. It is therefore difficult to place appropriate later groups of vessels in parallel with the contents of Fu Hao's tomb.

The elaborate vessel sets and angular articulated containers described must have continued at least for a century or so. The *fang yi* and owl *you* in the British Museum (nos 5 and 7) are products of such an industry and can be matched by similar vessels from tombs and in other collections. There is, however, no escaping the conclusion that a large part of the late Anyang production was very different. A dramatic change of style seems to have taken place in the third or fourth periods of Anyang occupation.

Vessels from tombs M51 and M53 at Dasikongcun are generally taken as illustrating the last part of the Anyang period.[13] The only problem in selecting these particular tombs is that their occupants' status may have been very low, and their simplified impoverished vessels may have been as much a product of this status as of the general artistic tenor of the time. However, other late Anyang tombs, including M1713 in the western sector of Yinxu (Fig. 8), demonstrate the wide currency of such vessels.

What late Anyang bronzes and ceramic imitations seem to illustrate is a complete change of aesthetic (Fig. 8). Rounded vessels often replaced angular ones; vessel types also changed in importance. *Ding* and *yan* remained present, but increasingly bronze *li* were used in place of ceramic ones and *gui* with handles became standard, not rare. Among the wine vessels *gu*, *jue* and *jia* continued in use but often changed in shape. Thus a *jia* with a lobed body was now popular. *You* were increasingly important, and a small squat vessel with a U-shaped handle became the major type. Shouldered *zun* were less common than before, being replaced in the main by a *zun* type that was simply an enlarged *gu*.

Few of these vessels occur in the rectangular or square-section forms popular in Fu Hao's tomb or

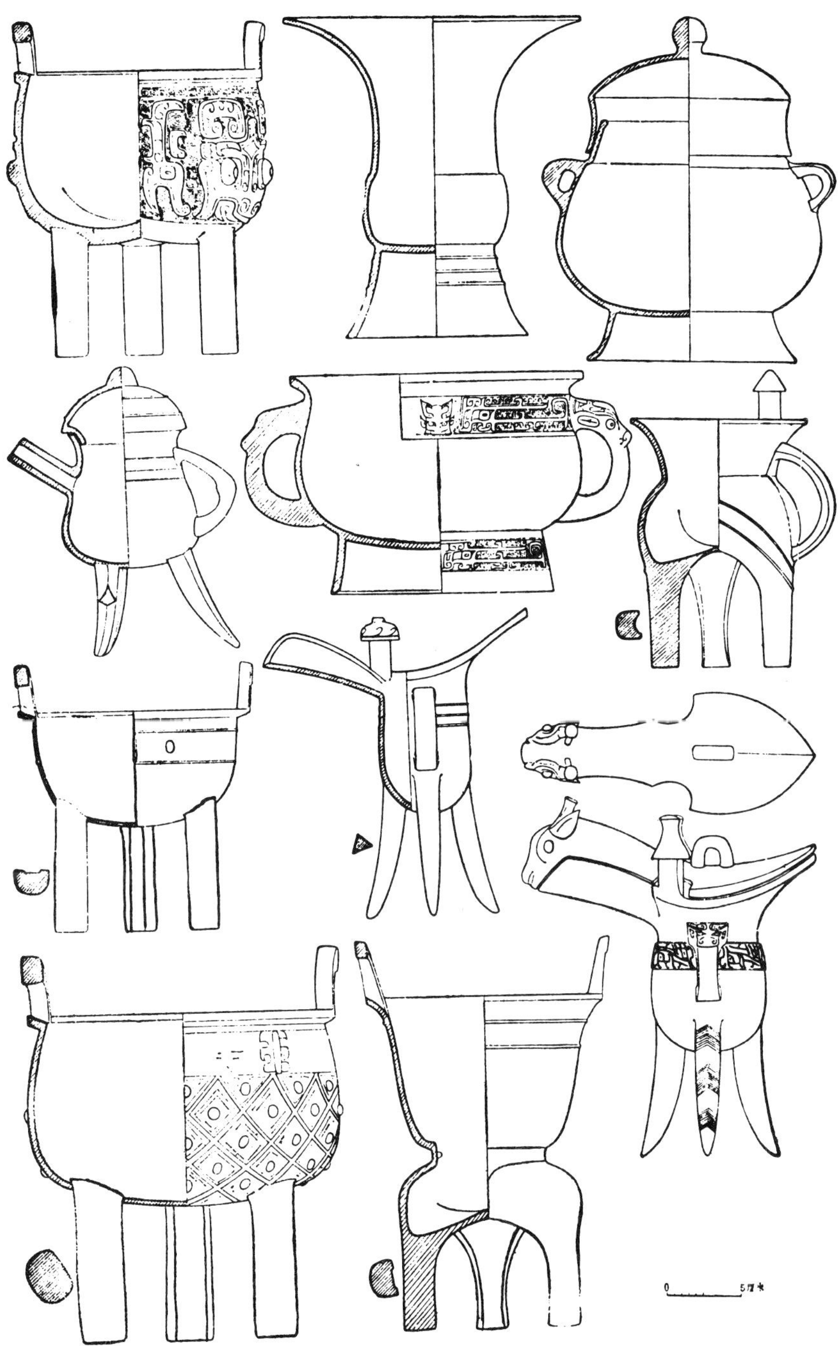

Fig. 8. Bronze vessels from tomb M1713 in the western sector of Anyang Yinxu. Shang dynasty, end of the Anyang period. H. of *li ding* (*top left*) 19 cm.

other contemporary burials, although *fang lei* and *fang ding* remained current into the early Western Zhou (no. 10). With the rectangular forms in decline, flanges also became less important, and high-relief and realistic zoomorphs were also casualties. Instead some of the Erligang and early Anyang motifs were revived. Such changes seem to suggest social and economic decline accompanied by a deliberate return to the past. Rounded containers with narrow bands of decoration (Fig. 8) contributed an essential ingredient to the early Zhou style.

The provinces

While bronzes from Anyang are regarded as the standard set by late Shang production, a large number of provincial centres cast other, very different bronzes; metropolitan Shang influence seems to have been circumscribed. In the Erligang period a single style pervaded most parts of China that made bronzes; in the Anyang period several styles existed side by side.[14] Underlying this diversity must have been a degree of independence that is reflected in the distinctions between the pottery types in several areas.

Surrounding the Shang to the north and west was an area, sometimes called the northern zone, which combined some aspects of Anyang culture with features from adjacent regions of eastern Asia; it also had its own characteristics. Weapons, notably axes with tubular hafts and animal-headed knives (no. 12), define the region, which runs approximately from Liaoning in the east to Shaanxi in the west.[15] A few quite remarkable vessels have come from different sites in this broad sweeping area. Particularly relevant to the British Museum's collection are *pan* from Qingjian in northern Shaanxi, not far from the Yellow River where it runs north–south. These *pan* are decorated with small intaglio fishes and turtles; the same concern with realistic creatures was also noted in connection with vessels of the transitional period, including the British Museum's *pou* (Fig. 6) and a *pan* from Pinggu Xian. A *pan* in the British Musuem (no. 11) resembles one from Qingjian in its proportions, intaglio decoration and the layered rim. Its fine precise casting also seems to be characteristic of the area.

The most exciting and innovative bronzes have been found in the southern provinces of Hubei, Hunan, Anhui and Jiangsu, and contrast not only with contemporary bronzes from Anyang but also with those from Panlongcheng, which are similar to examples from Zhengzhou, and other later transitional sites in the south. Later southern bronzes, on the other hand, are remarkably inventive, altering the shapes and motifs of Anyang vessels in unusual, unpredictable ways.

These southern bronzes display two major preoccupations: an interest in animal figures that far exceeds the concerns of Anyang casters and an enthusiasm for bells (and no doubt their music).[16] The bronzes have been found mainly in isolated deposits, which do not seem part of burials but may have been sacrificial offerings. As the vessels and bells have been found in relatively small numbers, there is no way of knowing whether their owners followed northern ritual practices or not. Their ancestors at Panlongcheng and other areas must have done so, but probably metropolitan Shang influence had waned at this date. The bronzes lack inscriptions, so there is no information to be gained from that source.

A large wine container, traditionally called a *zun*, cast in the shape of two rams is an example of a southern Shang bronze (no. 13). Two almost realistic rams' heads either side of the opening resemble four that encircle a *zun* found at Hunan Ningxiang. On both vessels the animals' horns were pre-cast so that they could be fitted into the mould assembly for the whole vessel.[17] Only in this way was it possible to make the horns stand away from the heads.

Bronzes representing other creatures equally realistically have been found, including vessels in the shape of buffaloes and several in the form of elephants.[18] Attributed to the south, but with less certainty, are several bronzes whose subject is a male figure grasped by a tiger. A small finial in the British Museum is an example (no. 15). One reason for looking to the south as the source is the very lifelike quality of the casting. Another is the discovery in Anhui province of a large shouldered *zun* that displays in its centre panel a man grasped by a tiger, which for reasons of symmetry has its body divided, branching to give two views either side of the single head.[19] Several other bronzes illustrating the same theme are attributed to the south.[20] At Anyang rare examples of the same theme occur: a single head appears between two tigers on an axe; the same subject fills the handles of a large, apparently royal, *ding*, known as the *Su Mu Wu fang ding* (now in the Historical Museum, Beijing).[21] However, these last two examples are almost flat, unlike the rounded realistic sculpture from the south.

If the south exploited northern technology but transformed its vessel shapes and zoomorphic ornament, other areas copied Anyang more slavishly.[22] Shaanxi province between Baoji in the west and Chang'an further east, for example, a region that was to give birth to the Shang's successors, the Zhou, was committed to late Anyang-style bronzes, often virtually indistinguishable from their prototypes.[23] However, even this area must have been considerably separated from Anyang, as like the northern zone and the south it did not share Anyang-style ceramics. At the fall of the Shang it was peculiarly receptive to influences from other parts of China, including both the southern and north-western cultures already described. Early Zhou bronzes were eclectic, borrowing features from all these different sources.

Notes

1. Li 1977, pp. 6–7.
2. Chang 1980, p. 6–19, lists the Shang kings, their capitals and additional information gleaned from texts.
3. Watson 1979, p. 70, quoting Miyazaki casts doubt on the status of Anyang as a capital.
4. For a description of archaeological work at Anyang see Li 1977 and Chang 1980. Essays in Chang 1986 are relevant, especially to the dating of Fu Hao's tomb.
5. For an introduction to the study of oracle bones and references to all the major works see Keightley 1978.
6. The oracle-bone periodisation is discussed in Li Xueqin 1977 and 1981 in connection with the discoveries in Fu Hao's tomb; see also Shaughnessy 1982.
7. For a description of pottery types see Chang 1980, pp. 105–6, fig. 28, and *Kaogu xuebao* 1979.1, pp. 27–120, table 4.
8. For a periodisation of Anyang bronze vessels see Zhang Changshou 1979.
9. The contents of the tomb are discussed in Zhang Changshou 1979, pp. 279–82; Chang 1980, p. 82, fig. 18; Thorp 1985.
10. The tomb is reported in Beijing 1980f; see also Chang 1986.
11. The functions of flanges are described in Bagley 1987, Introduction, Section 1.9.
12. See New York 1980, pp. 53–7, for a brief discussion of the royal tombs. Three large *he* in the Nezu Museum, Tokyo (Mizuno 1959, pls 42–4), are thought to come from tomb M1001, perhaps the tomb of Wu Ding, while the *Su Mu Wu fang ding* (Akiyama *et al.* 1968, pl. 10) is believed to come from a consort's tomb; see also Huber 1983.
13. For reports on the tombs see *Kaogu tongxun* 1958.10, pp. 51–61, and *Kaogu* 1964.8, pp.380–4; see also Zhang Changshou 1979, pp. 284–5.
14. This distinction was first noted by Robert Bagley (Bagley 1977, pp.210–13; New York 1980, p.112; Bagley 1987, Introduction, Section 1.12).
15. For discussion of the area see Watson 1971 and Lin 1986. Further consideration of this topic was given by Tong Enzheng in a paper presented to the British Association of Chinese Studies on 20 September 1986.
16. Southern casting is thus defined by Robert Bagley (New York 1980, p.112). For a study of southern bells see Kao 1986.
17. The four-ram *zun* is discussed in New York 1980, no. 20.
18. Finds of a buffalo *zun* from Hengshan and an elephant from Liling, both in Hunan province, are reported in *Wenwu* 1978.7, p. 88, and *Wenwu* 1976.7, pp. 49–50; see also New York 1980, no. 24, and Rawson 1983.
19. The *zun* is illustrated in Akiyama *et al.* 1968, pl. 43.
20. The *you* are illustrated in Hayashi 1984, vol. 2, pl. 288, *you* 15; Elisseeff 1977, no. 46.
21. For the axe see Beijing 1980f, colour pl. 13:1, and for the *ding* see Akiyama *et al.* 1968, pl. 10.
22. Bronzes found in Shandong and inscribed with the Ya Chou clan sign revive rectangular Anyang-style vessels. These bronzes were once thought to be Shang in date, but they are now usually dated to the early Western Zhou (*Kaogu xuebao* 1977.2, pp. 23–34).
23. Some authors have suggested that eccentric bronzes were typical of the western area (Watson 1962, p. 50; Loehr 1968, no. 50). Discoveries of large numbers of traditional Shang-period bronzes in Shaanxi, many of which are illustrated in Beijing 1979, have shown this view to be oversimplified.

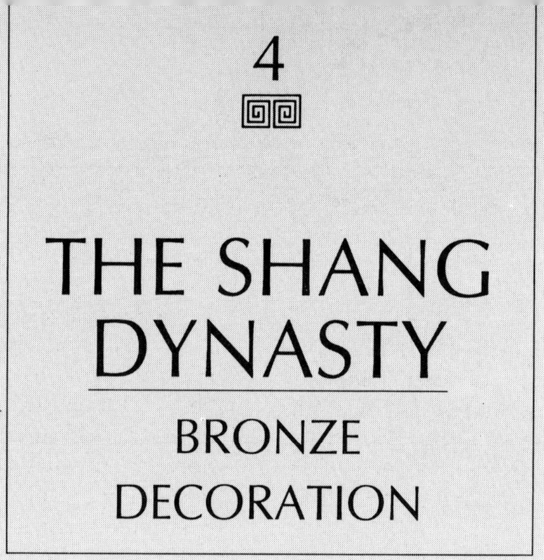

4

THE SHANG DYNASTY

BRONZE DECORATION

Shang-period bronze decoration has been discussed in two very different ways: some scholars have concentrated on meaning, others on design and technique. A search for meaning is stimulated by eyes that look out from so many bronzes. Intuitively we suppose that the casters must have intended to represent a particular creature, be it real or mythological. What is the strange monster that we now call the *taotie* with its large eyes, varied horns and two bodies (Fig. 9)? What was the name given to it by the Shang? What did it mean? We are used to creatures having names, habits and, indeed, meanings; we are baffled by one that falls into no known category.

Other easily recognised animals, birds and insects appear on Anyang bronzes. Their familiarity makes us think that the stranger *taotie* and dragons must also have been real to their creators; but we can recognise only a few of these strange beasts. The Chinese dragon, the *long*, can be identified on many bronzes (it appears on no. 21, for example), but that still leaves the much more common *taotie* unexplained and does nothing to help with other peculiar monsters, often also called dragons, that were conjured up from parts of the *taotie*, such as the creatures on no. 5, the *fang yi*.

Several explanations have been offered. The creatures have been described as totems, as symbols of families or clans. A few writers have gone much further and suggested that they were intermediaries between man and the spirit world. Such theories are based upon comparisons with other, often very different, societies. Alternatively it has been argued that the creatures and their arrangement on the bronzes symbolise relationships within society. The disciplines of anthropology and sociology are invoked to support such claims.[1]

Although these notions have been offered as solutions, they are really better understood as questions. Could the creatures represent totems or gods, spirits or shamans, lords and their vassals? A search for such meanings is perfectly understandable. After all, other peoples in other societies have represented animal spirits and clan totems in their art. The questions are worth while, but we do not yet know the answers to them.

Perhaps the greatest difficulty lies in the absence of contemporary texts that might support one or other of these suggestions. What is worse is that the majority of surviving ancient texts describing religious and ritual matters date from the Eastern Zhou, almost 1,000 years after the founding of the Shang city at Anyang. Not only many centuries but considerable changes in ritual practice separate these two periods. In the middle of the Western Zhou vessel shapes and zoomorphic decoration inherited from the Shang were virtually eliminated. If belief had orginally dictated the zoomorphic decoration, such beliefs must equally have become submerged, ceasing to wield power. When the Eastern Zhou ritual texts were composed, memories of the earlier religious preoccupations had probably all but disappeared.

In addition Shang and Western Zhou zoomorphic decoration varies so greatly over 700 or 800 years as to make any one of the notions proposed appear too simple. Very dramatic changes, for example, took place between the middle of the Erlitou and the end of the Anyang stages. Over this period abstract scrolling patterns centred on eyes alternated with very much more concrete and easily identified zoomorphs. Most commentators on symbolic questions ignore the very long periods of time when rather abstract motifs were current, concentrating on the dragons, birds and *taotie* of the Anyang period.[2] However, any account of bronze decoration must have explanations to offer that are relevant both to the abstract and to the concrete.

So far explanations that have concentrated on design and explained some, if not all, of the changes within the terms of the unusual casting technology adopted by the Chinese have endured best.[3] It is likely that technique and style are not the whole story, but as yet a secure and reliable method of determining the nature of the meanings expressed by the bronze decoration has not been found.[4] Furthermore, even if all or just some of the motifs do represent symbols of a complex religion, it is necessary to start with an analysis of form. Reasons why one rather than another form is chosen are of vital importance in the history of any art, and in making such choices artists and craftsmen are not always guided by meaning.

The first bronze vessels were undecorated. A few Erlitou vessels carry the simplest decoration – a row of projecting bosses and relief striations. At Zhengzhou the situation was transformed and a large number of patterns were used in which creatures, seen either in profile or full face, can be discerned. These faces descended from jade carvings and turquoise inlay found at Erlitou sites (Fig. 3); they must presumably have held some meaning for the jade carvers, but did they have the same import to the bronze casters? What can be established is not the meanings but the principles of design that the casters adopted. In particular, casters copied from jades a symmetrical arrangement of features. On *cong* and jade handles the corners divided the faces whose features filled the compartments on the flat surfaces either side. On bronzes faces were arranged about a vertical line at the centre of each mould section. Eyes, horns and the suggestion of a jaw had to stand either side of the central line. However, because the bronze-casting moulds were much wider than most of the jades, there was room within the width of each section for more than just the features of the face. On early bronzes this area

Fig. 9. Rubbings of *taotie* motifs on Shang and early Western Zhou bronzes to illustrate the chronological progression of designs: (a) Style I – Erligang period; (b) Style II – Erligang period; (c) Style III – Erligang period; (d) Style III – transitional period; (e) Style IV – Anyang period; (f) Style V – Anyang period; (g) triple band based on Style II – late Shang; (h) triple band based upon Style III – early Western Zhou.

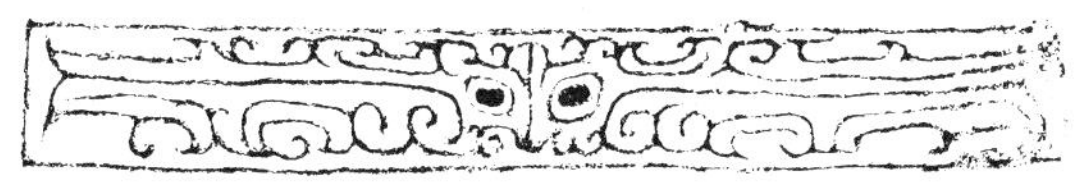
a

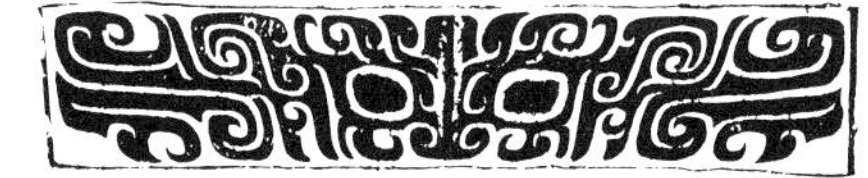
b

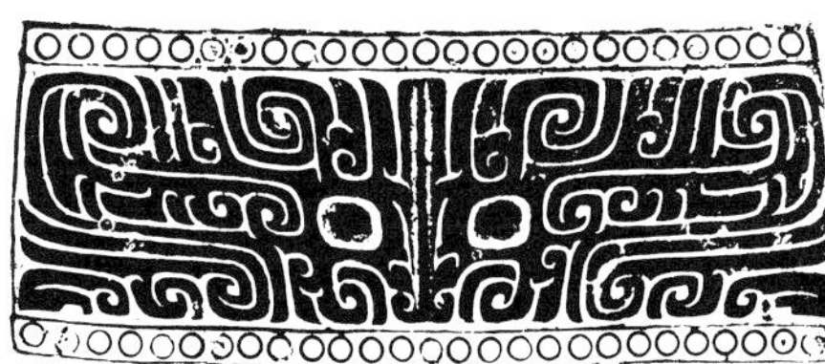
c

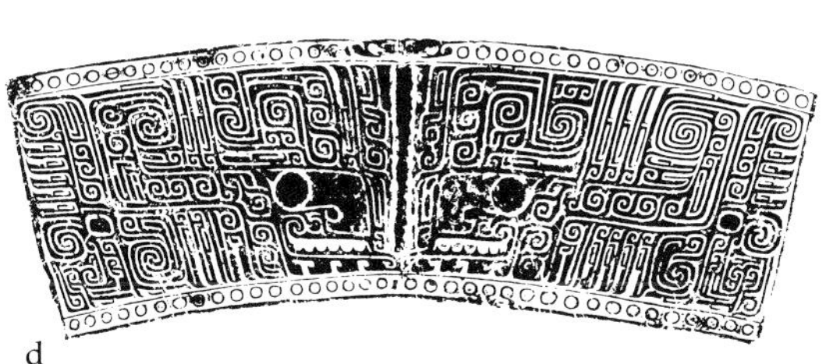
d

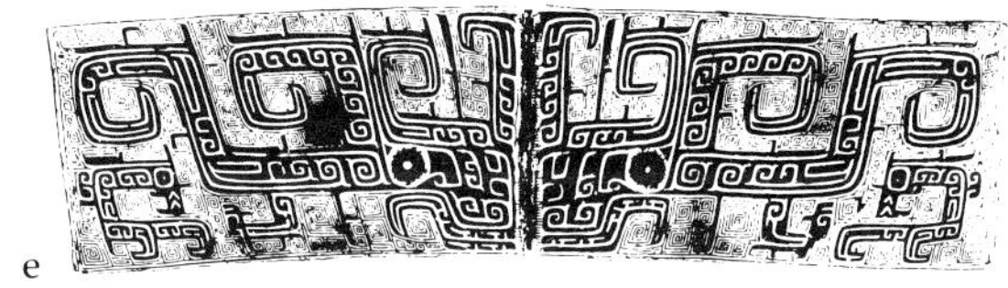
e

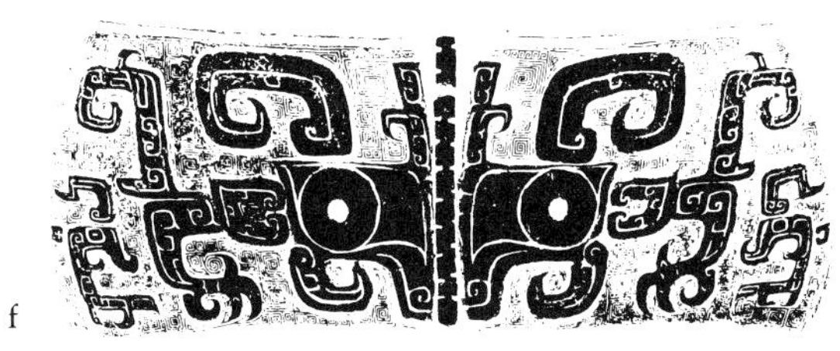
f

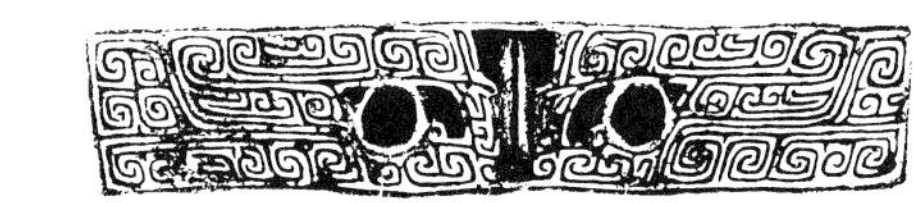
g

h

was filled with elegant scrolls and quills. In due course these fillers were treated as bodies. Because the areas either side of the faces were symmetrical, that is, equal in size, they were filled in time with two bodies (Fig. 9). To understand the two bodies of the *taotie* it is therefore necessary to look not to meaning but to the jade ancestry of the *taotie* and to an obsessive symmetry that that ancestry stimulated.[5]

The *taotie*'s double body has given rise to many theories. In particular, it is often suggested that the bodies were derived from two dragons confronted about the central line to produce a single image; but examination of the chronological evolution of *taotie* faces does not allow this explanation. The earliest types of *taotie* face (Fig. 9a) long pre-date any examples that could be understood as two confronted dragons.[6] On the other hand, some late *taotie* faces were cut apart so that they could be read as two dragons (for example, the creatures below the lip of no. 5).

The principal exponent of the priority of style is Max Loehr. His perspicacious account in 1953 of the chronological progress from simple to complex motifs in terms of five styles was later substantiated by excavation.[7] In Style I, as defined by Loehr, designs were executed in thin relief line (Fig. 9a); such lines could be drawn directly in the mould and were thus technically the easiest form of decoration to produce. In Style II closely related motifs were rendered in broad relief bands (Fig. 9b); such motifs were probably first produced on a model and were then impressed into a mould. Both styles appear on Erligang-period bronzes. None of these early motifs suggest particular creatures. Variation between one motif and another seems a matter of casting choice rather than a question of depiction.

Preoccupation with beautiful surface rather than representation seems to have sustained the development of Style III. This style elaborated Style II to cover vertically much larger areas (Fig. 9c). To do this successfully long upright quills were extended either side of the eyes, nose and jaw of the creatures. Still only very limited features were displayed. The majority of the surface was filled with decorative flourishes. When the space to be filled was large, quills might be relieved by adding another eye. A new creature had been created. In the fourth example illustrated (Fig. 9d) such eyes appear either side of the main *taotie*. We read, as no doubt the caster intended, the outermost quills and hooks as part of a second creature, perhaps an exotic bird, in profile. To date it has proved more useful to consider such additional profile creatures as artistic devices rather than as religious images (Fig. 6).

Similarly on vessels with handles, such as *jue* (no. 1) or *jia*, a Style II or III *taotie* would occupy a full unit diametrically opposite the handle, leaving two half units either side of the handle. On the *jue* (no. 1) such half units of the design are filled with scrolling flourishes and have no zoomorphic content. On later vessels similar scrolls were given an eye, and the viewer could thus interpret them as mythical beasts. Such flourishes were sources of some strange Shang monsters. If they were credited with a meaning, it must have been secondary, being given to an already existing shape.[8]

At Anyang *taotie* faces became almost concrete, and their features and outlines were distinguished from a background of spirals. Separation of the motif from the background had begun in the transitional perod and can be seen in some Style III patterns where small spirals were inserted among the quills. At Anyang spirals were essential features of the design. *Taotie* motifs belong to Loehr's Style IV if they are flush with the background spirals, and to Style V if they are in relief.

The *taotie* faces in Figures 9e and 9f illustrate typical Anyang forms of the beast. Both are symmetrical designs with two bodies conjured out of a maze of scrolls and quills that had extended either side of the face in the earlier patterns. A wide variety of horns could be used, many of these invented by using parts of the *taotie*. In addition, a large number of closely related strange creatures were based upon parts of the *taotie* (no. 5). The variety was almost endless, and none of these creatures seem to have represented known or mythical beasts. They were also quite distinct from the *long*, a dragon that can still be identified because the motif resembles the character in its oracle-bone and bronze inscription forms.[9] A coiled version of the *long* is illustrated on no. 21.

These invented zoomorphic motifs seem to have been devised to fill compartments of different shapes and proportions on angular and highly articulated vessels. Imaginary beasts were much easier to use in this way than real creatures, as they could be extended or compressed, and could be given new heads or different bodies as the shapes of the vessels demanded.

Bronze design benefited immeasurably from such flexibility. Vessel shapes were derived from a reper-

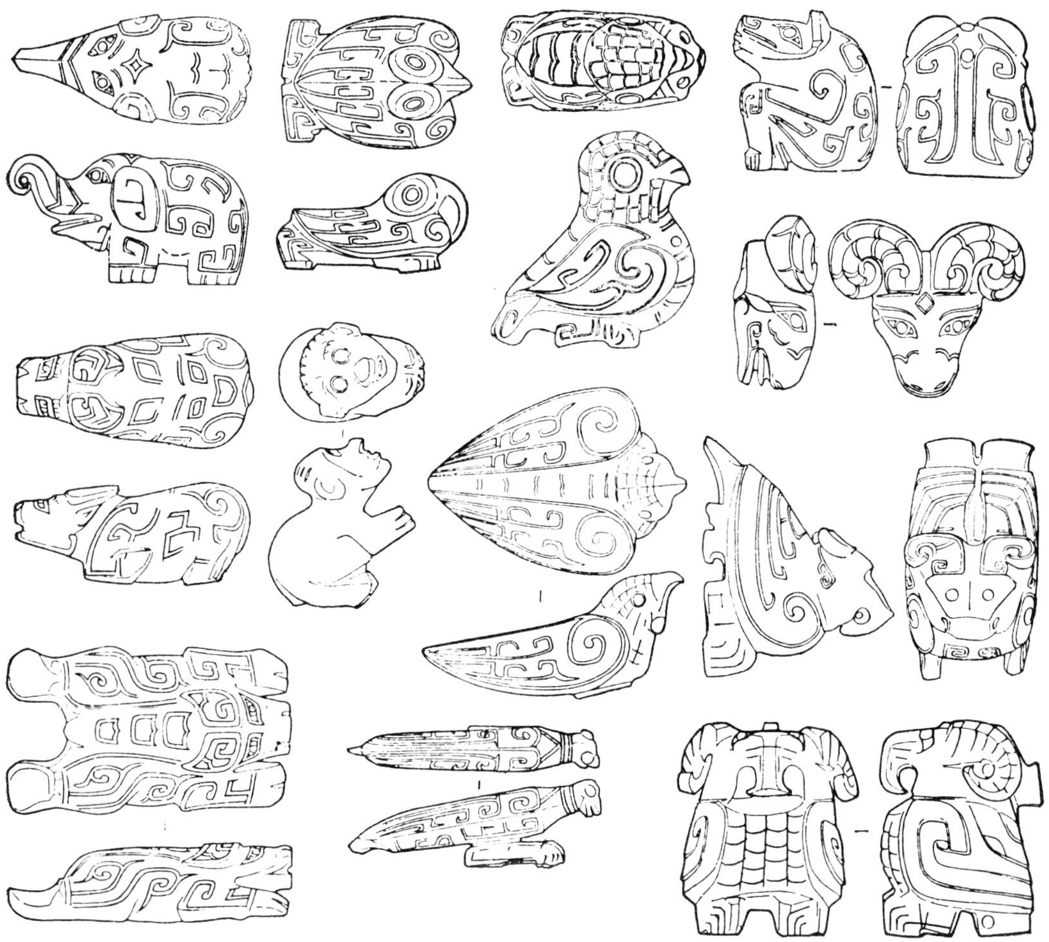

Fig. 10. Jade carvings from Fu Hao's tomb, M5, at Anyang Xiaotun. Shang dynasty, Anyang period. L. of elephant (*top left*) 6.5 cm.

tory of neolithic ceramic forms. To these were added angular forms articulated by flanges, features that were easy to cast in piece-moulds. Flanges in combination with horizontal breaks in the pattern framed compartments and so focused attention on the creatures within them. Advances from rather indistinct *taotie* and dragons to more concrete motifs displayed against a clearly defined ground, invention of new angular vessel shapes, and the use of flanges to articulate the compositions can all be explained within the logic of the casting technology.[10]

Animal-shaped vessels and motifs representing real creatures cannot be explained on technical grounds alone. Anyang casters seem to have become interested in semi-realistic creatures rather suddenly and adopted a bronze-casting tradition first observed in transitional vessels from the north. Turtle, fish and birds appeared on a *pan* from Pinggu Xian at Beijing and on a slightly later *pou* in the British Museum (Fig. 6, rubbing no. 1).[11] Both animal- and bird-shaped containers have come from Fu Hao's tomb (Fig. 7). While clearly depicting imaginary beasts, these vessels are nevertheless convincing. They are also covered profusely with small semi-realistic creatures.

A new interest in zoomorphs that had an existence, real or mythological, outside bronze-casting design is also apparent in jade carving. Small jades from the Fu Hao tomb, for example, illustrate mythical birds, *long*-dragons, tigers, elephants, oxen, sheep and insects, such as cicadas, that invaded the bronzes (Fig. 10). What the jades did not represent were *taotie* motifs with double bodies and dragons based upon parts of the *taotie*, for such designs seem to have been specific to the surfaces of bronzes, determined by their shapes, their techniques and their traditions. Rather limited versions of the *taotie* do appear, but almost invariably only the face, and certainly not in the variety and inventive forms known in bronze. A distinction between two types of bronze motif was therefore expressed in jade.[12]

The connection with jades seems to point to the north-east. In the Hongshan neolithic culture of Liaoning province birds, turtles and dragons appear at a very early date, *c.* 3000 BC, according to present theories.[13] Pinggu Xian, where the very first zoomorphs were noted, is also in the north-east. In addition realistic representation of animals is also a feature of such areas as Shilou in Shanxi and Qingjian in Shaanxi (see Chapter 3). It is possible that all these sites were part of a continuum of a northern culture distinct from the main Anyang tradition that came into contact with it from time to time. Small animal-headed knives found in Fu Hao's tomb are direct evidence of this contact (compare no. 12). In addition *pan* in Fu Hao's tomb decorated with *long*-dragons, fish and birds seem to follow a northern custom. Anyang casting at the time of Fu Hao therefore benefited from two contrasting traditions: non-representational *taotie* motifs and related zoomorphs based on their parts were derived from Henan casting; depictions of creatures, both real and mythological, shown in vessel shapes, surface decoration and small jade carvings seem to have been borrowed from the north.[14]

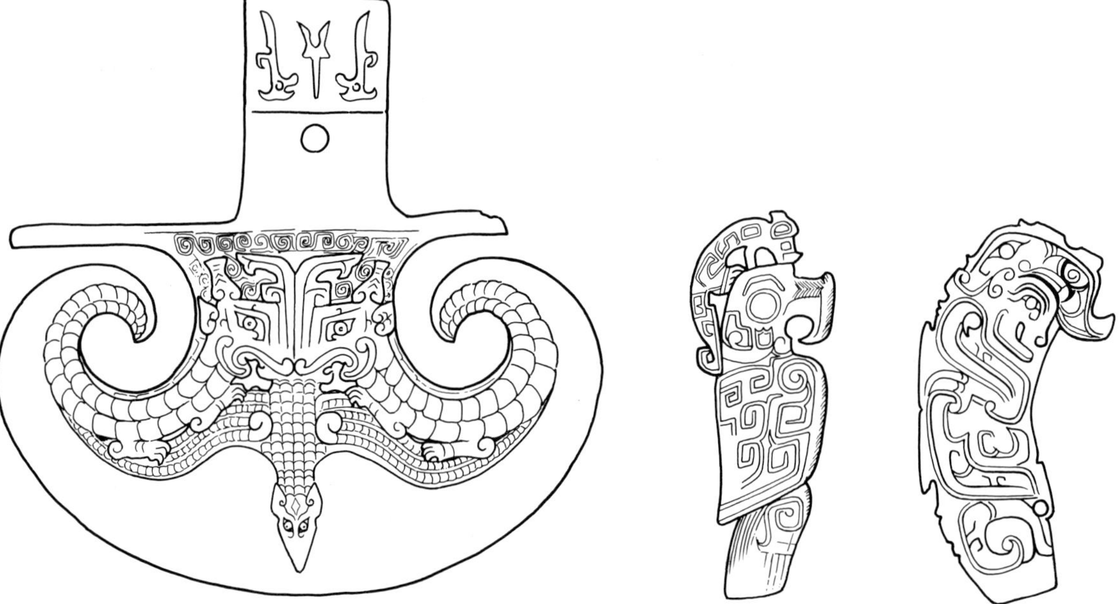

Fig. 11. Animal motifs with one creature grasping another: *left*, on a bronze axe, Shang dynasty, 17.7 × 16.7 cm; *centre*, on a jade carving, Shang dynasty, H. 9 cm, Sackler Collections; *right*, jade carving, Western Zhou, H. 8.3 cm, Sackler Collections.

The enthusiasm for realistic representations lasted only a short time, then the new creatures were tamed and stereotyped; animal-shaped vessels were either abandoned or greatly simplified. In place of the four-legged animal *zun*, jugs with animal-headed lids (known as *gong*, no. 6) seem to have been preferred; bird-shaped vessels gave way to the symmetrical owl *you* (no. 7). Motifs in the shape of birds, dragons and tigers gained fixed forms and fixed usages. They do not, for example, occupy main panels on vessels such as shouldered *zun* or *fang yi*.

Small sculptural figures were similarly limited. Animal heads in the round could stand on the shoulders of vessels and make up handles; a tiger or dragon grasping a figure of a bird was especially popular. The latter motif was peculiarly persistent and survived into the Western Zhou on such vessels as the *Kang Hou gui* (no. 22). While this motif could not appear on a vessel's surface, it occasionally decorated weapons. A curved axe, a shape particularly associated with western China, displays a rare example (Fig. 11). Here a dragon with a scaly body grasps in its jaws what may be a reptile but may equally well be a bird.[15] Related motifs were rendered in jade (Fig. 11). In later times also motifs which seem to have been excluded from vessel surfaces by tradition or rule were employed on small bronzes, such as weapons, and on jades. These practices are not easy to define; however, limitations on what was or was not suitable for ritual vessel decoration are slowly being revealed.

A link with provincial rather than metropolitan areas persistently recurs in the discussion of the most vivid of late Shang-period zoomorphic motifs; for only in the south were vessels in the shape of animals further exploited and explored. Here they survived and flourished. As on the Fu Hao bronzes, their bodies continued to be covered with a multitude of smaller animals. Rams, which were restricted to rectangular panels or small terminals on Anyang bronzes (no. 8), were cast realistically in the round (no. 13).

It is interesting that in the south the *taotie* was less influential and perhaps less well understood than at Anyang. On the ram *zun*, for example, a *taotie* face fills the area below the lip of the container. Its eyes are clear but its other features have dissolved in a maze of lines. On southern bells also *taotie* features were swamped by surrounding intaglio lines; their purposes forgotten, the lines were multiplied, as were the eyes, making the eighteen bosses of the traditional bell (no. 28).[16] This disintegration of the *taotie* at the hands of some southern casters is perhaps the strongest evidence for arguing that Anyang casters and their patrons saw special significance in *taotie* motifs.

But even at Anyang fully developed *taotie* (Figs 9e, 9f) seem to have suffered something of a decline. In the second half of the Anyang period routine copies of much earlier semi-abstract patterns enjoyed a new vogue. These borders are illustrated in Figures 9g and 9h. Their narrow widths and the use of eyes in an otherwise indeterminate pattern of scrolls and quills are features descended directly from the designs developed at Zhengzhou, Panlongcheng and Gaocheng Xian. Such motifs, often designated triple bands, are in effect descendants or revivals of Erligang motifs.

What gave rise to this reversal of the previous hundreds of years of development? Why did the Shang prefer to look backwards rather than forwards, inwards rather than outwards? The answers probably lie in social and economic conditions. We must now consider bronze technology, traditional design practices, contacts with neighbours and possibly economic and political prosperity and decline if we are to elucidate the puzzling motifs of Shang bronze design. Its transformations owe as much to these factors as to the precepts of a religion, or religions, as yet unknown.

Notes

1. The fullest consideration of the symbolism of Chinese bronze motifs is found in Chang 1983; see also Glum 1982 and *Wenbo* 1985.3, pp. 23–8, 13. Hayashi 1986 has a rather different perspective, linking the relationship between different motifs to the relationship between lords and their vassals.
2. Chang has approached the contrasting Shang types of motif by returning to Karlgren's A and B categories (Karlgren 1937). He has postulated two different lineages that were responsible for different types of design (Chang 1964). At present the archaeological evidence does not fully support such an analysis.
3. The principal accounts of the importance of style and technique are given by Loehr 1953 and 1968 and Bagley in New York 1980 and Bagley 1987. Loehr has taken his arguments beyond a discussion of style and also suggested that the bronze motifs have no discernible meaning (Loehr 1980).
4. Sarah Allan in an unpublished paper presented to the Early China Seminar at the School of Oriental and African Studies, London, on 4 March 1986 suggested that the zoomorphic images were not representational but should be approached through a methodology derived from studies of primitive art in other societies. These ideas will be expanded in future publications. However, even this approach shows a tendency to ignore important regional and chronological differences in Shang and Western Zhou bronze art.
5. Throughout this account I am indebted to Bagley 1987.
6. For fuller discussion see Bagley 1987, Introduction, Section 1.5.
7. The five styles are described in Loehr 1953; see also Rawson 1980, p. 67.
8. For a discussion of this phenomenon see Bagley 1987, Introduction, Section 1.5.
9. For discussion of the *long* see Rawson 1983; *Wenwu* 1982.7, pp. 70–5; *Wenwu* 1984.1, pp. 75–83, 29. A clear distinction should be made between the *long* and the various single-eyed beasts assembled from parts of the *taotie*. Such dragons are often called *kui*-dragons, although most authors who discuss *kui* fail to separate them from *long*. The term *kui* only confuses the issue. It is a much later term defined in the *Shuo wen* (compiled *c.* AD 100) as a dragon-shaped spirit with one foot. This description of the single foot clearly refers simply to profile dragons in bronze decoration, most of which are *long*. The rest were derived from parts of the *taotie*.

10. These topics are fully covered in Bagley 1987, in several sections of the Introduction.
11. For the *pan* from Pinggu Xian see *Wenwu* 1977.11, pp. 1–8, fig. 5, and Rawson (forthcoming), fig 55. For decorated sherds from Erlitou see Soper 1966, fig. 7; *Kaogu* 1965.5, pp. 215–24, pl. 3.
12. The jades are illustrated in Beijing 1980f, pls CXXXII–CXLVII.
13. Jades of the Hongshan culture are illustrated in *Wenwu* 1984.6, pp. 1–5; *Wenwu* 1984.11, pp. 1–11; *Kaogu* 1986.6, pp. 497–510; *Wenwu* 1986.8, pp. 1–17. The very early dates given are somewhat surprising. However, even if the Hongshan culture proves to be considerably later, its jades indicate a clear contact between the north-east and Anyang at the period of Fu Hao's tomb.
14. For discussions of the northern zone see Watson 1971 and Lin 1986. Before the date of Fu Hao's tomb *pan* decorated with realistic motifs were already in use (Chang 1980, p. 85, fig. 18).
15. Compare two axes from western China (Li Xueqin 1985b, nos 92, 98).
16. Southern bells are discussed in New York 1980, no. 19, and Kao 1986.

5

THE WESTERN ZHOU PERIOD

The Zhou defeated the Shang in battle and gained their empire. The date of this conquest is hotly debated; the effectiveness of their military action is not in doubt. Before the conquest the Zhou had occupied what is today part of Shaanxi province. Shang oracle-bone texts mention the Zhou both as an enemy and an ally. Bronze-casting had spread to this region in the Erligang period, and the inhabitants of the area continued to adopt Shang practices throughout the Anyang period, making some of their own variations to the metropolitan tradition. Finally the Zhou came to the fore and were able to take advantage of declining Shang power to seize the centre themselves. Dates given in historical sources for the conquest vary considerably between the mid-twelfth and the second half of the eleventh centuries. It is usual to accept a date of *c.* 1050 BC on present evidence.

The history of the Zhou conquest and the subsequent activities of their kings are recounted in one of the earliest surviving Chinese texts, the *Shu jing*. Yet even this work and the other famous early Zhou classic, the *Shi jing*, or 'Book of Poetry', are not contemporary with events described. The Zhou annals in the *Shi ji* are even later. However, both newly discovered oracle-bone texts and bronze inscriptions assembled over several centuries support the bare historical outline recounted in these later texts.

The founder of Zhou fortunes was Wen Wang, a wise and just ruler in traditional accounts. Wen Wang is named in oracle-bone texts recovered at Zhouyuan to the west of present-day Xi'an, where remains of buildings, tombs and hoards have been excavated in recent years. Wu Wang, Wen Wang's son, conquered the Shang, and under his direction the centre of Zhou power shifted eastwards. Cheng Wang, Wu Wang's son, succeeded as a child and ruled at first under the regency of Zhou Gong (the Duke of Zhou), one of the brothers of Wu Wang. A rebellion of that period by the remnants of the Shang peoples was suppressed, and gradually land was handed out to many of the relatives of the royal family and their advisers, establishing control over regions as far north as Beijing. Of the reign of Kang Wang little is known. His successor Zhao Wang is largely famous for having to campaign in the south against peoples known as the Chu and the Jing. He is said to have died on one of these campaigns.

Zhao Wang's successor was Mu Wang, whose reportedly long reign occupied the first half of the period designated as the middle Western Zhou. Legends tell of his fabled journey to the west, but firm historical evidence for such an expedition or for military campaigns is lacking. Mu Wang was followed by Gong Wang, Yi Wang and Xiao Wang. Bronzes that can be dated to this time sometimes bear inscriptions which hint at profound economic and social changes. Among the later kings Li Wang is possibly the best known. The difficulties of his reign resulted in his flight southwards and the establishment of the Gong He regency. The last two Western Zhou kings were Xuan Wang and You Wang. The reign of the Zhou from their western capitals came to an end in 771 BC, when they were forced to flee in front of the invading Quan Rong. This flight signalled the end of the period we now call the Western Zhou to distinguish it from the second half of Zhou rule, which is known as the Eastern Zhou because from 770 BC the Zhou capital was sited in the east near Luoyang.[1]

Excavation has greatly enlarged this picture of the

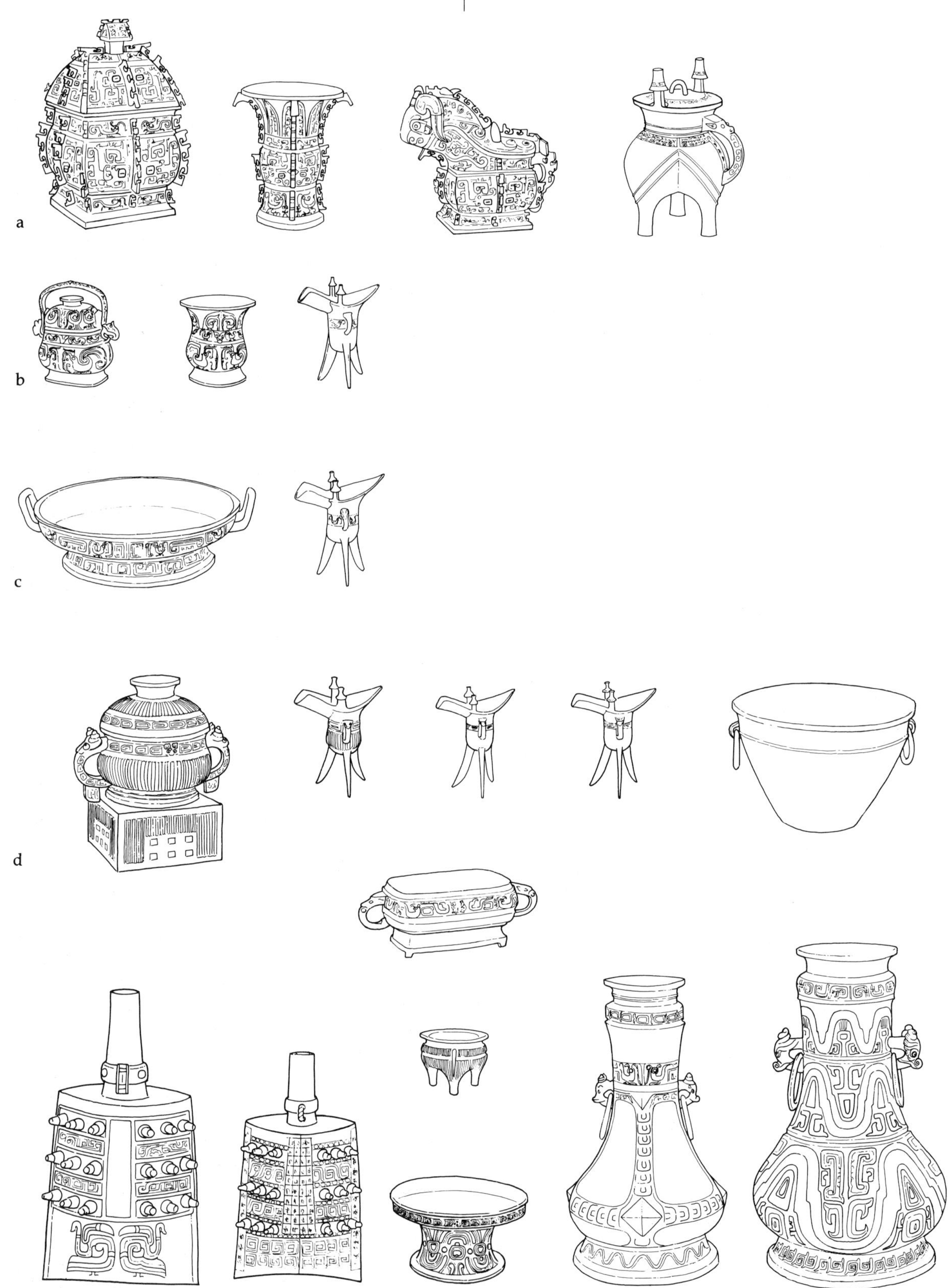

a
b
c
d

Western Zhou. Extensive archaeological discoveries have been made at Zhouyuan, an area that spans the present counties of Qishan and Fufeng Xian in Shaanxi province. Royal tombs have not come to light in this area, but many smaller burials have been excavated. In addition, when the Zhou were forced to flee from this area in 771 BC they seem to have buried many bronzes in the crisis; these hoards have provided rich finds. A large number of sites have also been excavated at the secondary capital constructed by the Zhou near Luoyang and named Chengzhou. Evidence of the smaller states or fiefdoms has come from several parts of China north of the Yangzi.[2]

Many bronze vessels have been revealed. They had now assumed a more political role than their Shang counterparts. Long inscriptions cast in them commemorate political events and record gifts between monarchs and subjects. Vessels for religious ceremony were used to sanctify temporal events and political relationships. A long inscription on a basin known as the *Li gui*, excavated at Lintong in Shaanxi, describes a sacrifice carried out at the time of the Zhou victory over the Shang.[3] The *Kang Hou gui* inscription (no. 22), on the other hand, recounts the granting of land to the Kang Hou (or Marquis of Kang), one of the brothers of Wu Wang, following a successful campaign against the Shang rebels. From such grants small states or fiefdoms, sometimes called lords' states, were established. These grants were an essential to Zhou control of the extensive territory they commanded.

A later inscribed bronze in the British Museum's collection, the *Xing Hou gui*, refers to such petty states (no. 25). It records the casting of the *gui* to commemorate a grant to the Xing Hou of three groups of retainers, and with these men came presumably land. The Xing Hou were descendants of Zhou Gong and held their territory in what is today Hebei province. Another four-handled *gui*, decorated like the *Xing Hou gui* with strange elephant-like monsters, also bears an inscription that names the Xing Hou. It was found in Hebei province.[4]

More information about early Zhou historical events and the bronze styles contemporary with them has come from a hoard of bronzes buried at Zhuangbai, a village in Fufeng Xian at the heart of the Zhouyuan area. This hoard of 103 items included several bronzes cast by members of successive generations of the same family. An account of both the fortunes of the Zhou dynasty and of the affairs of the family is set out in the inscription on a *pan* cast by the archivist Shi Qiang. The family had moved to the west from the Wei territory near Anyang, and their fortunes were evidently mixed up with those of the Zhou court.[5]

The inscription on the *Shi Qiang pan* identifies his ancestors by their posthumous titles – Zu Xin, Fu Jia, etc. – which correspond with the ancestors named in dedications on other vessels in the hoard, and the following chronological sequence of vessels has been established. The earliest vessels belonging to the clan were cast by one Zhe. The surviving items included a *fang yi*, a *zun* and a *gong*, all highly decorated with neatly hooked flanges, and a much more unassuming *jia* (Fig. 12a). Zhe's descendant was Feng. The Feng bronzes are a complete contrast: they are smoothly shaped without flanges and decorated with birds (Fig. 12b). The Shi Qiang vessels which followed belong to the same artistic tradition and are also decorated with birds, but these had started to turn into abstract motifs (Fig. 12c). The bronzes of the following generation have also been identified. These are the Wei Bo Xing or Xing bronzes (Fig. 12d). They illustrate a remarkable change: old vessel shapes have gone, new ones have been established, and new types of decoration have been invented.

Early Western Zhou

As mentioned in Chapter 4, the Zhou inherited the very diverse styles current in various parts of China at the end of the Shang period. These included rounded vessels decorated with narrow registers based on ancient patterns, often known as triple bands (Figs 9g, 9h). Such vessels were ancestral to the *Zhe jia*, for example (Fig. 12a). Also prevalent were stereotyped bronzes with angular shapes, modelled on such vessels as the *Yin Guang fang ding* (no. 10), whose neat rectangular body and restrained relief decoration of snakes and bosses were repeated in many Zhou bronzes. Such standard vessels contributed to the style of the *Kang Hou gui* (no. 22).

However, the *gui*'s large handles crowned by animal heads with vertical horns exemplify a bold

Fig. 12. Vessels cast by several generations of one family, found in a hoard at Shaanxi Fufeng Zhuangbai: (a) the Zhe vessels; (b) the Feng vessels; (c) the Shi Qiang vessels; (d) the Wei Bo Xing vessels. H. of the *Zhe fang yi* (*top left*) 40.7 cm.

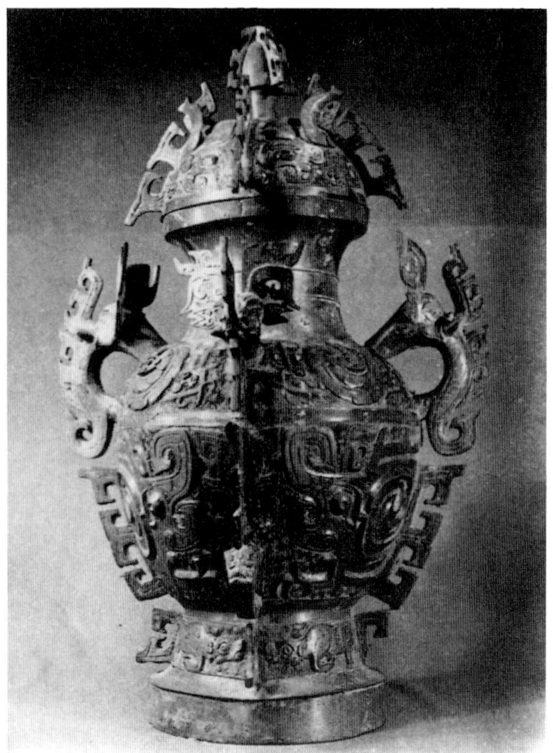

Fig. 13. Bronze ritual vessel *lei* from Sichuan Peng Xian Zhuwajie. Early Western Zhou. H. 70.2 cm.

sculptural style that the Zhou also enjoyed. This forceful quality has caused much speculation. Several scholars have suggested that the style was developed in Shaanxi well before the conquest. Also attributed to pre-conquest Zhou casting are unconventional motifs such as the coiled dragon on no. 23 and the spiky birds on no. 24. However, as yet there is no evidence that this style was prevalent in Shaanxi much, if at all, before the conquest.[6] Most of the Anyang-period bronzes excavated in Shaanxi were highly conventional.

Instead, the unconventional sculptural style seems to derive from both bronzes made in southern China and preoccupations of northern and western China with realistic animal motifs. The southern bronze style that produced the ram *zun* (no. 13) may have penetrated westwards up the Yangzi River to Sichuan, where it was perhaps assimilated to local depictions of both real and fantastic creatures. Several quite extraordinay *lei* are products of this western industry (Fig. 13).[7] These round vessels (derived from ceramic containers) are decorated with small birds on the lids, handles sporting large animal heads, and hooked flanges; their bodies carry coiled dragons as well as *taotie* motifs. Hooked flanges had generally disappeared from Henan and Shaanxi provinces, leaving only a few southern bells and vessels as possible models for these bristling appendages. Bronzes of southern type have been found in Shaanxi and may have stimulated a revival of flanges.[8]

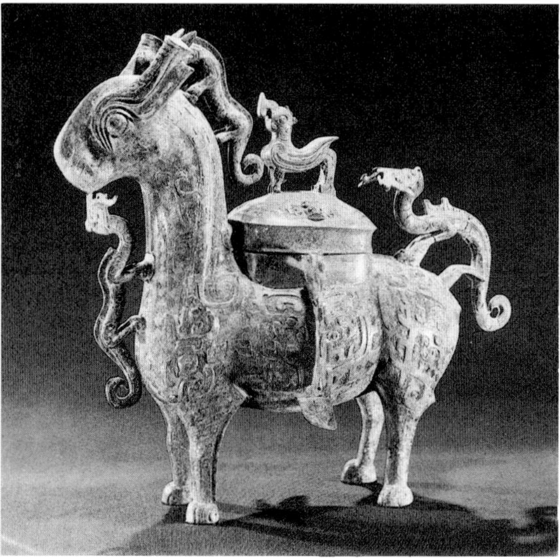

Fig. 14. Bronze ritual vessel *zun* in the shape of an imaginary animal from tomb M163 at Shaanxi Chang'an Zhangjiapo. Early Western Zhou. H. 38.8 cm.

Some support for this view is gained by the recent discovery of an animal-shaped vessel in a tomb at Chang'an Xian outside Xi'an (Fig. 14). The creature is covered with a profusion of smaller animals, giving the container a fractured silhouette. On either side of the body hooked flanges are cast in the shape of birds. At Anyang such animal-shaped vessels had flourished in Fu Hao's tomb, but had declined thereafter; in the south, on the other hand, animal-shaped *zun* seem to have been made for a much longer period. While animal-shapes may have been borrowed from the south, small creatures applied to the back of the *zun* (Fig. 14) came perhaps from north-western casting. Early Zhou vessels thus combined features from several sources.

During the second half of the early Western Zhou this flamboyant style was wedded to more conventional late Anyang design to produce such vessels as the *Zhe fang yi, zun* and *gong* (Fig. 12a). These

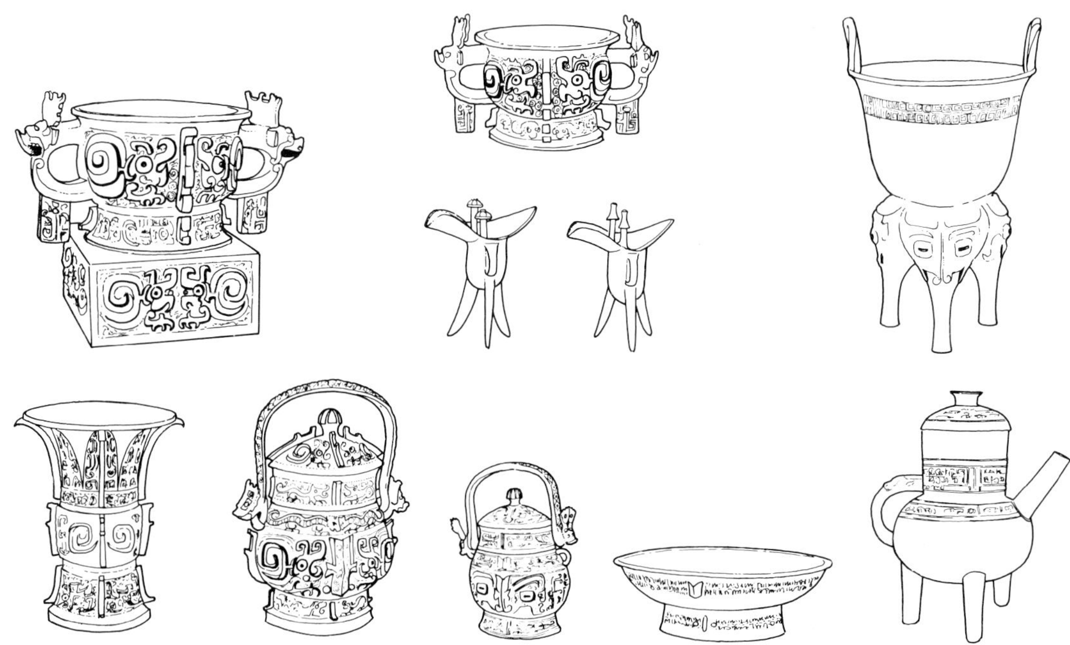

Fig. 15a. Vessels recovered from a tomb at Shaanxi Jingyang Gaojiabao. Early Western Zhou. Two *gui*, two *jue*, a *yan*, a *zun*, two *you*, a *pan* and a *he*. The tomb also held two *ding*, a *gu* and a *zhi* which were too damaged to be restored. H. of *gui* on base 34.5 cm.

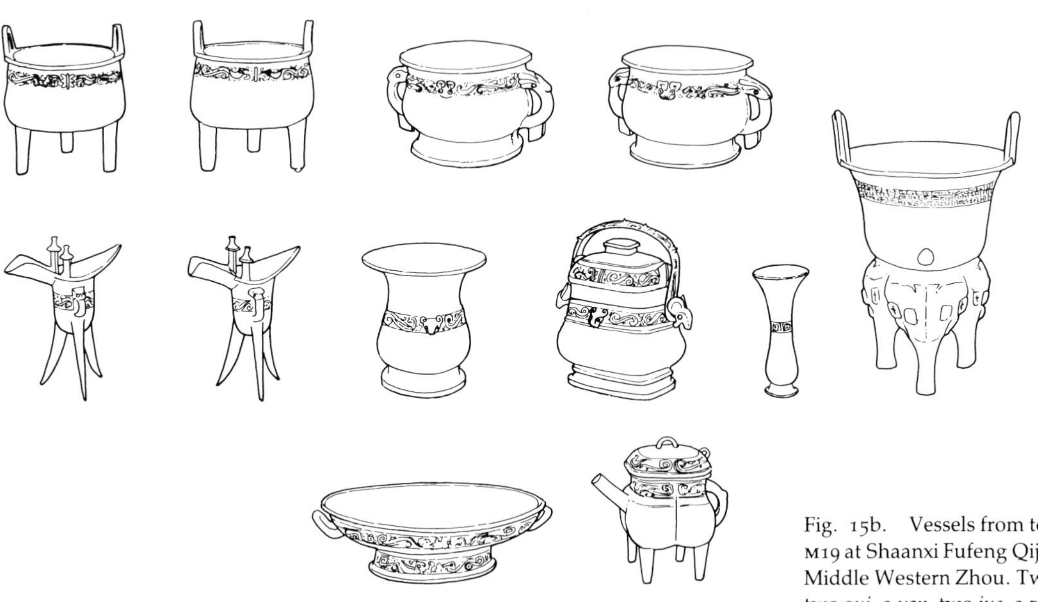

Fig. 15b. Vessels from tomb M19 at Shaanxi Fufeng Qijiacun. Middle Western Zhou. Two *ding*, two *gui*, a *yan*, two *jue*, a *zun*, a *you*, a *zhi*, a *pan* and a *he*. H. of the *ding* 20.4 cm.

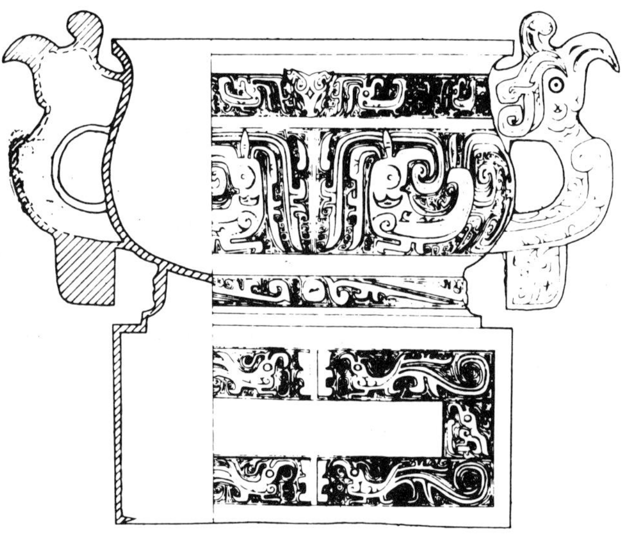

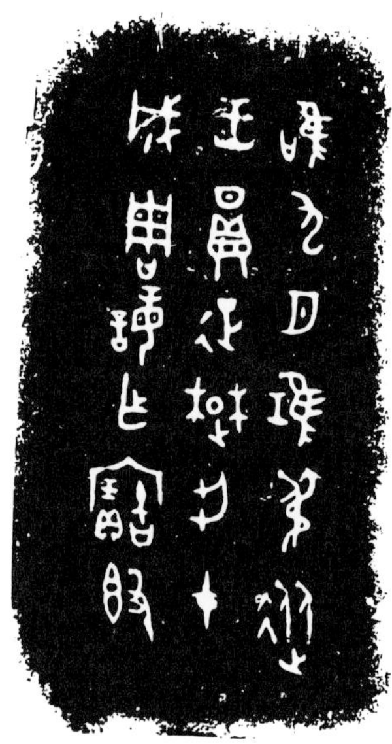

Fig. 16. Bird-decorated *gui* on a square base and its inscription from tomb M17 at Shaanxi Chang'an Huayuancun. Middle Western Zhou. H. 25.5 cm.

bronzes bear hooked flanges developed on early Zhou vessels and carry unusual motifs such as plumed dragons around the foot-rings. The vessel shapes, however, belong to the Anyang tradition. Neatly divided fields of design were inherited from the same source.

Although the Zhou use of inscribed vessels to commemorate political and ritual events had departed from Shang practice, they otherwise followed Shang example in their range of vessel shapes. Bronzes from a tomb in the west at Shaanxi Jingyang Gaojiabao are decorated with coiled dragons typical of the early Western Zhou (Fig. 15a). The assemblage in the tomb included two *gui* on square bases (very popular with the Zhou), two *ding* (now damaged) and a *yan*. The wine vessels comprised two *you*, a cylindrical *zun*, two *jue*, a *gu* and a *zhi*, the last two now damaged. A *he* and a *pan* were probably both used for water.[9] The Zhou emphasis on *gui* is obvious here, but otherwise the set closely resembles a Shang ritual tomb group. Ritual practices must have passed from the Shang to the Zhou with only a few changes.

Middle Western Zhou

For convenience this account of bronze styles is divided at the moment when decoration of large birds was introduced, and this is designated as the start of the middle Western Zhou. Two *gui* from tomb M17 at Chang'an Xian Huayuancun are useful in locating this moment (Fig. 16). These *gui* bear inscriptions that mention the southern campaigns, against Chu and Jing, during which Zhao Wang is thought to have died. The *gui* were probably made during Zhao Wang's reign, or just possibly soon after his death, in the succeeding reign of Mu Wang.[10]

The *gui* carry handles in the shape of birds and stand on square bases. Both bases and basins are decorated with large plumed bird motifs. Their long crests and tail feathers flow evenly across the surface of the bronze, filling out the compartments of the vessels and obscuring the breaks in the design which traditionally fell at the junctions of the mould sections. Such decoration accorded well with the smoothly contoured bronzes of the period, illustrated by the *zhi* (no. 26).

These vessels descended from earlier rounded bronzes decorated with triple bands (Fig. 8) rather than from more angular containers with hooked flanges (Fig. 12a). Bird-decorated bronzes combined simple shapes with elaborate surfaces. The first bird designs were probably contemporary with late forms of exotic elephant, seen, for example, on the *Xing Hou gui* (no. 25), and with an extraordinary plumed dragon. Like the birds, these motifs covered the vessel surfaces continuously.[11]

Often large-scale birds, elephants and dragons were omitted and the vessels carried only narrow registers enclosing small birds or dragons, taking the place of the earlier triple bands. These narrow registers appear on vessels from tomb M19 at Shaanxi Fufeng Qijiacun.[12] Contents of this tomb illustrate the continued survival of early Zhou ritual vessels based upon Shang types (Fig. 15b). Functions had remained the same, but the style was very different. As at Jingyang pairs of *ding* and *gui* are accompanied by a single *yan* as food vessels; the wine containers comprise a *zun*, a *you*, two *jue* and a *zhi*, and the water vessels are a *he* and a *pan*.

This continuity is deceptive. The middle Western Zhou must have been a time of change, upheaval even. Vessels of this period from Shaanxi Qishan Dongjiacun dedicated by one Wei bear long inscriptions recording transactions in which land was exchanged for goods.[13] Such practices deviated from the earlier systems in which land was granted in return for service. Other inscriptions of the time hint at social upheaval.

A tomb of similar date in the middle Western Zhou at Puducun in Chang'an Xian indicates that ritual vessel sets were changing. This tomb contained a new form of *li*, based upon pottery containers, and three bells of a type imported from the south.[14] Such developments had started further west at Baoji. The tomb of a Yu Bo, ruler of the petty Yu state, dated to the beginning of the middle Western Zhou, contained several innovations: anticipating the Puducun tomb, it held *li* based on pottery vessels and bells, *zhong*, introduced from the south. In addition it contained a new vessel type called a *ying*, which replaced the *he*, and a *dou*, rarely made in bronze. In a second chamber within

Fig. 17. Selected vessels from the tomb of a Yu Bo and accompanying burials at Shaanxi Baoji Rujiazhuang. Beginning of middle Western Zhou: five *ding* and four *gui* from tomb M1(1); a *li*, a *ying*, a *dou*, and three bells from tomb M1(2). H. of largest bell 31.7 cm.

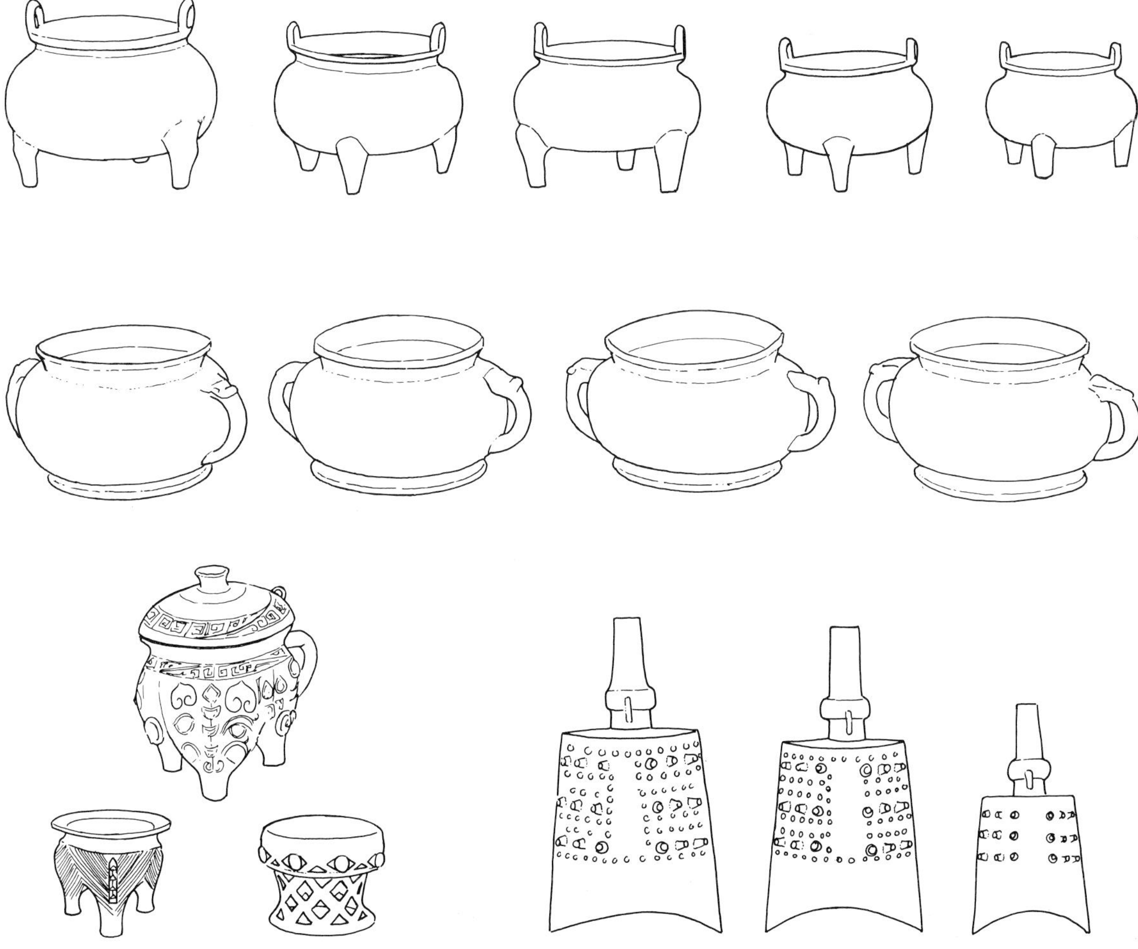

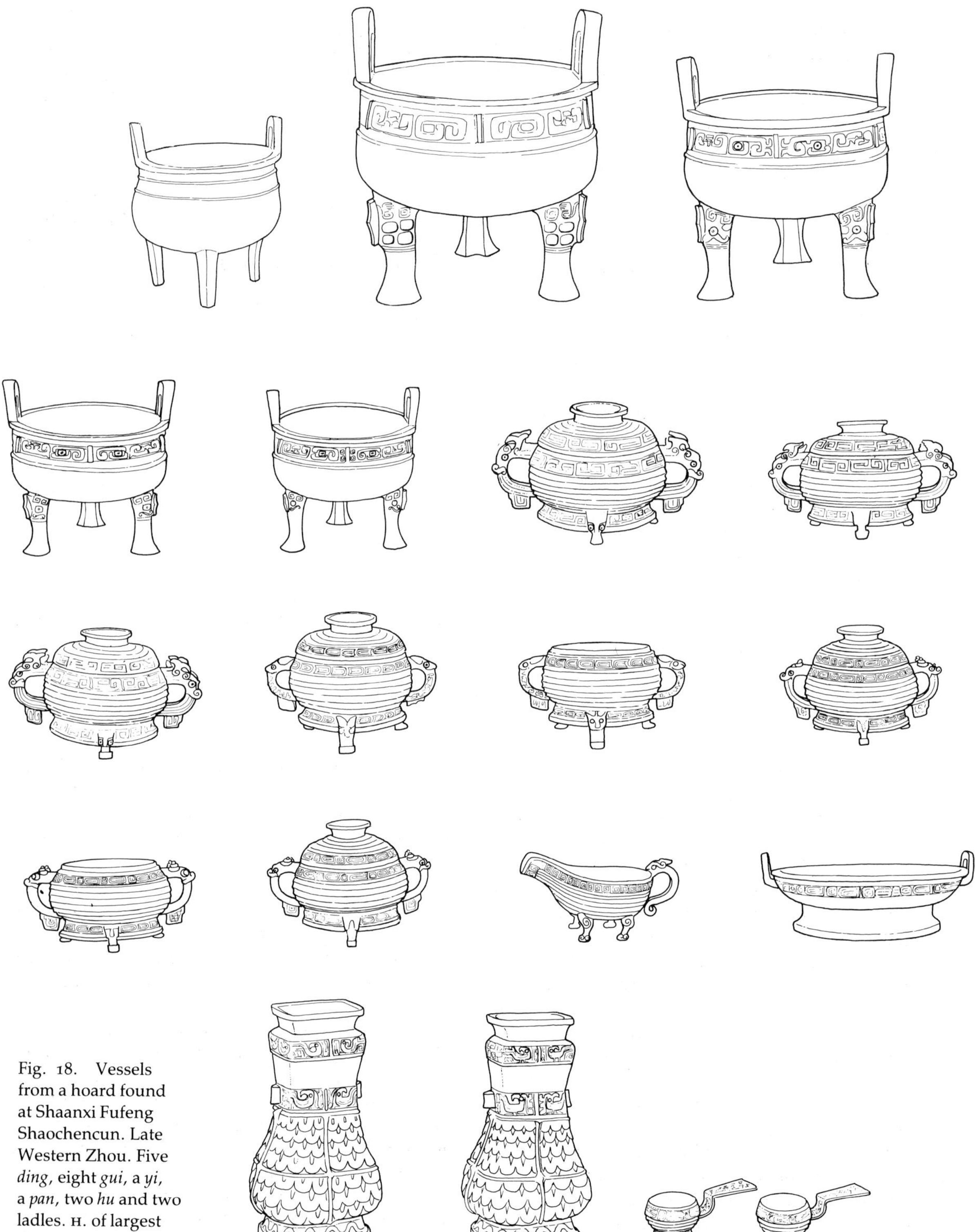

Fig. 18. Vessels from a hoard found at Shaanxi Fufeng Shaochencun. Late Western Zhou. Five *ding*, eight *gui*, a *yi*, a *pan*, two *hu* and two ladles. H. of largest *ding* 47.2 cm.

the tomb another burial was supplied with matched sets of *ding* and *gui*, a new departure in ritual vessel practice that was to be extended across much of China and taken to indicate rank (Fig. 17).[15]

These changes culminated in the manufacture of the Xing vessels, found in the Zhuangbai hoard, which stand at a turning-point in the history of Chinese ritual bronzes (Fig. 12d).

Late Western Zhou

Late Western Zhou is deemed to start when these new vessel types were established as the ritual paraphernalia for sacrifices to the ancestors. The end of the middle and beginning of the late Western Zhou is marked by the Xing bronzes among which new forms predominated. The Xing *jue* are the last remnant of earlier practices. A fully established late Western Zhou vessel set is illustrated by vessels excavated at Fufeng Shaochencun (Fig. 18).[16]

This hoard lacks the wine cups used without a break since the early Shang, the *jue*, the *jia*, the *gu* and the *zhi* (added in the Anyang period). In addition the very popular *you* and cylindrical *zun* had disappeared. Such changes alone effected a complete revolution. The only wine vessels left were pairs of large *hu*. These tall vessels, which were either circular in cross-section, as in the case of the Xing bronzes, or rectangular, as in the case of the Shaochencun vessels, had been invented by enlarging the *you*. However, their use must have differed from that of the *you*.

In place of wine vessels food containers were now dominant. Sets of *ding* and *gui* were used to indicate rank. A feudal lord was entitled to nine *ding* and eight *gui*, a high official to seven *ding* and six *gui*, and lesser officials to ever-decreasing numbers down to one of each. The Xing bronzes include eight *gui* and were presumably matched with nine *li* in place of *ding* or in addition to *ding*.[17]

New vessel types include the *xu*, a rectangular form of *gui*, a *dou* based upon ceramic or more usually lacquer examples, and a rectangular vessel called a *fu* (now sometimes known as a *gu*) which seems to copy containers made earlier in bamboo. Not only were these vessels added to the bronze repertory, but alternative shapes were invented that replaced many existing types.

Li based upon ceramics have already been mentioned. Two other vessel types copying ceramics are illustrated in Figure 19 – a *gui* and a *ying*. It is necessary to emphasise how unusual it is for a cheap material, ceramic, to be copied in an expensive one, bronze. Commonly, goods made first in costly materials are afterwards reproduced in cheaper ones, so that commodities originally beyond the purse of most aspiring customers later become widely available. The reverse process was always less usual. It had happened, of course, when bronze-casting was first invented in China, for at that time the principal models available to casters were neolithic ceramics. It happened again when bronze-casting spread to areas where it had been previously unknown or little used. However, the metropolitan bronze-casters of middle and late Western Zhou were the inheritors of an ancient tradition and of a repertory of well-established shapes; they did not need to look to ceramics for want of other and presumably more prestigious models. Some fashion or fad may have led to the copying of ceramic vessel shapes in middle Western Zhou. It was very probably started in the west where bronze was less well established. Thereafter, the co-existence of old and new that seems to have

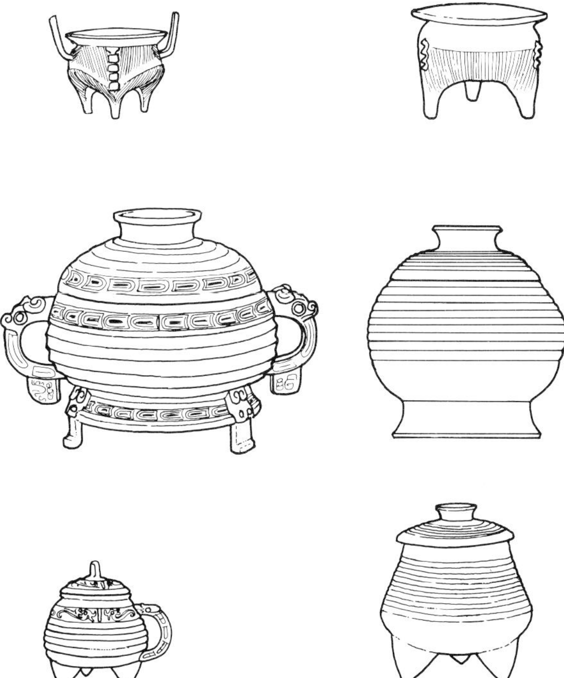

Fig. 19. Drawings to illustrate the derivation of late Western Zhou bronze *li*, *gui* and *ying* from middle Western Zhou ceramic containers. *Left*, three bronze vessels from the Sackler Collections; *right*, ceramic *li* from Shaanxi Chang'an Puducun; ceramic *gui* from Beijing Fangshan Liulihe M51; ceramic vessel with pointed feet from Shaanxi Chang'an Puducun.

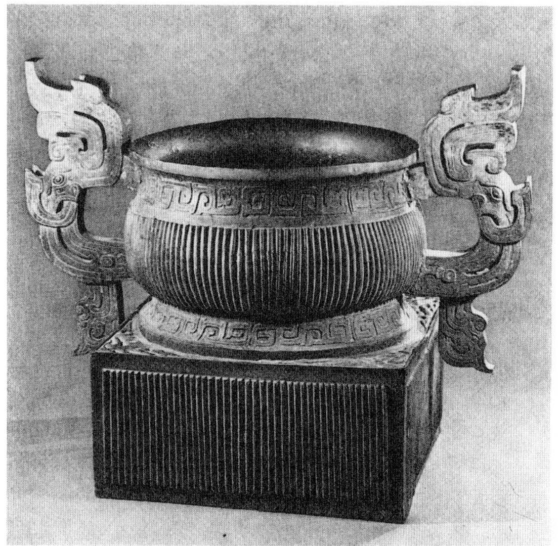

Fig. 20. *Hu gui* and its inscription from Shaanxi Fufeng Famen Qicun. Late Western Zhou. H. 59 cm.

obtained would have been a natural state of affairs. The complete predominance suddenly attained by the new shapes in the late Western Zhou suggests deliberate policy and some centrally made decision to discard the older vessels and adopt the new. A reforming spirit may have valued the newer vessel shapes – even those with humble antecedents – more than those associated with a long Shang pedigree.

Other new shapes seem to have been based on a revival of early Zhou vessels. *Gui* on square bases decorated with vertical ribbing were popular, as the Xing bronzes illustrate. Among the most spectacular is the *Hu gui* cast in the reign of Li Wang (Fig. 20). It combines a square base with ribbing and elaborate handles. All three features revived early Western Zhou characteristics; neither such handles nor the ribbing had been employed in the middle Western Zhou, and square bases also had been relatively uncommon. Ribbed *gui* on bases, therefore, hint at a marked interest in earlier traditions. Some of the same arguments apply to the *yi*, which seems to have been dependent on the *gong*.

At the same time the many zoomorphs so popular on Shang and Western Zhou vessels virtually disappeared. Birds, dragons and *taotie* had become progressively simplified and were finally replaced by almost completely abstract designs. Only small dragons survived. If the *taotie* or bird had had symbolic roles, those roles were now evidently forgotten. Even the surviving dragons seem anonymous fillers of spaces.

Of the abstract patterns a wave design developed from much more ancient blade-shaped ornament proved the most effective. This feature appears round the *Xing hu* (Fig. 12d) and on the *Shi Wang hu* in the British Museum's collection (no. 29). On this second *hu* the design is sunk in great concave bands which were to survive into the Eastern Zhou (Fig. 25). Such textures enliven decoration lacking the compelling eyes that had animated earlier schemes. The wave pattern also had the unique quality of overriding the compartments into which vessel surfaces had been divided by mould sections. From early Shang until middle Western Zhou the casters had observed the logic of these mould sections and had not drawn parts of the pattern across their boundaries. Now that constraint was abandoned. This change paved the way for continuous horizontal borders in place of decoration divided vertically around vessel bodies. Horizontally continuous ornament was to be an essential element of Eastern Zhou bronze style. Indeed, although many late Western Zhou bronzes lack technical or artistic quality, their rigidly controlled shapes and decoration were influential models for casters of the succeeding period.

In addition to the changes enumerated so far Western Zhou casters invented interlace patterns, which were to become a prominent feature of Eastern Zhou design. Interlace is ornament in which motifs, or parts of motifs, were laid over one another or interwoven. If one motif lay over another, a third dimension was implied. Interlinking added further visual interest, as the part which had lain in the background was brought forward towards the viewer. Under the Shang design tradition, in which a single motif was placed within a small or large rectangular compartment defined on the vessel surface by vertical divisions between the mould sections and set horizontal lines, interlace was most unlikely to occur. The motifs were separated from each other by boundaries which the casters did not seem to have considered breaching.

However, during the early and especially the middle Western Zhou animal figures were combined in more intricate compositions in small three-dimensional bronze sculptures and on flat jade ornaments. Small-scale bronze sculpture was an ancient tradition. One animal grasping another in its jaws occurs on both Shang and early Western Zhou bronzes, as illustrated by the handles of the *Kang Hou gui* (no.22). Although such handles were less common in the middle Western Zhou, sculptur-

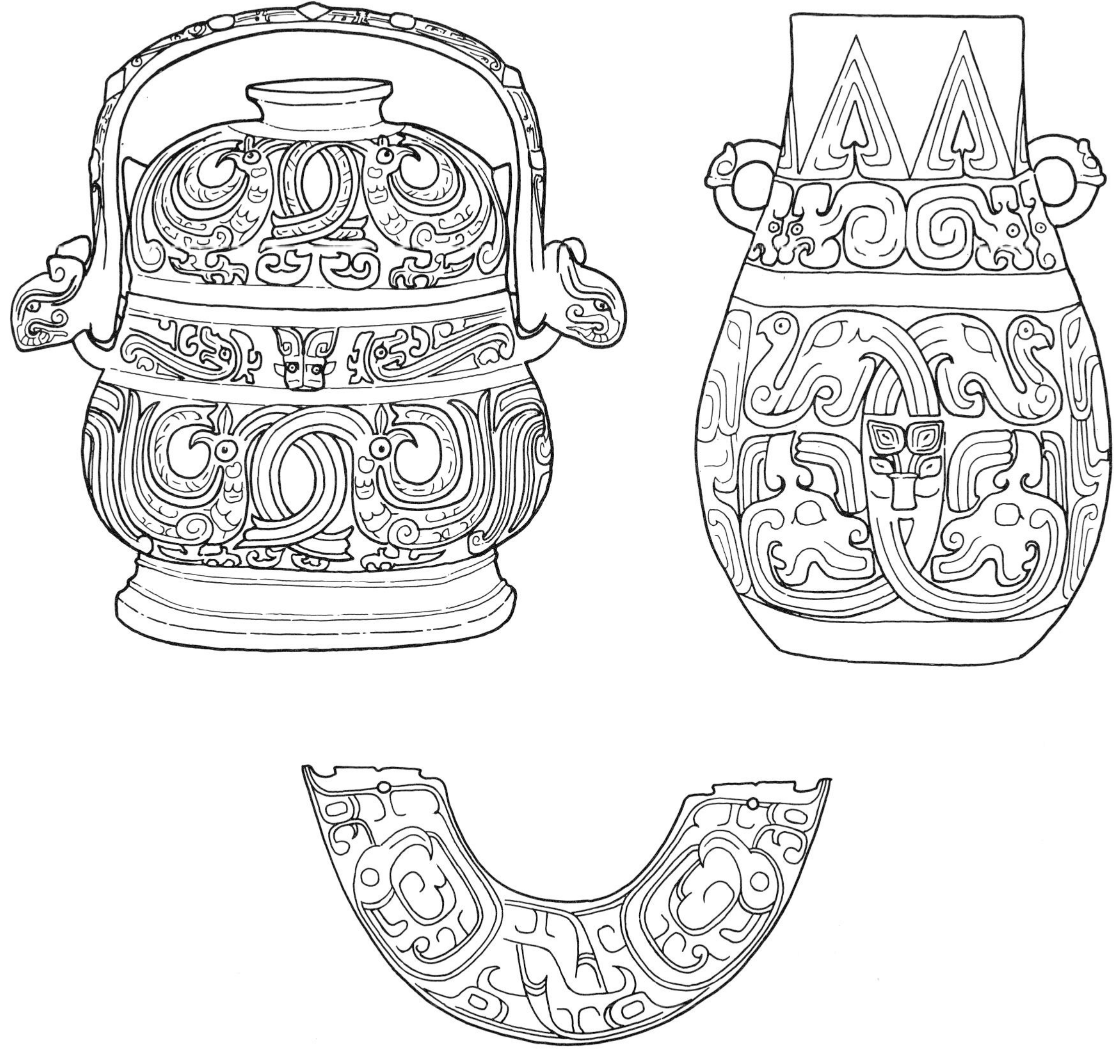

Fig. 21. Early interlace designs: *left*, bronze ritual vessel *you* from Anhui Tunxi, middle Western Zhou, H. 23.5 cm; *right*, bronze ritual vessel *hu*, early Eastern Zhou, H. 25 cm, British Museum, Seligman Bequest (1973.7–26.24); *below*, jade *huang*, middle Western Zhou, W. 14.1 cm, Harvard University Art Museums, Arthur M. Sackler Museum.

al compositions of creatures were revived on bronzes such as the *Hu gui* (Fig. 20). Because such castings are made in the round, the fact that one creature lies over another tends to be overlooked. However, when similar compositions were carved on flat pieces of jade, overlapping and interlinking were much more conspicuous.

A middle Western Zhou jade which shows a figure of a man grasped in the jaw of a tiger is illustrated in Figure 11. Many similar jades are known.[18] On a very few jades the creatures are not just overlapped, they are interlinked. A small jade pendant in the Winthrop Collection in Harvard University Art Museums (Fig. 21) carries a pair of plumed birds similar to those used on no. 26, the *zhi*; it is probably of the same period – the middle Western Zhou. But unlike the bronze, on which each bird is confined to its own rectangular section bounded vertically by the mould joints, the jade carver has interlinked the plumes on the jade. He was not after all constrained by such considerations as mould seams. Indeed, the very small spaces available on jade pendants seem to have inspired carvers to develop such overlapping and interlinking, as this made it possible to cram more on to a surface.

On only a very few bronzes is this interlinking used on the main decorative surface of the vessel. A *you* from a southern site at Tunxi in Anhui province is one of these exceptional pieces (Fig. 21).[19] Its shape and high technical quality are characteristic of metropolitan Zhou casting; so too is its inscription. However, the birds' crests interlinked across the mould joint are unorthodox and suggest that the piece may have been made in the south-east, perhaps by a caster brought there from metropolitan areas further north and west. As described in Chapter 6, the south-east seems to have been unaffected by the revolution in ritual vessel types and designs experienced at the centre, and thus middle Western Zhou vessel shapes and motifs were preserved in the south-east long after they disappeared from metropolitan centres. Plumed bird motifs, both separate and interlinked, survived in the local industries of Anhui and Jiangsu.[20]

These provincial interlaced motifs were probably essential intermediaries in the history of Chinese interlace,[21] for late Western Zhou metropolitan bronzes were singularly drab: the motifs employed were very limited indeed, and it seems that interlace was not allowed to intrude upon the main areas of vessel bodies. Only a very few major late Western Zhou vessels carry interlace, and then usually only in subordinate positions. On the *Da Ke ding* in the Shanghai Museum, for example, dragons are interlaced on the outer edges of the handles – a relatively inconspicuous position. The *ding* body itself bears a wave pattern.[22] Interlace was much more freely employed on some small bronzes, such as ladle handles.[23] In this respect its use on vessels seems artificially restricted. Such restraint hints at the existence of rules or a code for ritual vessels that was perhaps connected with the revolution in ritual practice.

In the Eastern Zhou these limitations were ruptured. Competing politically independent states patronised different foundries. Provincial areas came into their own, standing in parallel with descendants of the metropolitan Western Zhou casting. Out of this medley of traditions a new wealth of bronze-casting styles was developed.

Notes

1. For the history of the Western Zhou see Creel 1970 and Xu Zhuoyun 1984.
2. Excavation reports are listed in Rawson (forthcoming), Appendix 1.
3. The *Li gui* is described in New York 1980, no. 41, where publication of its inscription is cited.
4. The *gui*, known as the *Chen Jian gui*, is discussed in *Kaogu* 1979.1, pp.56–9, 88. Although the *Xing Hou gui* and the *Chen Jian gui* are dated by Li Xueqin and other scholars to the early Western Zhou, they may be as late as the first part of the middle Western Zhou. Their depressed silhouettes are similar to that of the *Ban gui* and other vessels of that time (Hayashi 1984, vol. 2, pls 107–8).
5. For discussion of the inscriptions on the vessels from the hoard see *Kaogu xuebao* 1978.2, pp. 139–48, 149–58; *Gu wenzi yanjiu* 7, 1982, pp. 87–101.
6. Attention has been concentrated on the so-called Baoji sets (Watson 1962, p. 50; Loehr 1968, no. 50).
7. The *lei* have come from two separate caches reported in *Wenwu* 1961.11, pp. 28–31; *Wenwu* 1980.12, pp. 38–47; *Kaogu* 1981.6, pp. 496–9, 555. A very similar *lei* has been found in Liaoning province (*Wenwu* 1977. 12, pp. 23–33, pl. 2:2). A further example from Shaanxi Qishan Hejiacun shows that the manufacture and use of these exotic *lei* were shared by all three regions (*Wenwu* 1972.6, pp 25–9, fig.4).
8. For vessels in southern style found in Shaanxi see *Kaogu* 1980.3, pp. 211–18, pl.2:4; *Kaogu yu wenwu* 1986.5, pp. 12–22, fig.5:4. This contact was first noted by Robert Bagley (New York 1980, p. 201).
9. The excavation of the bronzes is reported in *Wenwu* 1972.7, pp. 5–8.
10. For a report of the excavation of the *gui* and discussion of their inscriptions see *Wenwu* 1986.1, pp. 1–43.
11. The plumed dragon appears around the foot-rings of the Zhe vessels, on the *Yan Hou yu* (New York 1980, no. 53), and on a basin formerly in the collection of J. T. Tai whose inscription refers to the thirty-fourth year of a king, who is probably Mu Wang (Cheng 1963a, pl. 17b; Barnard and Cheung 1978, no.156).

12. The excavation is reported in *Wenwu* 1979.11, pp. 1–11.
13. The Wei vessels are discussed in *Wenwu* 1976.5, pp. 26–59, 63.
14. The excavation report is found in *Kaogu xuebao* 1957.1, pp. 75–85.
15. The excavation of the Yu Bo's tomb is described in *Wenwu* 1976.4, pp. 34–56; for discussion of the terminology of *dou* and *fu* see *Wenwu* 1982.6, pp. 70–3, 85.
16. For the excavation report see *Wenwu* 1972.6, pp. 30–5.
17. For the early history of vessel sets see Yu Weichao and Gao Ming 1978. Li Xueqin 1985c, pp. 463–4, describes the system of ranks and the numbers of *ding* and *gui* appropriate to each.
18. Rawson 1980, fig.98.
19. *Wenwu* 1965.6, p. 52.
20. For local copies of the metropolitan style of the *you* see *Kaogu xuebao* 1959.4, pp. 59–90.
21. An early Eastern Zhou *hu* from Tai'an in Shandong province is an example of the reuse of a formula known since the middle Western Zhou in eastern China (*Wenwu* 1986.4, pp. 12–14, pl. 1:4).
22. Shanghai 1964, no.47. The only major Western Zhou vessel whose body is covered with interlaced dragons is the *Song hu* (Rong Geng 1941, 2.724).
23. Examples are found on two ladles from the Zhuangbai hoard (Rawson (forthcoming), fig.163; Beijing 1980b, nos 82, 83).

6

THE EASTERN ZHOU PERIOD

In 771 BC Zhou centres of power in the west near Xi'an fell to the invading Quan Rong; the first half of the Zhou rule, known as the Western Zhou, was over. The following period, known as the Eastern Zhou, with the Zhou capital at Luoyang, is divided into two sections: the Spring and Autumn period (770–475 BC) and the period of the Warring States (475–221 BC). These names are taken from two texts that describe events of the time.[1] The Zhou period ends when China was finally unified under the western state of Qin.

Nominally the Zhou kingdom survived after 770 BC, established at what had previously been the secondary capital. In practice, however, power passed to lords of large and small states. Subdivision of Zhou-dominated lands had always been a danger inherent in Western Zhou rule. The kings had ruled by delegating powers to their relatives and members of other great families, who, over the second half of the Western Zhou, must have become increasingly independent. Disruption of the Zhou court inevitably gave authority to new states formed in the aftermath of the flight from the west. Some of the states endured a few centuries; others thrived during the whole of the Eastern Zhou. In discussions of the history of the bronze vessels a few of these states are particularly relevant.

Bronzes from the Zhou capital near Luoyang are not always impressive. A chronologically arranged series of excavated bronzes from Zhongzhoulu at Luoyang is useful as a yardstick against which to measure some bronze-casting developments.[2] Centres of interest, however, shift just as the centres of power moved. Bronzes from the state of Zeng in Hubei and Guo in Henan illustrate the survival of Western Zhou styles. Development of this inheritance can be plotted in central and southern Henan, in the lesser states and fiefdoms of Zheng, Huang and Fan. In due course this area came under the control of the great southern state of Chu, whose power marched alongside that of the northern state of Jin. Gradually Chu swallowed up more and more territory, annihilating in the east Wu and Cai, states which contributed bronzes important to the discussion. Jin, on the other hand, was subdivided between the families of Han, Zhao and Wei, a position formally acknowledged by the Zhou king in 403 BC.

To the east and north were the states of Qi and Yan. Both areas have produced many bronzes, but there is not space to consider them separately here. Qin industry in the west was for some centuries rather conservative. As the state's power grew in the fourth and third centuries, its bronzes became more influential, leading rather than following prevailing trends.[3]

Spring- and Autumn-period ritual vessels appear in sets similar to those employed under the Western Zhou. *Ding*, *gui* and pairs of *hu* survived, although the *gui* became gradually less important. New shapes were added, especially a large basin or *jian*, a jar with a constricted neck and lid called a *fou*, and a vessel of circular cross-section in two parts, each of which could stand independently of the other, known as a *dui*. Despite these changes, which were accompanied by considerable regional variation and startlingly different artistic styles, the ritual vessel repertory remained fairly static; nothing like the Western Zhou revolution took place.[4] A relatively new development was the high value placed on bells. Large sets were buried in many tombs, and their fine casting is often pertinent to the progression of decorative styles.

Bronzes document inter-state rivalry, bargains and marriages. Examples from one state turn up in burials of another because marriages or conquests brought vessels or weapons of one state into the hands of a new owner. In place of gifts and grants from the Zhou king described in Western Zhou bronze inscriptions, Eastern Zhou bronzes illuminate alliances and contests between the states. Above all they represented the power and prestige of their owners.

Early Eastern Zhou; eighth to early sixth centuries

Early Eastern Zhou bronzes descend directly from those of the Western Zhou. The Guo state cemetery excavated at Shangcunling near Sanmenxia in Henan province provides numerous examples. The Guo ruling house had moved eastwards in parallel with the Zhou court. Since Guo was conquered by Jin in 655 BC, the bronzes must have been made before that date. The largest tomb excavated, tomb M1052, contained seven *ding*, six *li*, one *yan*, six *gui*, one *dou*, two *hu*, a small jar known as a *guan*, a *he* and a *pan*.[5] Such a set might have graced a late Western Zhou burial.

Other early eastern Zhou vessels, perhaps also associated with the Guo state, have been excavated at Jia Xian Taipuxiang.[6] A small *hu* in the British Museum resembles one from this site and is probably contemporary with it (Fig. 21). Large-scale interlaced patterns in broad, rather slack ribbons decorate the *hu* and some of the vessels from Taipuxiang. As discussed in Chapter 5, interlace woven across principal vessel surfaces may derive from eastern provincial casting.[7]

Over about a century large interlace patterns diminished in size until they covered the vessels in a dense even texture, on which tiny dragons' heads and bodies were hardly visible. Mid-way between the British Museum's *hu* (Fig. 21) and the tiny interlace of the sixth century (illustrated on no. 32) stand the contents of the tombs of a lord of the Huang state and his wife near Xinyang in Henan province. Huang was overcome by Chu in 648 BC, and thus the tombs must date before the mid-seventh century.[8]

Man and wife were buried side by side in lacquered coffins. The tomb of the Huang lord contained two *ding*, two *dou*, two *hu*, two *guan*, a *pan* and a *yi*; that of his wife held rather more bronzes – two *ding*, two *dou*, two *hu*, two *guan*, two *he*, two *li*, another single *guan*, a *pan* and a *yi*, and some smaller bronzes. Both tombs were well supplied with jades, the wife's containing rather more than her husband's. Patterns on the vessels are confined to fairly narrow registers, within which various dragon motifs, inherited from the Western Zhou, overlap and intertwine (Fig. 22c).[9]

Tight and dense motifs occur on bronzes excavated in 1923 from a tomb at Lijialou at Xinzheng Xian in southern Henan attributed to the small state of Zheng. The bronzes are extremely diverse in type and decoration and have provoked much debate. However, Li Xuequin's proposed date for the burial in the first quarter of the sixth century seems likely.[10]

The special interest of the Xinzheng bronzes is their diversity. Several vessels carry very large-scale ornament. Two *hu* are covered with raised interlace embellished with intaglio lines. Other *hu* bear straps defining rectangular compartments filled with deeply sunken motifs. Both these *hu* types and their textured relief patterns have Western Zhou counterparts.[11] A large round jar with a constricted neck, known as a *fou*, from the same site is decorated with sunken patterns of Western Zhou origin and also displays writhing snakes of much more unusual type, perhaps derived from the southern state of Chu (Fig. 22a). The snakes are intertwined and distinguished from one another by the different patterns on their bodies; these same snakes turn up again among bronze decoration from the Jin state.[12]

The Jin state

The lords of Jin, descendants of one of the brothers of Cheng Wang, were established in southern Shanxi well before the fall of the western capital. After the Zhou flight eastwards, Jin and Zheng became powerful supporters of Zhou. Several capitals were occupied by Jin. In 585 the Duke of Jin moved the capital to Xintian, which has now been identified at Houma in Shanxi province. Workshops littered with bronze-casting mould fragments were discovered south of the city site. This find located in Jin a bronze style that had been recognised first in a group of vessels discovered much further north at Liyu near Hunyuan. Liyu-type bronzes are, however, only one of many varieties for which moulds are known from Houma.[13]

Within the history of the Liyu style and the Houma foundries the *Zhao Meng jie hu* (no. 34) are key items: their inscriptions are essential to the

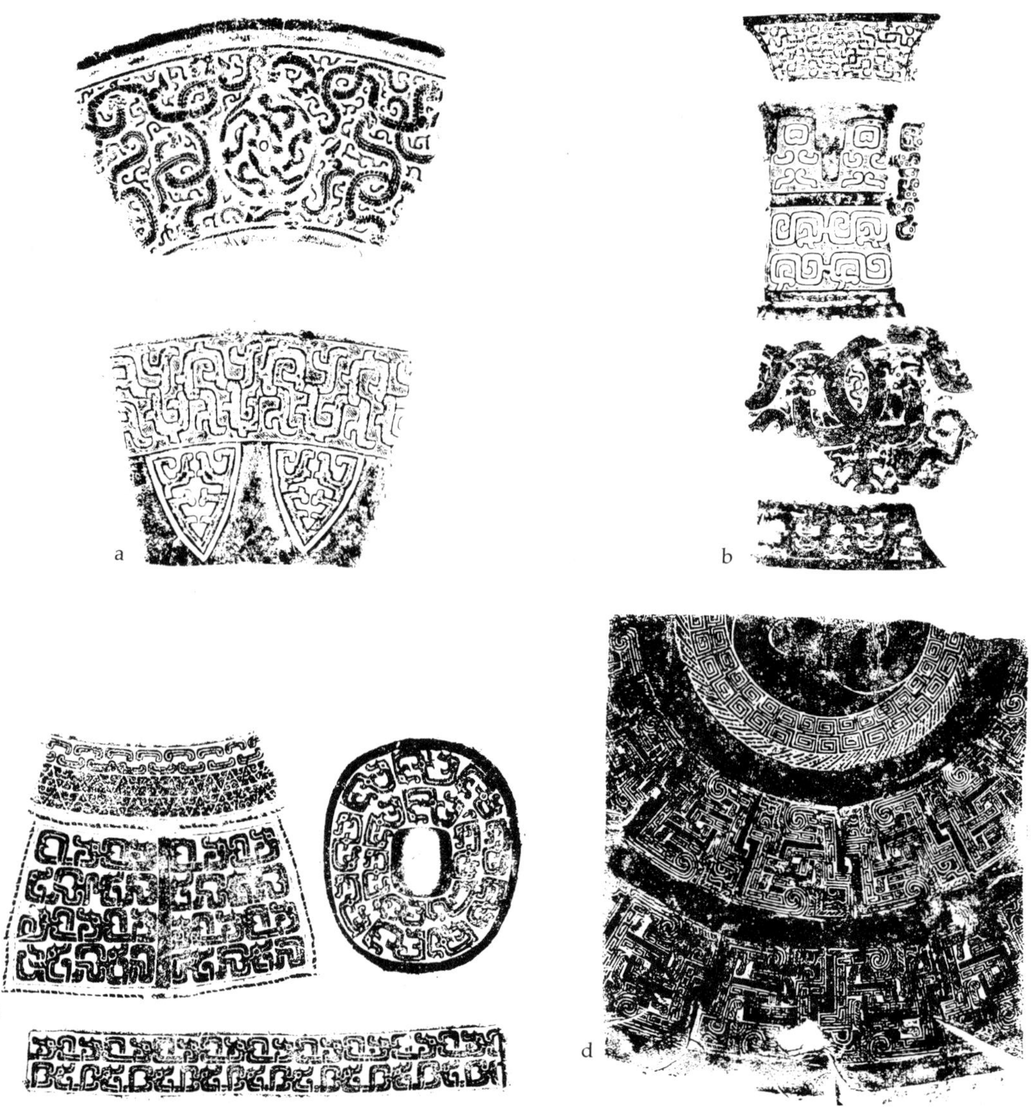

Fig. 22. Interlace on early Eastern Zhou bronzes: (a) snake motifs and abstract sunken ornament both on a *fou* from Henan Xinzheng Lijialou, Zheng state, 6th century BC; (b) interlaced snakes and abstract motifs on a large *hu* from tomb M13 at Shanxi Houma Shangmacun, Jin state, 6th century BC; (c) on bronzes from tombs at Henan Xinyang, Huang state, 7th century BC; (d) on a *ding*, proto-Liyu type, from tomb M269 at Shanxi Houma Fenshuiling, Jin state, 6th century BC.

dating of the Liyu style. The sequence that culminated in the decoration of these *hu* started in the sixth century with the diverse bronze styles noted on the Xinzheng vessels. Tomb M13 at a cemetery at Houma Shangmacun contained bronzes that parallel the Xinzheng find. Large *hu* are decorated with interlocking dragons in relief (Fig. 22b); around the neck and lid are sunken Western Zhou-type motifs; openwork enlivens the lids, the handles and the foot-rings. Other vessels from the tomb display the tiny interlace of the sixth century.[14]

Later stages of Jin casting are revealed by the

contents of tombs M269 and M270 at Changzhi Fenshuiling. On these bronzes sunken motifs seen on the Shangmacun *hu* have been reduced in size, small interlace is present, and a new type of textured interlace is introduced. This design is based upon the small interlace, lying flat with the surface of the bronze; the strands of intertwined dragons have been pulled apart and the vacant space filled with striations. The design is sometimes called proto-Liyu (Fig. 22d).[15]

Proto-Liyu designs date from the mid-sixth century or slightly later and were followed by a wide variety of interlace in which the strands were raised in relief, textured with intaglio lines, and punctuated with dragon heads or rounded studs.[16] Out of these experiments arose the classic Liyu dragon pattern. One high-relief variety is illustrated on the *Zhao Meng jie hu* (no. 34) dated to *c.* 482 BC. This strap-like ornament is often thought to have been preceded by varieties in low relief, but this is by no means certain, especially as low-relief and flat varieties certainly survived in the Warring States period, long after the high-relief type had disappeared.

Taotie interlinked with dragons on the *Zhao Meng jie hu* hint at regional contacts that contributed to these high-relief designs. A sequence of development within Jin bronze-casting alone cannot account for the faces or indeed the fractured sections of interlace (proto-Liyu motifs are continuous). As central designs on vessel bodies, *taotie* faces had disappeared during the middle Western Zhou; they were victims of the dramatic revolution in vessel shape and design. Eastern provincial foundries, however, seem to have been immune to these radical changes – for example, plumed bird motifs survived in the south-east (Fig. 21). In the same way *taotie* motifs seem to have been preserved in the east. Excavation of an early Eastern Zhou tomb at Shandong Yishui Liujiadianzi has revealed a *ding* decorated with a *taotie* face and surrounded by fractured sections of relief (Fig. 23). Sharp brows over the eyes recall much earlier *taotie* faces.[17]

The faces on the *Zhao Meng jie hu* suggest that the casters knew something of such eastern relief designs; they combined the eastern *taotie*, however, with the snake patterns of the Xinzheng *fou*. Between the *fou* (fig. 22a) and the *hu* (no. 34) stands the set of Lü bells from the Jin state, of which one is in the British Museum (no. 33). In place of the usual Western Zhou-derived dragon patterns at the lip of the bell, a blind *taotie* is composed of small snakes

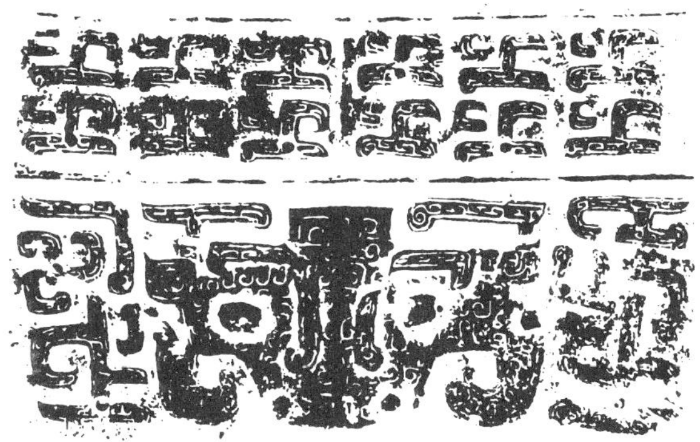

Fig. 23. Rubbing of a *taotie* face on a *ding* from Shandong Yishui Liujiadianzi. Early Eastern Zhou.

(rubbing no. 14).[18] Along the backs of the creatures which form the horns v-shaped patterning mimics snake designs on the *fou*. These snakes are repeated on the *hu*, where they make the horns of the *taotie*, being hooked into its brows and then coiled with the dragon interlace.[19] While the sources of the motifs on the Liyu bronzes can be traced to Shandong and Xinzheng, emulation of the extraordinarily inventive relief decoration on Chu state bronzes may have motivated these various restless experiments.

Both the *hu* (no. 34) and the bells (nos 33 and 35) belong to the apogee of Houma production. Later bronzes decorated with dragon interlace declined in quality. In the north invention passed to inlay decoration discussed below.

Southern China: the states of Wu, Cai and Chu

Although the bronzes from Luoyang and the Jin state are sometimes treated as the metropolitan styles of the sixth and fifth centuries BC, discoveries in the south have somewhat altered this perspective. To understand the casting traditions of central and south-eastern China it is necessary to review their contact with those of the Western Zhou. The interaction of the south-east and that of the centre of China with the Western Zhou capitals in the west and at Luoyang were surprisingly different. These separate developments contributed to the diversity of Eastern Zhou casting.

The south-eastern provinces of Jiangsu and Anhui had been familiar with ritual vessels from at least the transitional period of the Shang. Later Shang bronzes from this area seem to have deviated from northern models.[20] Little contact seems to

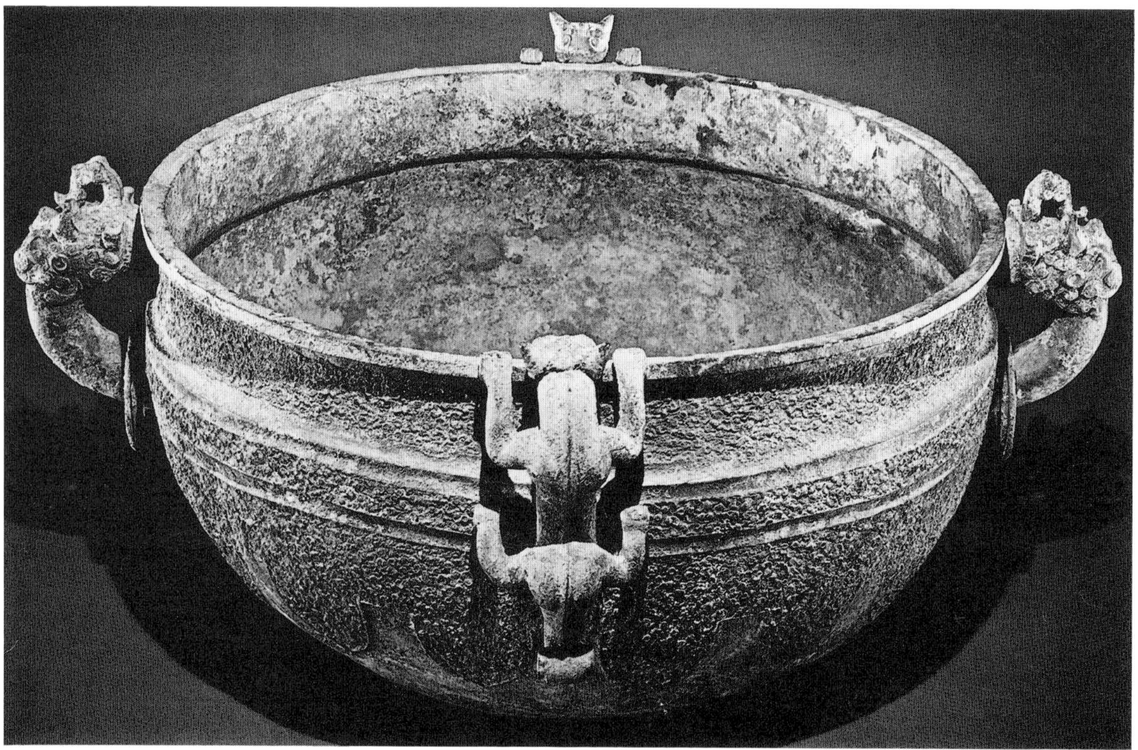

Fig. 24. *Fu Zhai jian*. Wu state, 5th century BC, said to have been found at Henan Hui Xian. H. 45 cm. Shanghai Museum.

have existed in the early Western Zhou, and so far no examples of tombs or vessels have been found. However, from the beginning of the middle Western Zhou there was direct communication with metropolitan centres. The first Western Zhou bronzes appear in hoards or in a local tomb type called a *dun*, constructed not underground in a shaft but above ground under a mound. In one such tomb appeared a *gui* with a long inscription describing the movement of a Wu Hou named Ze to Yi. The inscription is in impeccable northern style and was presumably cast in the north or, if in the south, by a metropolitan caster. The *gui* is dated to the end of the early or beginning of the middle Western Zhou; it is now treated as evidence of the growth of the Wu state.[21]

At this time many bronzes were introduced to Jiangsu and Anhui with the result that metropolitan Western Zhou bronze styles became current. While the ritual revolution in Shaanxi and Henan subsequently obliterated vessel shapes and designs at the principal Zhou centres, they survived here in the south-east. Thus *taotie* and plumed birds, and also vessel shapes, especially *you*, cylindrical *zun* and *gui* on arched bases, and hooked flanges – giving rise to filigree openwork – all had a new lease of life in the south-east.

A *gui* decorated with birds from Jiangsu Dantu Dagang Muzidun confirms that the end of the early or beginning of the middle Western Zhou was the moment when metropolitan styles entered the area. This *gui* resembles in almost every detail that from Huayuancun discussed above (Fig. 16).[22] These metropolitan bronzes stimulated local copies, of which the *you* (no. 27) is a formidable example, combining a metropolitan shape with local decorative motifs: large coiled snakes and a small reptile are southern in taste, and the background of criss-cross striations is based upon the impressed pottery of the area. Such relief texturing was to be fundamental to Eastern Zhou bronze design.[23]

Repeated textures were exploited in what is now called the Huai style, well illustrated by several basins or *jian* inscribed by kings of the Wu state. They are densely covered with small relief curls that lie over small dragon heads ultimately derived from Western Zhou motifs (Fig. 24). However, the curls are not contained in strict horizontal borders found on Western Zhou metropolitan bronzes; they flow across the basins like the criss-cross patterns on the *you*. Relief curls and a lack of dividing registers are two of the defining features of the Huai style. A number of east-coast bronzes illustrate experiments with relief textures, linking vessels like the *you* and the *jian*. However, the plastic curls of the Huai were probably a local variant of the relief styles invented in the Chu state in central China, for both politically and artistically Chu dominated southern China.[24]

None of the basins under discussion came from Wu state tombs. Their dispersal illustrates ambitions of the states, especially those of Chu, and the exchange of bronzes that distributed and intermingled the varied regional styles. One pair, commissioned by Guang, King of Wu (r.514–496 BC), was excavated from a tomb of a Marquis of Cai in Anhui province. Marriage between a daughter of the Wu king and the Marquis of Cai brought them into the Cai family. This marriage was part of a futile attempt to keep the powerful state of Chu at bay, but Wu was overrun in 473 BC and Cai in 447.[25] Four other basins, of which one is illustrated in Figure 24, were commissioned by Fu Zhai, the last king of Wu (495–474 BC), and were retrieved at Hui Xian in Henan province.[26]

In Hubei, the heart of the territories of Chu, contact with metropolitan Western Zhou bronze styles followed a quite different pattern. Early Western Zhou bronzes were well known in the area: tombs at Huangpi Lutaishan, for example, followed metropolitan style and contained early and early to middle Western Zhou vessels.[27] However, contact with the north seems to have died away. Middle Western Zhou bronzes imported and copied in the south-east were not known here. At the end of the Western Zhou, on the other hand, rulers of the small state of Zeng cast vessels that replicated the vessel sets and designs of the late Western Zhou. Their close adherence to the late Western Zhou vessel sets is in complete contrast to the east coast where middle Western Zhou shapes and motifs survived and later Western Zhou bronzes had initially little influence.

Vessels inscribed by the second son of a marquis of Zeng include standard *ding, gui, dou, yi, he, pan* and large *hu* typical of their Western Zhou predecessors.[28] The *hu* (Fig. 25) are also interesting for their deep concave banding characteristic of earlier bronzes, such as the *Shi Wang hu* (no. 29). It seems that here Western Zhou traditions inspired textured

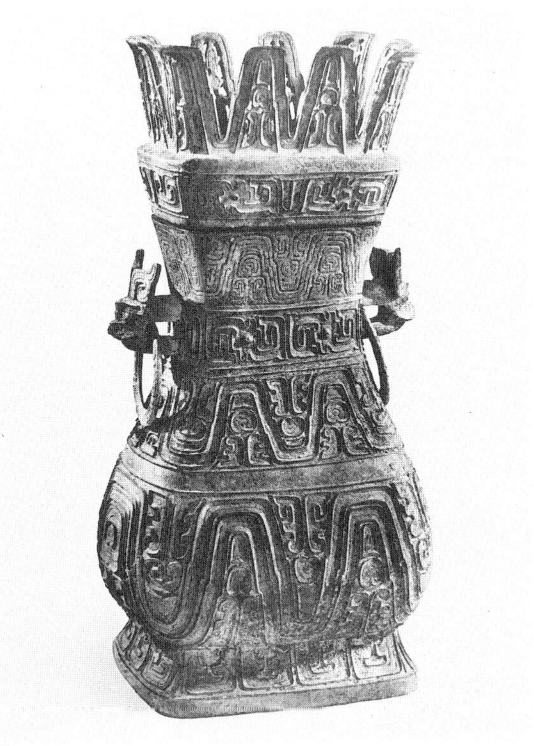

Fig. 25. *Zeng Hou You Fu hu* from Hubei Jingshan. Early Eastern Zhou, 8th century BC. H. 66 cm.

relief culminating in the Xinzheng vessels already described.

As important was the exploration of relief effects on vessels from tombs M1 and M2 at Xichuan Xiasi in Henan province. Tomb M2 is thought to be that of Yuan Zifeng, who held the office of Lingyin of Chu and died in 548 BC: tomb M1 is thought to be that of his wife. This latter burial contained vessels conventionally decorated with tight angular interlace typical of the sixth century, seen on vessels from Xinzheng and Fenshuiling. However, they also carry much more unusual knobbly relief. In the tomb of Yuan Zifeng this style had progressed much further: a *li* bears conventional interlace overwhelmed by large openwork appendages of massed curls. On the *ding* from the two tombs, seven from tomb M2 and two from tomb M1, the curls have invaded the surfaces of the containers themselves (Fig. 26); borders of relief scrolls and curls alternate with sunken motifs.[29] Like Western Zhou patterns, but unlike the Huai bronzes, the ornament is divided into horizontal registers.

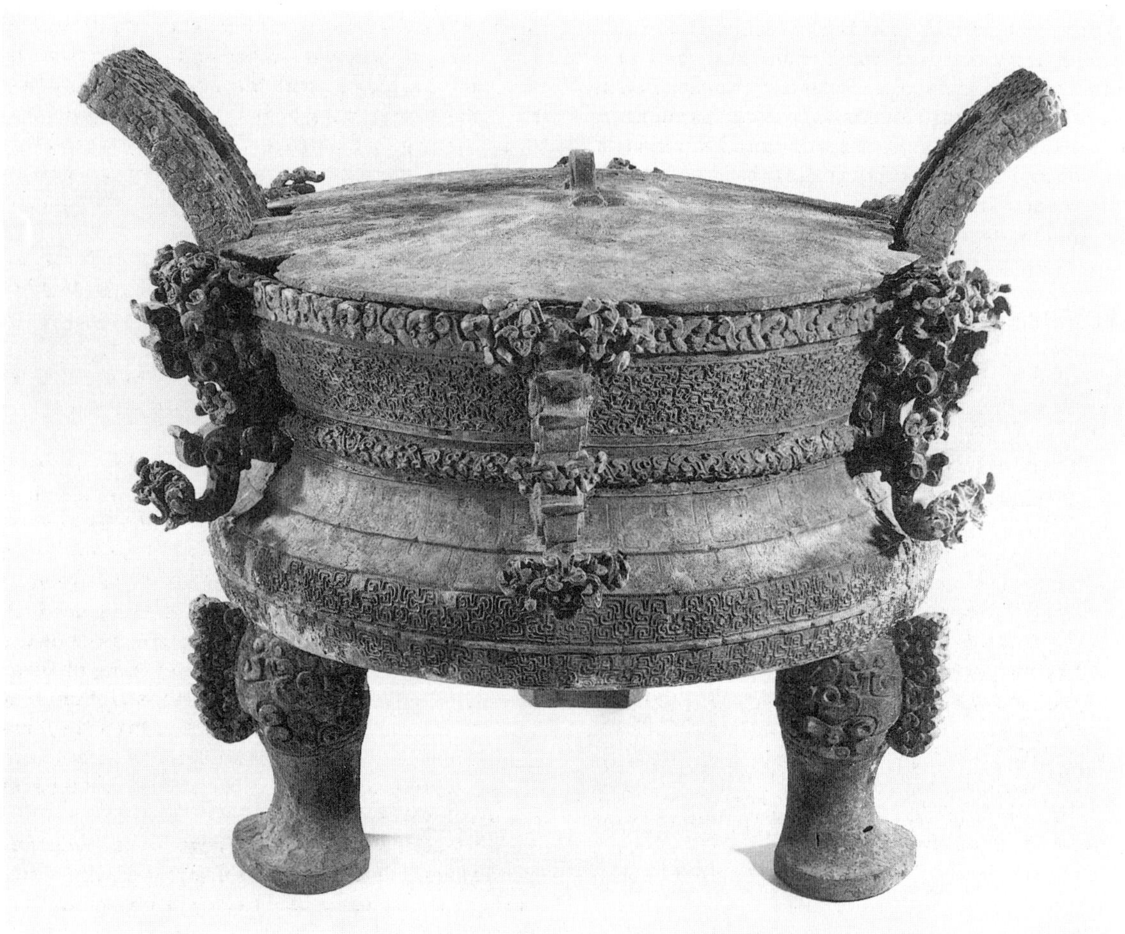

Fig. 26. *Ding* from tomb M2 at Henan Xichuan Xiasi. Eastern Zhou, 6th century BC. H. 67 cm.

Another spectacular find, the tomb of the Marquis Yi of Zeng excavated at Sui Xian Leigudun in Hubei province, illustrates the culmination of this style. This tomb dates to *c.* 433 BC on the evidence of an inscribed bell cast for the funeral ceremonies by the king of Chu. It hung with sixty-four other bells on a large wooden frame supported by figures standing on a writhing mass of dragons in bronze. Vessels in the tomb were also enlivened with a wealth of dragons, curls and various types of interlace. Gold vessels and jades echoed such design.[30]

A cylindrical *zun* standing in a basin, or *pan*, was one of the most remarkable items (Fig. 27). Its filigree appendages must have been cast in the lost-wax process, a technique also used for the relief appliqués on the Xichuan vessels. Cylindrical *zun* were not known in early Eastern Zhou times in Hubei but had been widely used along the east coast.[31] East-coast casting contributed a few vessel shapes and probably also filigree openwork to the Chu tradition; from Chu the east coast had probably derived the plastic curls which were essential to the Huai style (Fig. 24).

The inlay style

At the time that cast designs were elaborated and refined on Jin and Chu bronzes a relatively new method of embellishing bronze with inlay was developed. The Shang had inlaid weapons with turquoise, but with a few exceptions this art seems to have died out in the Western Zhou. No later than the sixth century inlay was once again in use.

Copper and gold are found on vessels from the mid-sixth-century Xichuan tombs just described. The sources of these types of inlay are much debated: was inlay a Chinese invention, or was it stimulated at least in part by the decoration of woodwork, textiles and bronze of China's northern and north-western neighbours? Scholars in the West, notably So, Bunker and Mackenzie, have argued for some influence from techniques or styles prevalent among China's neighbours. Chinese scholars, especially those concerned with the exhibition 'The Great Bronze Age of China' held in New York in 1980, have contested this view.[32]

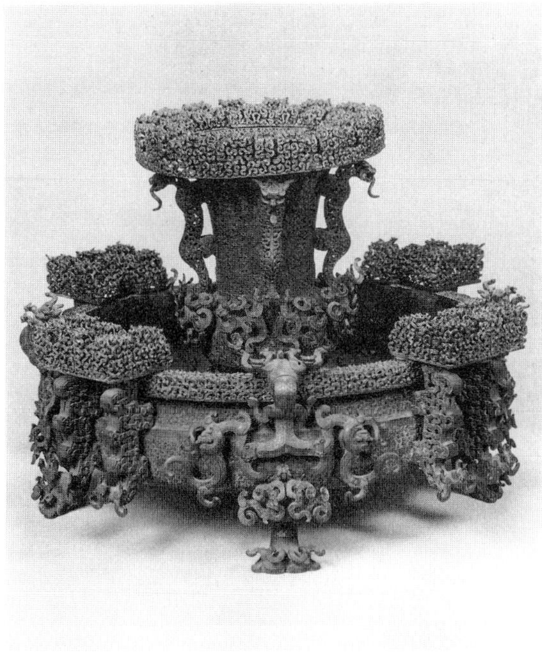

Fig. 27. *Zun* standing within a *pan* from Hubei Sui Xian. Eastern Zhou, 5th century BC. H. 33.1 cm.

Pictorial designs

Large S-shaped creatures inlaid in copper on vessels from tomb M2 at Xichuan Xiasi are typical of the first stages of copper inlay and the beginnings of pictorial designs in the sixth century (Fig. 28a). The animals are crouched, their heads turned back to look over their tails. This stance was developed in China to depict *long*-dragons, especially as vessel handles. Similar forms were used for small jades and were later borrowed by the nomadic peoples to the west for their bronze animal-shaped fittings.[33] If such early inlay was stimulated by outside influences, it is likely that the impetus came either from the north through Henan or from the west, being transmitted perhaps through Sichuan down the Yangzi; most of the early copper-inlaid vessels have been discovered in the south – for example, in the tomb of the Marquis of Cai.[34]

The inlay technique was unusual and can be examined in a damaged bronze bowl in the Victoria and Albert Museum. Here crouched felines in copper were inserted into the moulds prepared for the bowl. Chaplets were used to hold the copper felines in place while the bronze was cast around them.[35]

Even if the foreign origins of these first stages of copper inlay are not yet proved, the subsequent development of pictorial scenes on the bronzes is highly unusual.[36] Later vessels are decorated with densely packed registers, often filled with men or strange man-like creatures hunting animals. Such vessels seem to be inlaid in the same manner as the bronzes decorated with large felines. One of these vessels, a *hu* (Fig. 28c), has an inscription that records the acquisition of the vessel from the Xian Yu peoples on the northern borders, also known as the Di, who became rulers of the state of Zhongshan during the Warring States.[37]

The scattering of animal figures in a non-symmetrical manner is foreign to Chinese design examined so far. It resembles most closely some rock carvings found in the north, west and south-western borders, and a piece of inscribed bone also from the extreme north (Fig. 28b). While the date of the rock carvings is difficult to establish – they may be as late as the Ming and Qing in some cases – the bone carving certainly belongs to the Eastern Zhou period, although within that span its date is not clear.[38] It is likely to be a remnant of a much larger industry or style that perhaps contributed to the pictorial vessels.

Another piece of evidence to support arguments that the style was foreign is found in the way in which such pictorial bronzes were gradually modified. Hunting scenes with animals tumbling in all directions were in due course replaced either by animals neatly arranged in horizontal rows, subdivided by paired triangles or by scenes of daily life and of court ritual. In the example illustrated in Figure 28e several activities are neatly depicted. Regulated designs had replaced the random rather foreign hunting scenes.[39]

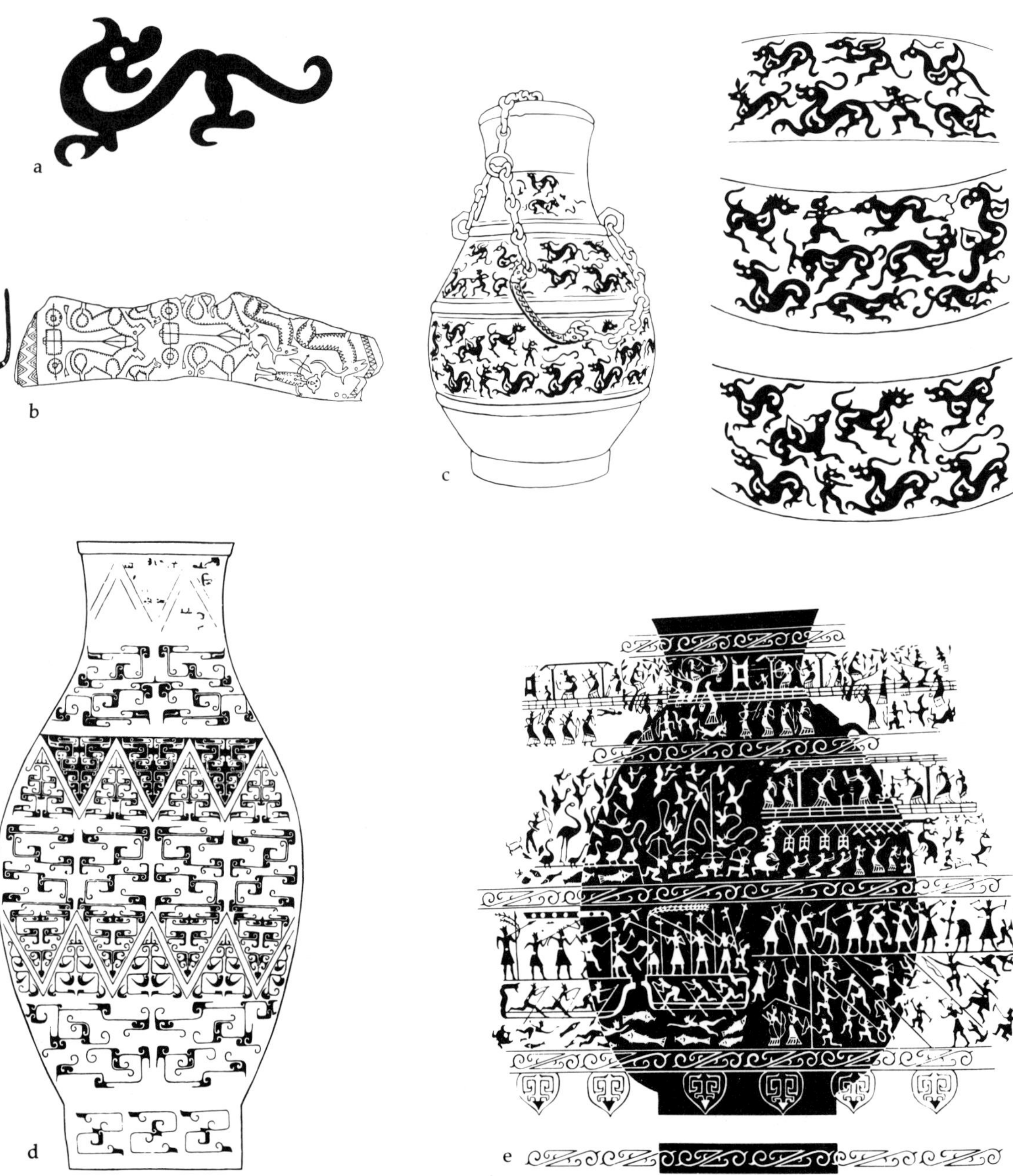

Fig. 28. Eastern Zhou inlay patterns: (a) a feline in copper on a box from tomb M2 at Henan Xichuan Xiasi; (b) figures and chariots incised on a bone fragment from tomb M102 at Inner Mongolia Ningcheng Nanshangen; (c) *hu* inlaid with scattered figures and animals in copper, H. 37.9 cm, Ethnographical Museum, Berlin; (d) *hu* inlaid with geometric patterns in gold and silver, from Henan Hui Xian Liulige, H. 57.8 cm; (e) *hu* inlaid with figure designs, H. 31.6 cm, Palace Museum, Beijing.

Calligraphic designs

What is here described as the calligraphic style originated in gold-inlaid inscriptions, particularly on bronzes from Chu and the eastern states of Wu and Yue. Gold-inlaid inscriptions on *ge* from Xichuan are sixth-century examples of this technique. Although gold is often correctly associated with China's nomadic neighbours, there is no other reason to regard the genre as foreign, especially as gold inlay was so frequently employed in writing Chinese. Many bronzes are inlaid with extraordinarily elaborate bird script characters, which display alternating thickness and thinness in the strokes, imitating brushwork. Alternating thin and thick inlaid lines define the calligraphic style.

A spearhead in the British Museum is a fine example of the type (no. 36); its inscription records the name of the Yue king, Zhou Ju (r. 448–412 BC). Refined but exceedingly elaborate characters lie against a lozenge-patterned ground produced by an unknown technique. The socket is inlaid in turquoise bounded by triangles. This mixture of turquoise and gold inlay, the calligraphic lines of gold and the triangular organisation of the socket design were the elements exploited in the mainstream of the calligraphic inlay discussed here.[40]

While most of the gold inscriptions are found on southern bronzes, occasional inlaid inscriptions appear on bronzes from the Jin state, such as a bird-shaped vessel now in the Freer Gallery, Washington. The technique may have been inspired by the southern weapons, several of which have been found in Shanxi, including a sword inscribed with the name of King Guang of Wu (514–496 BC).[41]

In Shanxi calligraphic gold inlay replaced the relief dragon interlace typical of the Houma foundries, as illustrated by decoration of a *dou* from Shanxi Changzhi Fenshuiling tomb M126 and an almost identical vessel in the Freer Gallery (Fig. 29). Here a band of dragon heads is outlined in thin line with thicker areas where the line changes direction, as in lacquer painting or calligraphy.[42]

Dragon heads were shortly replaced by abstract patterns of alternating thick and thin lines, first arranged in rows and then frequently in triangular or diagonal configurations following the triangular shapes noted on the spearhead. Many of the early northern designs were inlaid in copper, but they retained the calligraphic line and turquoise of their southern models. A fifth-century *hu* from tomb 60 at Liulige illustrates this geometric arrangement (Fig. 28d).[43]

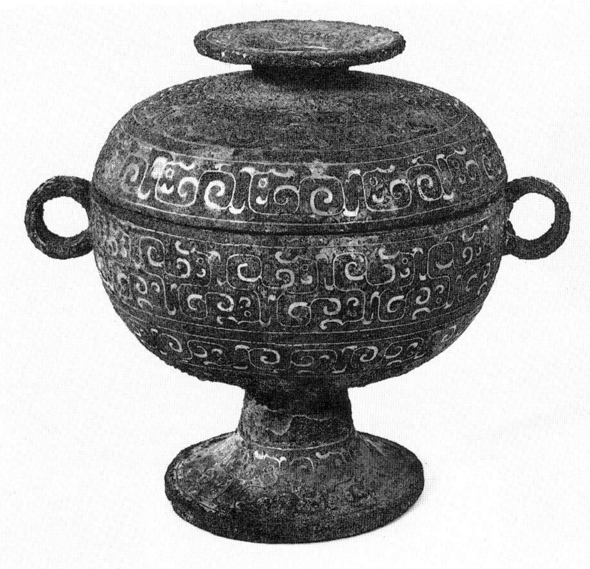

Fig. 29. Bronze ritual vessel *dou* inlaid with dragon heads in gold. Eastern Zhou, Jin state, 5th century BC. H. 15.5 cm. Freer Gallery of Art, Washington.

By the fourth century gold and silver had almost universally superseded copper. Fittings from Jincun, illustrated in nos 37 and 38, are typical of the flowering of this later inlay phase. It has been argued that the tombs at Jincun belonged to the Zhou royal family, and this is thought to explain their sumptuous contents. The fittings combine geometric patterns inherited from the fifth century with flowing lines undoubtedly stimulated by the example of lacquer decoration.[44]

The extraordinary richness that inlay imparted to bronze surfaces is well illustrated by the contents of the royal tombs of the small state of Zhongshan, excavated at Pingshan Xian in central Hebei (Fig. 30). This small state had been founded by a non-Chinese people, the Di, who had recently given up their nomadic life and settled in northern China. Their tombs, dated to the end of the fourth century, contained both typically Chinese castings and some more exotic bronzes. Two *fang hu* inlaid with lozenge patterns filled with precious stones, gold and silver stand at the end of a long sequence of calligraphic and geometric designs initiated by the Changzhi *dou* (Fig. 29) and elaborated in the Liulige *hu* (Fig. 28d). Inlay on a pair of winged animal figures (Fig. 30) resembles the decoration of bow fittings from Jincun (no. 38).[45]

These creatures are beautifully modelled in the

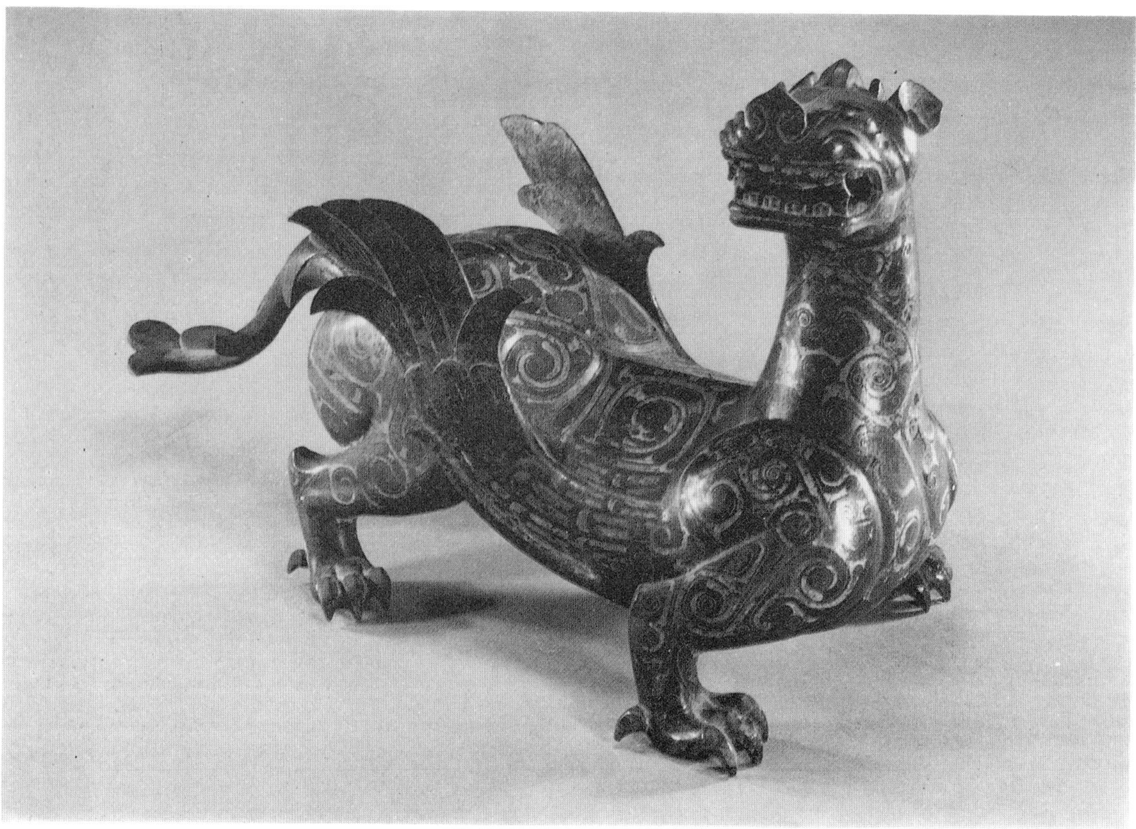

Fig. 30. One of a pair of winged beasts inlaid in silver from a royal tomb of the princes of Zhongshan buried at Hebei Pingshan Xian. Eastern Zhou, 4th century BC. H. 24 cm.

round, illustrating the excellent use of bronze for sculpture from the fourth century. A small fitting in the British Museum showing a tiger and boar in combat (no. 40) is a product of the same concern and skill. Both bronzes display exotic foreign elements. Wings on the creatures from Zhongshan are foreign to the Chinese tradition, as is the theme of two animals in combat. Both preoccupatons derive distantly from Western Asia, being borrowed perhaps by the Di from their neighbours further west. The elements are illustrated, for example, on textiles from tombs at Pazyryk in the Altai.[46]

Inlay undoubtedly created sumptuous bronzes, but the tombs at Zhongshan also exhibit the growing use of plain undecorated vessels. Indeed, ritual vessels – the *ding*, *gui* and *hu* – had ceased to be the centre of attention; in succeeding centuries they were replaced by utilitarian vessels for daily use. Small furniture fittings, chariot parts and belt-hooks were, however, decorated with increasing complexity. Inlaid weapons had initiated this trend, which had intensified throughout the Warring States. Bronze was inventively used for sculpture and for architectural fittings, but these items were no longer part of solemn state and family rituals. Rather than serving dead ancestors and their needs, bronzes glorified the power and prestige of monarchs and great families in this life.

Although the ancestral sacrifices of the Shang and Zhou died with their dynasties, the legacy of their ritual bronzes was and is formidable. During the succeeding dynasties of the Qin (221–206 BC) and Han (206 BC–AD 220) possession of *ding* vessels previously belonging to the Zhou was deemed evidence of the legitimacy of the dynasty and of Heaven's approval. Tomb reliefs illustrated Qin attempts to retrieve ancient *ding*, and the Han historian Sima Qian described at some length the auspicious discovery of a tripod in 113 BC.[47] More than 1,000 years later interest in ancient bronzes was revived as the Song emperors (AD 960–1279) sought to restore what they believed to be ancient rituals; once again the august religious and political associations of the bronzes ensured their veneration and respect.[48] Inscribed bronzes were particularly prized as avenues of communication with the past. From the Song period inscribed bronzes in particular were essential components of Imperial art collections, conferring status, even legitimacy, on their owners. These collections were soon emulated outside the Chinese court and later fuelled Western interest in Chinese art. Today ancient Chinese bronzes cast for religious ritual and to proclaim political might have become revered as one of the world's great art forms.[49]

Notes

1. For a survey of Eastern Zhou history and archaeology see Li Xueqin 1985c.
2. For a report on the excavations at Luoyang Zhongzhoulu see Beijing 1959c.
3. For an outline of Qin history and achievements see Li Xueqin 1985c, pp. 222–39; New York 1980, pp. 353–68.
4. Vessel types and their evolution have been analysed for some areas. For central China, especially Henan, see *Kaogu yu wenwu* 1981.3, pp. 84–103; for Qin in the west see *Kaogu yu wenwu* 1981.1, pp. 83–93; for Chu in the south see *Kaogu xuebao* 1982.2, pp. 155–82.
5. For the tombs at Shangcunling see Beijing 1959b.
6. For a *hu* from Jia Xian Taipuxiang see Hayashi 1984, vol. 2, pl. 315, *hu* no. 3; compare Beijing 1972a, no. 64.
7. Watson 1977, pl. 50b, deems such decoration archaistic. However, the archaeological evidence and technical examination of the British Museum's *hu* does not support this view. A similar *hu* was excavated in Shandong province and is likewise decorated with interlace (*Wenwu* 1986.4, pp. 12–14).
8. The two Huang tombs are reported in *Kaogu* 1984.4, pp. 302–32; see also Li Xueqin 1985c, pp. 182–4.
9. Similar designs are found on bronzes from tombs of a Fan lord and his wife; see *Wenwu* 1981.1, pp. 9–14, and Li Xueqin 1985c, p. 183.
10. The Xinzheng bronzes are illustrated in Sun Haibo 1937 and discussed in Li Xueqin 1985c, pp. 85–7.
11. The *hu* are discussed in So 1983.
12. So 1983 discusses parallels between wood and bronzes in the art of the fifth century. It is possible that similar inspiration was available at this rather earlier period.
13. For reports on the discovery of the Houma moulds see *Wenwu* 1960.8–9, pp. 6–10; see also Weber 1973, pp. 507–38; Keyser 1979.
14. Excavation of the tombs at Houma Shangmacun is reported in *Kaogu* 1963.5, pp. 229–45.
15. The tombs are reported in *Kaogu xuebao* 1974.2, pp. 63–85. For a definition of proto-Liyu and the classic Liyu styles see Loehr 1968, nos 63, 64.
16. These patterns are illustrated on vessels and bells from tomb 60 at Henan Hui Xian Liulige (Guo Baojun 1959); see also Rawson 1980, fig. 122.
17. Compare a *gui* in the Harvard University Art Museums (Chen Mengjia 1977, no. A251). The openwork fringes on the *gui*'s handles link the bronze to vessels from Tunxi and other south-eastern sites (Beijing 1972a, no.56). The Harvard *gui* also shares the Shandong *ding's* combination of *taotie* face and fractured relief ornament, thus suggesting that the south-eastern bronze culture dependent on middle Western Zhou was linked to a similar phenomenon in Shandong. Lawton 1982, p. 19, quoting Huber, also suggests connections with Shandong may have influenced the direction taken by the Liyu style.
18. These *taotie* patterns were anticipated on bells from Shanxi Changzhi Fenshuiling M269 (*Kaogu xuebao* 1974.2, pp. 63–85, pl. 3:4).
19. Snakes combined with small *taotie* faces appear on a *jian* from Henan Hui Xian (Guo Baojun 1981, pl. 76).
20. For transitional vessels see New York 1980, nos 15, 16.
21. For the excavation of the *gui* see *Wenwu* 1955.5, pp. 58–61; comments on the inscription are found in Li Xueqin 1985a.
22. The excavation of the tomb at Muzidun is described in *Wenwu* 1984.5, pp. 1–10. The *gui* is also illustrated in Li Xueqin 1985b, no. 185.
23. Impressed ceramics were found in the tomb at Muzidun cited above (cf. n. 22). Middle Western Zhou vessel types with local forms of decoration were not superseded in this area by late Western Zhou bronzes.
24. Attention concentrated on the Huai style at the expense of the central Chu industry because bronzes from the east-coast areas were discovered first. Some authorities have misleadingly suggested that the Huai style was descended from the Liyu style; it existed, however, in parallel. Its roots lay in a combination of middle Western Zhou motifs with relief derived from impressed ceramics. An intermediate stage is exhibited by a set of bells, one of which is in the Shanghai Museum (Shanghai 1964, no. 77). Such designs were then combined with features of Chu bronzes (Mackenzie 1982).
25. For history of the states see Li Xueqin 1985c, pp. 184–5. The contents of the tomb of the Marquis of Cai are reported in Beijing 1956b.
26. New York 1980, p. 268.
27. The bronzes are reported in *Jianghan kaogu* 1982.2, pp. 37–61; see also *Wenwu* 1982.12, pp. 51–7.
28. See *Wenwu* 1972.2, pp. 47–53; New York 1980, no. 62, and Rawson (forthcoming), fig. 153.
29. For discussion of the Xiasi tombs see *Wenwu* 1980.10, pp. 13–20; *Kaogu* 1981.2, pp. 119–27; Li Xueqin 1985c, pp. 156–7. Mackenzie 1982 identifies the relief style exhibited by the bronzes at Xichuan as the source of the plastic curls of the east coast known as the Huai style. However, it should also be noted that some influences must have gone the other way. Large curly openwork on the Xichuan bronzes may have been derived from the filigree handles on east-coast bronzes, which are possibly a local variant of hooked flanges inherited from the Western Zhou.
30. For the contents of the tomb see Beijing 1980d, Qian Hao *et al.* 1981, pp. 44–63; Li Xueqin 1985c, pp. 175–81.
31. This contact was first observed by Colin Mackenzie in 1982.
32. For So's views see New York 1980, pp. 305–11; compare Bunker 1983, Mackenzie 1984. For contrary views see New York 1980, pp. 374–6.
33. Rawson (forthcoming), no. 93.
34. *Wenwu* 1980.10, pp. 13–20, p. 2:2. For similar inlay see Beijing 1956b, pls 10, 11, 12; *Wenwu* 1981.1, pp. 1–8; *Wenwu* 1984.1, pp. 10–26. These southern inlaid designs are paralleled by lacquer patterns; compare *Kaogu xuebao* 1982.1, pp. 71–116, fig. 28.
35. The bowl is illustrated and discussed in Hayashi 1980.
36. Colin Mackenzie (1984) has supported his case for the foreign origins of this type by noting the unusual, possibly foreign, shape of a *hu* so inlaid from Hui Xian (Guo Baojun 1981, pl. 75:6).

37. This category of bronze is discussed by Weber 1968, pp. 113–150; see also New York 1980, no. 70.
38. For rock drawings see *Wenwu* 1972.12, pp. 42–6; *Wenwu* 1980.6, pp. 1–11; *Kaogu yu wenwu* 1981.2, pp. 87–93; *Kaogu yu wenwu* 1986.5, pp. 59–67. The bone carving is reported in *Kaogu* 1981.4, pp. 304–8. The northern, western and south-western areas shared some aspects of a common culture (Tong Enzheng 1986). It is possible, therefore, that copper-inlay designs originated in this border area and entered central China both down the Yangzi towards Hubei and Hunan and then eastwards, and also from the extreme north.
39. For further illustrations see Weber 1968, figs 51–8; New York 1980, no. 91.
40. The British Museum's spearhead is by no means the earliest weapon of this type. Several items can be dated to the second half of the sixth century (see Hayashi 1972, pp. 502–15).
41. For the Freer vessel see Pope *et al.* 1967, no. 112; Lawton 1982, no. 3; Li Xueqin 1985c, pp. 47–8. See also Li's comment on the *Luan Shu fou*, also inlaid with a gold inscription and dated to before 573 BC (Rong Geng 1941, 2.806). If genuine, the *fou* appears to bear the oldest gold inscription identified to date. Notwithstanding this evidence, at present the majority of inlaid inscriptions of the sixth century appear to be southern.
42. The excavation of the *dou* is reported in *Wenwu* 1972.4, pp. 38–46; for discussion of the Freer Gallery vessel see Lawton 1982, no. 8.
43. This inlay type is discussed by Jenny So in New York 1980, pp. 305–7, nos 73, 74, 75. See also Weber 1968, figs 34, 35.
44. For lacquer designs relevant to the evolution of inlay see Beijing 1984c and *Kaogu xuebao* 1982.1, pp. 71–116. For swirling inlay based on lacquer see New York 1980, no. 76 and fig. 100; see also Watson 1973, no. 130.
45. For the bronzes from Zhongshan see *Wenwu* 1979.1, pp. 1–31; Paris 1984; Li Xueqin 1985c, pp. 93–107.
46. Rudenko 1970.
47. See Barnard 1973 and Wu 1984.
48. Watson 1973b.
49. Ledderose 1983 comments on the links between religious and aesthetic values in Chinese landscape art. See also Ledderose 1978 for the status of Imperial art collections.

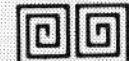

CATALOGUE

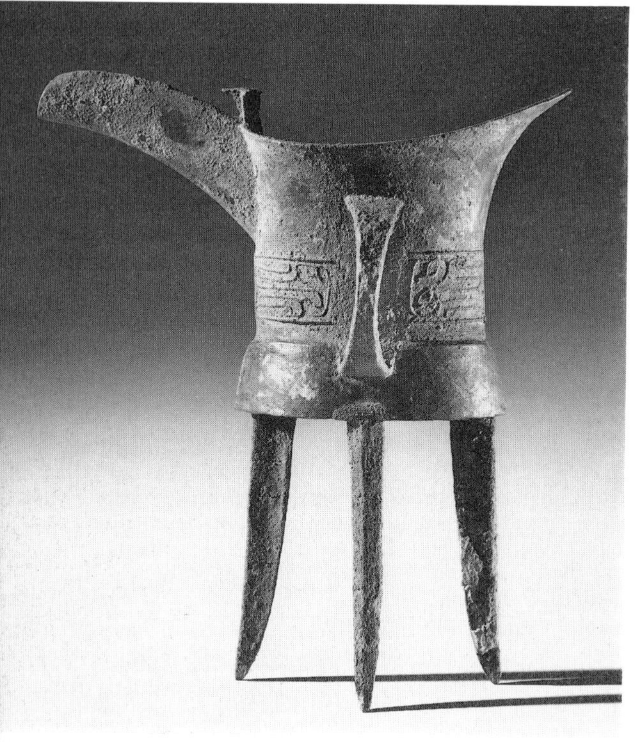

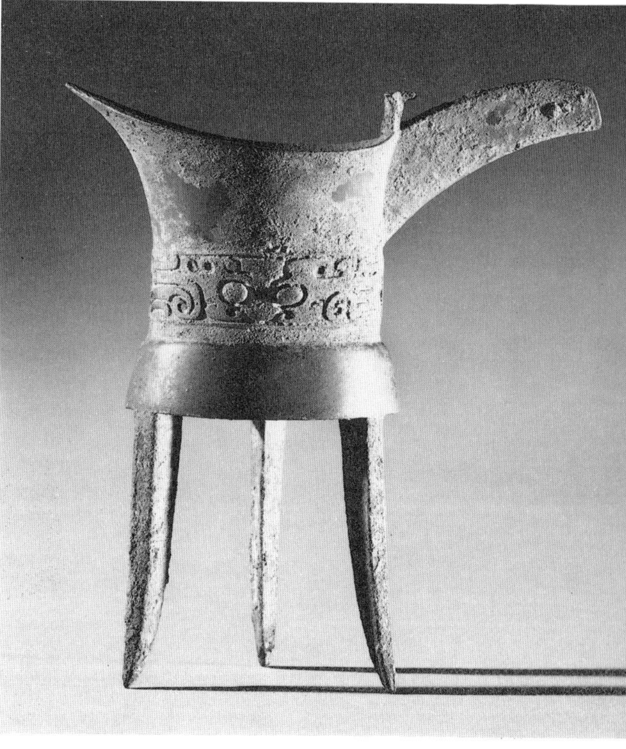

1

1 *Jue*

Shang.
H. 14.6 cm; L. at spout 13.5 cm.
1960.10–14.1; Brooke Sewell Fund.

Jue are the earliest-surviving bronze vessels. Many have been found at Erlitou-period sites. They have long spouts, narrow waists and slender slightly splayed legs. This neat *jue* is more restrained in proportion, with a short spout, an oval body and a slightly flared skirt above three short slight legs, features typical of the Erligang period.

All surviving *jue* were cast in piece-moulds, whose joints left marks down the centre of each leg and along the corresponding parts of the body. Two posts at the corners of the spout and rim and curved handles are standard in this vessel type. The posts are elementary, being little more than small vertical extensions with flattened tops; their function has been much debated – it is possible that they are simply the remnants of sprues. However, as all other extraneous traces of the casting process have been smoothed away, this view does not seem entirely plausible.

An early feature is the slight ridge of bronze inside the lip. Again there is no agreement as to its purpose. It has been argued that it imitates a folded lip on a wrought bronze vessel. These views have been hotly contested, but alternative suggestions are no more plausible.[1]

On one side of the vessel is a simple *taotie* face in Style II, while two shorter sections on the other side, bisected by a handle, contain abstract flourishes in thread relief designated as Style I. In due course such abstract motifs were given eyes and so could be interpreted as some sort of creature in profile.

1. Skeueomorphs in ceramics and bronze are discussed in Bagley 1987, Introduction, Section 1.1.

2 *Li* *(illustrated in colour)*

Shang.
H. to handles 25.9 cm; DIAM. at lip 16.8 cm.
1953.12–14.1; given by P. T. Brooke Sewell.
Literature: Watson 1963, pl. 2b; Lienert 1979, no. 159; Hayashi 1984, vol. 2, pl. 52, *li ding* no. 20.

Li took their wide lobes from neolithic-period ceramics, and in both the Shang and early Zhou periods ceramic *li* were often preferred to bronze ones. Bronze *li* of the Erligang period have come from tombs at Zhengzhou in Henan and Panlongcheng in Hubei. These early *li* have bodies that run in a continuous line to just below an everted lip and bear narrow registers of decoration.[1] The British Museum's more advanced vessel is articulated by a recessed neck between the lobed body and the everted lip and by short narrow legs below wide lobes.

Multiplied, narrow relief bands fill the entire surface. Similarly dense configurations are found on bronzes of the period transitional between Erligang and Anyang. Despite eyes on the lobes, the pattern of scrolls and quills does not resolve into a representation of a known or mythical creature. A smaller-scale repeating design around the neck is entirely abstract, lacking eyes which animate so many early Shang motifs.

1. Beijing 1981a, colour pl. 2; *Wenwu* 1976.2, pp. 26–41, fig. 11.

3 *Zun*

Shang.
H. 23.7 cm; DIAM. at lip 21.7 cm.
1986.4–17.1.

An expansive, trumpet-shaped mouth, angular shoulder and deep rounded body are features borrowed from high-fired ceramic vessels (Fig. 4); examples in low-fired ceramic are also known. An outward sloping, slightly stepped foot-ring has been added. Three cross-shaped holes were probably left by projecting ceramic spurs used to separate the moulds and the foot core during casting. The holes are aligned with the seams of the moulds, which divide major areas of decoration around the belly and bisect small projecting animal heads on the shoulders. The lower part of the vessel and the foot-ring are repaired.

The three relief buffalo heads on the shoulder contrast with *taotie* embedded in Style III scrolls and quills on the belly. Around the vessel's shoulders similar scrolls and relief bands resolve themselves into birds. This register is bordered by small circles, an early feature. Below the shoulder diagonal lines and scrolls enclose eyes that cannot be read as belonging to creatures.

Similar *zun* have been found at Zhengzhou, decorated both in early thread relief and with relief bands, as here; rare examples carry large curling flanges.[1] The British Museum's vessel probably belongs to a slightly later time; it resembles vessels from early tombs at Anyang.[2] In the second half of

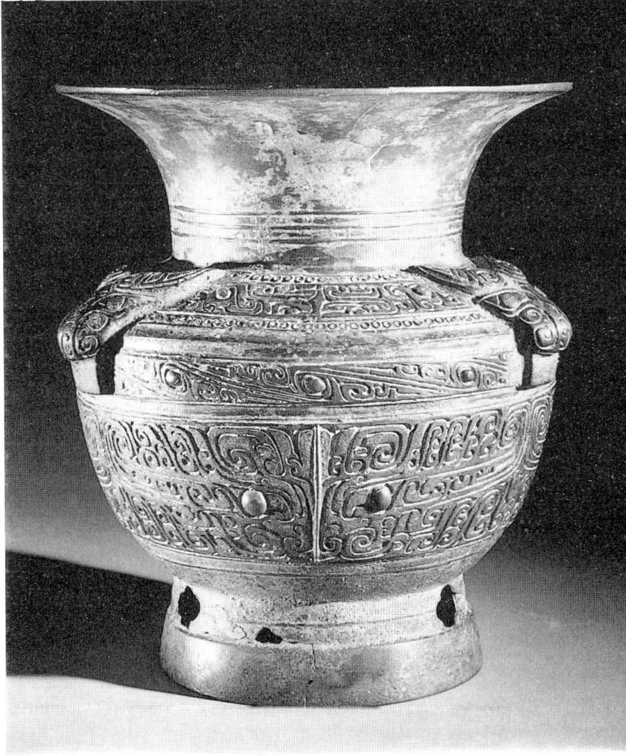

3

the Anyang period shouldered *zun* were often replaced by cylindrical vessels based upon the *gu*. However, the earlier shape did not entirely disappear, and late Shang examples can be identified both by their inscriptions and by their late types of decoration.[3]

1. Beijing 1981a, no. 76.
2. Li Ji and Wan Jiabao 1972, pls XXXIII, XXXIV.
3. *Wenwu* 1985.3, pp. 1–11, pl. 2:5.

4 *Hu*

Shang.
H. 29.8 cm; W. at lip 22.8 cm.
Inscription: rubbing no. 2.
1983.3–18.1; ex-Luboshez Collection.
Literature: Griffin and McNamee, 1972, pp. 9, 35–6.

Like the previous vessel, this wine container is paralleled in earlier ceramics. Several examples decorated with narrow horizontal bands have been found at Zhengzhou.[1] Although bronze Erligang-period *hu* have not yet come to light, a *you* vessel of a related form has been found (Fig. 5).[2]

While the vessel's shape harks back to the Erligang period, both the inscription, which consists of a pictograph of a hand holding a staff above a boat, and the background to the motifs of tight spirals (*leiwen*) and quills belong to the Anyang period. The principal motif is a large *taotie*, appearing once on the front and once on the back of the vessel. It has enormous compelling eyes. Horizontal bands and quills lying either side of the eyes now read as a body, repeated twice for reasons of symmetry.

Two different types of dragons fill the narrow borders. Creatures lying between the lugs are derived from single-eyed profile monsters on either side of *taotie* on Erligang and transitional bronzes (Figs 6, 9d). From such sources come their overlarge eyes, long trunks and profusion of quills. The small dragons in the next register are altogether more credible. This sort of dragon was composed by combining the beaked heads of Erligang-period creatures with simple bodies and claws borrowed from Anyang *taotie*. Neither dragon, however, resembles the *long*, known from oracle-bone script and depicted on no. 21.

The vessel has a bright grey-green patina and is quite heavily repaired. The background *leiwen* and the intaglio lines on the motifs are filled with a black substance that gives the bronze a much darker tone in these areas.

1. Beijing 1959a, pls 4:1, 4:8; for an Erlitou example see *Kaogu* 1965.5, pp. 215–24, pl.2:2.
2. *Hu* and *you* were closely related; the early *you* from Zhengzhou is reported in *Wenwu* 1983.3, pp. 49–59, fig. 14.

5 *Fang yi* *(illustrated in colour)*

Shang.
H. 27 cm; W. (max.) 16 cm.
1973.7–26.1; Seligman Bequest.
Literature: Hansford 1957, A1.

Fang yi occur in Fu Hao's tomb (Fig. 7) and perhaps originated slightly before that date. The British Museum's example is later, its decoraton belonging to an advanced stage of the Anyang period.[1] Faces, their main features in relief, appear on both lid and body. They lack a bounding line: eyes, brows, nose, jaws and horns stand out in a sea of *leiwen*. Whereas the two previous *taotie* had distinctly animal characteristics, here neat pupils filling the eyes hint at a semi-human being. However, the dragon-shaped horns are completely fantastic.

Additional dragons fill space either side of the faces. These profile dragons carry small bottle-horns and sharply angled tails converted from a *taotie*'s body, such as that on no. 4. A similar transformation made the dragons in the register just below the lid. They consist of half a *taotie*, employing both half its face and one of its bodies. This device of reusing elements first designed for one creature to make another has contributed misleadingly to the notion that the *taotie* can be understood as being made up of two confronted dragons.

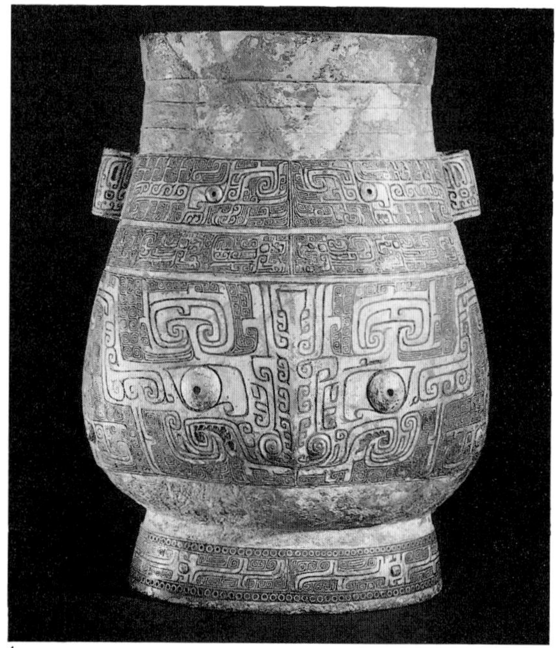

4

The vessel's decoration is articulated both by vertical flanges and by narrow horizontal divisions. These breaks in the surface focus attention on the motifs displayed within the compartments of the vessel.

1. For a chronologically arranged sequence of *fang yi* see Hayashi 1984, vol. 2, pls 249–53.

6 *Gong*

Shang.
H. 23 cm; L. 30 cm.
1968.4–22.1; Sedgwick Bequest.
Literature: Hayashi 1984, vol. 2, pl. 371, *yi* no. 1.

The vessel is shaped like a sauce-boat with a lid. Its body, oval in cross-section, stands on an oval foot-ring; the jug is waisted where body and handle join. This junction is covered by a bottle-horned dragon head; a diamond-patterned body lies each side of the vessel. Other creatures decorate the lid. Large *taotie* faces in relief cover the two ends, their

6▷

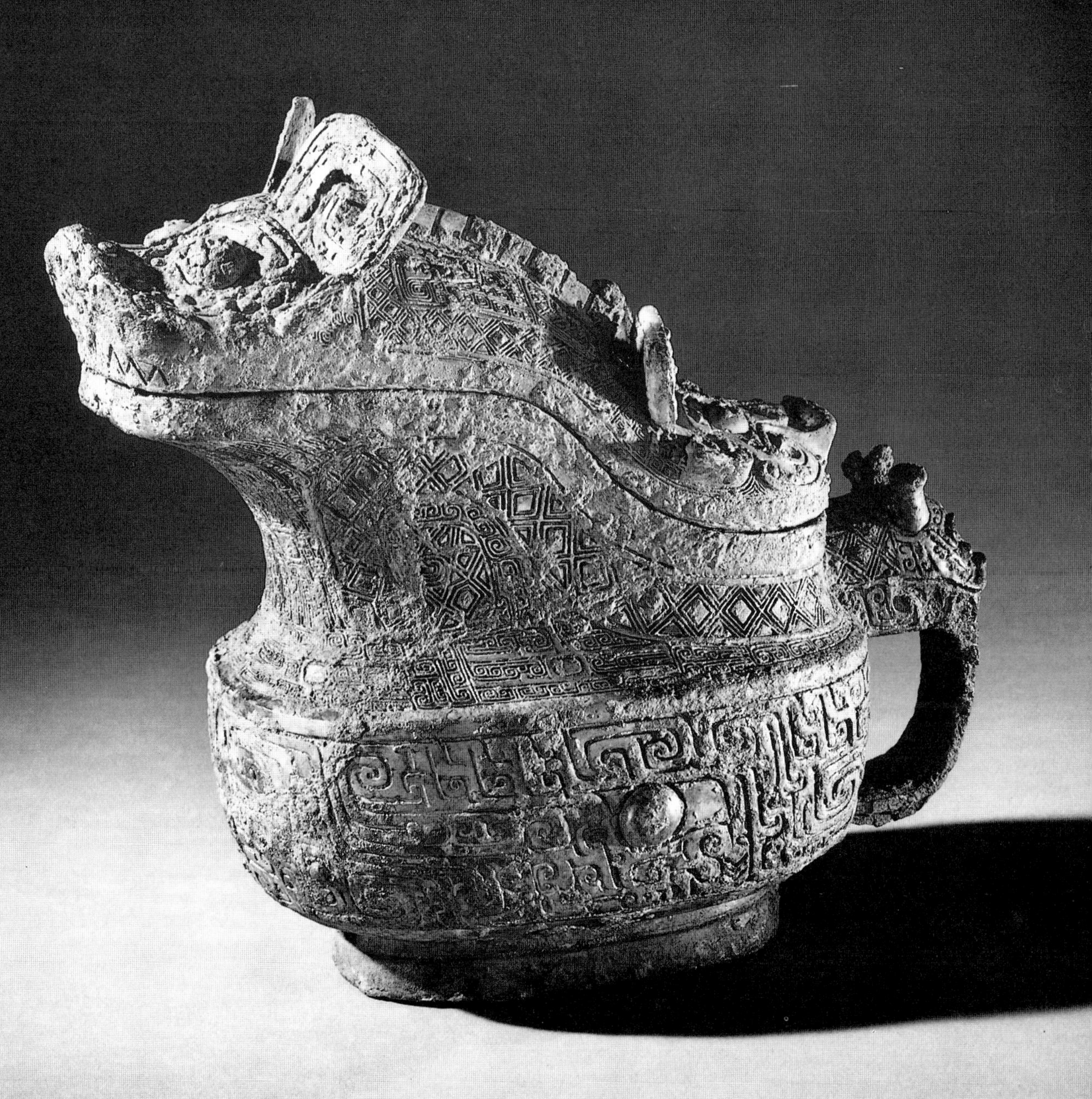

openwork horns standing upright. In the space between the heads small snake-like dragons lie against a fine *leiwen* ground either side of a dividing flange. The decoration around the lower part of the body is in complete contrast. Creatures in profile, one on each side of the vessel, are suggested by large eyes surrounded by a maze of scrolls and quills without a background of *leiwen*. Erligang and Anyang bronze styles are linked somewhat surprisingly on this bronze.

This *gong* is altogether rather unorthodox. *Gong* appeared at about the same time as animal-shaped vessels: both are present in Fu Hao's tomb (Fig. 7). One type of *gong* simply had a lid with a bottle-horned dragon head at the front on a rather ordinary body neatly divided by flanges. The other type combined a bird at the rear and a tiger at the front, rather as though it was made of an animal-shaped *zun* joined to an owl-shaped *you*.[1] The British Museum's *gong* conforms to neither of these major types, and it is possible that it is an early experimental vessel, standing, as Hayashi suggests, at the beginning of this vessel type's development.

1. Beijing 1980f, pls XXVI, XXVII.

7 *You* *(illustrated in colour)*

Shang.
H. 16 cm; W. at lip 11.2 cm.
1936.11–18.4; ex-Eumorfopoulos Collection.
Literature: Yetts 1929, A21–A23; Watson 1963, pl. 4; Hayashi 1984, vol. 2, pl. 287, *niao shou xing you* no. 19.

Two birds back to back make this wine container. Up-turned triangles on the lid, decorated with small intaglio insects, represent beaks; below them the birds' breasts are covered with scale-like feathers, with large wings either side of vertically dividing flanges. Tiny tails are tucked in under each wing. Each bird has two feet, giving the vessel four in all.

The *you* is quartered by flanges indented by short lines. Just below the lip, on the long axis of the *you*, lie two vertical loops that formerly held a handle. A small truncated pyramidal knob on the lid was used to lift it off the body. The areas bounded by the flanges, loops and lip are packed with small birds and dragons against a *leiwen* ground. Large birds occupy the four quarters of the lid, taking over the eyes of the main birds as their own. The surface of the bronze is a rusty-brown colour with green patches.

You, wine-containers with lids and handles, were used from the Erligang period, as illustrated by examples of circular cross-section with tall necks and rounded bodies from Zhengzhou (Fig. 5) and Panlongcheng.[1] In the Anyang period such tall *you* were sometimes decorated with birds' features in high relief, inspired perhaps by vessels in animal and bird forms (Fig. 7).[2] Squat *you* in the shape of a pair of birds back to back seem to be contemporary with the tall-necked vessels to which birds' features were applied.[3] Over the Anyang period such decoration was greatly simplified.

1. *Wenwu* 1983.3, pp. 49–59, fig. 14; New York 1980, no. 9.
2. Hayashi 1984, vol. 2, pl. 256, *you* nos 7, 8.
3. Beijing 1985a, fig. 59; *Kaogu xuebao* 1986.2, pp. 153–97, fig. 13.

8 *He*

Shang.
H. 22.9 cm; W. at lip 11.8 cm.
Inscription: rubbing no. 3.
1973.7–26.5; Seligman Bequest.
Literature: Hansford 1957, A4; Hayashi 1984, vol. 2, pl. 206, *he* 28.

Lobed ceramic wine vessels, later known as *he*, regularly occur in Erlitou-period burials with bronze *jue* and *jia*. It is possible that even at this early stage ceramic *he* were paralleled by bronze vessels, but that the bronze ones were too precious to bury. Bronze *he* are known from the Erligang period; rare examples also occur in early Anyang, as in Fu Hao's tomb. At that date egg-shaped vessels on three cylindrical legs were also made.[1]

The British Museum's *he* has four cylindrical legs above a lobed body of four sections. Each lobe is decorated with a *taotie*'s head bearing ram's horns in relief. The horns are neatly flattened against the vessel's sides, as on a rectangular *hu* from Fu Hao's tomb (Fig. 7), but the vessel is probably somewhat later in date. The pictograph cast in relief on vessel and lid has not been deciphered; it occurs on a number of other vessels.[2]

1. *Wenwu* 1976.2, pp. 26–41, pl. 4:3; Beijing 1980f, pls XXXIX, XL.
2. Bagley 1987, no. 8.

9 *Gu*

Shang.
H. 20.6 cm; DIAM. at lip 13.3 cm.
Inscription: rubbing no. 4.
1939.5–22.2; given by Walter Hochstadter.

After *jue*, *gu* were perhaps the most common Shang bronze ritual vessels. This *gu* has a relatively early shape, being rather short in proportion to its height. 8▷

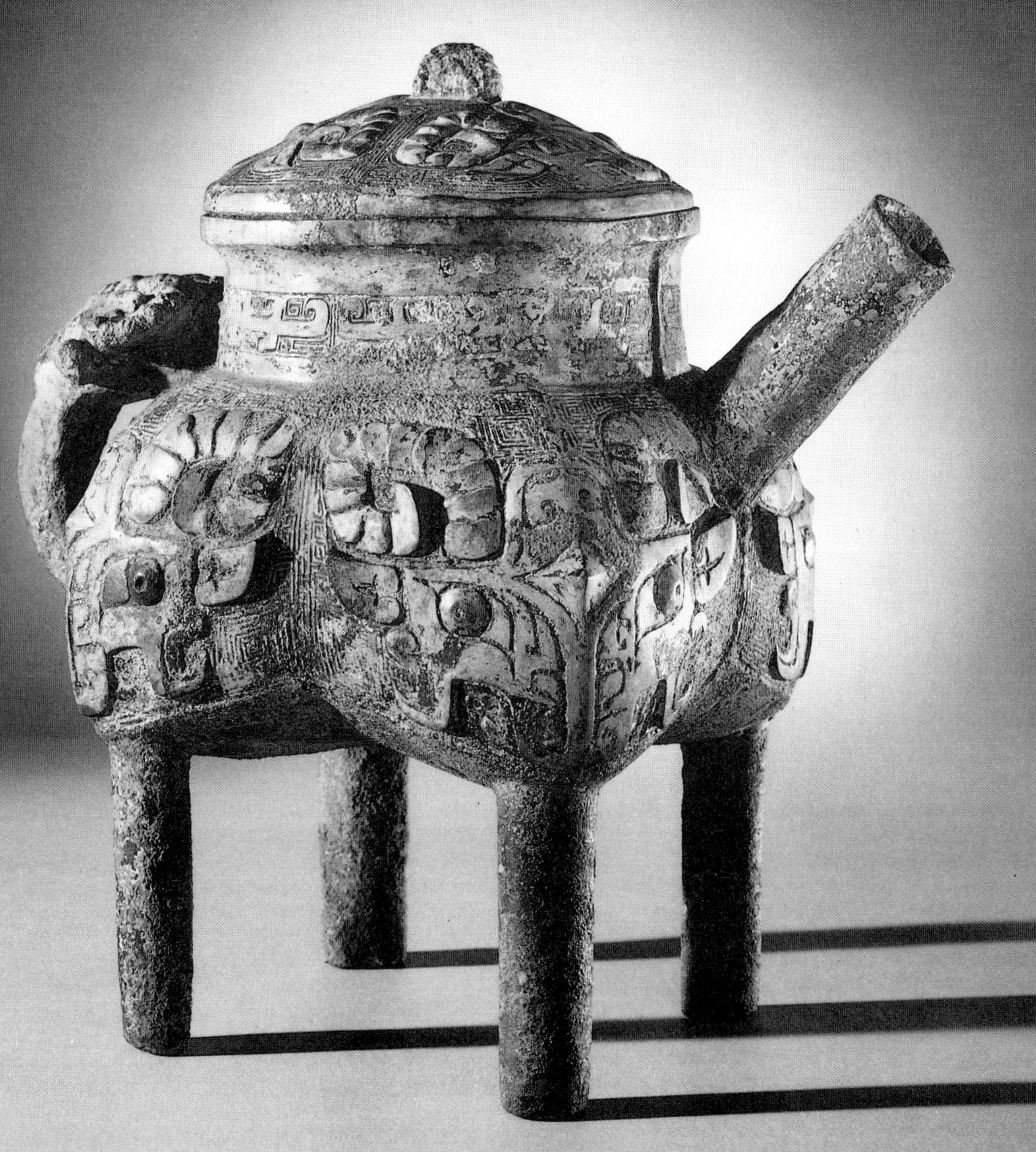

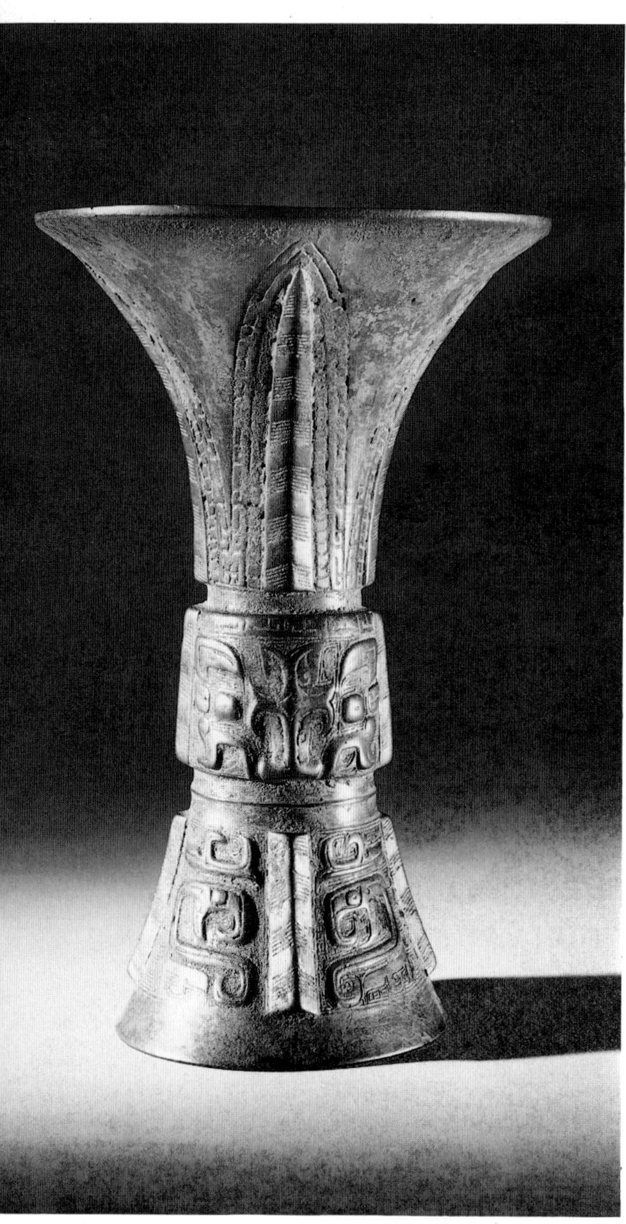

9

The shape notwithstanding, both the inscription and the decoration are typical of the late Anyang period. At the centre, front and back, are fairly conventional *taotie* faces without horns; in their place eyebrows lie above eyes completely filled by their pupils. Pairs of comma-shaped confronted dragons around the foot are more unusual.

Vertical divisions of triangular ridges, banded with closely packed intaglio lines alternating with smooth areas to make a chevron pattern, are the most distinctive features of the *gu*. Similar *gu* include a vessel from tomb M856 in the western sector of Yinxu at Anyang, a *gu* in a Chinese collection and a third vessel in the Fujii Yūrinkan in Kyoto. A number of other vessels with this distinctive banded decoration are known, including a *jue*, also from Yinxu (Fig. 8).[1] Inside the foot the *gu* carries an inscription starting with the graph for dagger-axe (*ge*), here a clan sign, and followed by the ancestor designation *Zu Gui*.

1. Bagley 1987, no. 49, describes the vessels; see also *Kaogu xuebao* 1979.1, pp. 27–146, pl. 15:1; Beijing 1981a, no. 238; Hayashi 1984, vol. 2, pl. 328, *gu* nos 136, 137.

10 *Yin Guang fang ding*

Shang.
H. to handles 24 cm; W. 18.5 cm; D. 14.7 cm.
Inscription: rubbing no. 5.
1981.5–30.1.
Literature: Wu Dacheng 1885.4; Liu Tizhi 1935, 3.2.4; Luo Zhenyu 1937, 4.10.2; Rong Geng and Zhang Weichi 1958, fig. 17; Yang Shuda 1959, p. 165; Zhou Fagao 1977, no. 879; Shirakawa 1963, 1.88.

Fang ding had an ancient pedigree. Both shape and decoration descend from bronzes of the Erligang period (Fig. 5); even earlier the shape appears among Erlitou ceramics.[1] Double-bodied snakes in the upper border also had a long history beginning in the Erlitou period.[2] On this *ding* and many like it the motifs were used with almost no variation, making one of the most stereotyped vessels of the late Shang and early Western Zhou. Among inscribed Shang and Zhou examples the most famous are the Zuo Ce Da vessels in the Freer Gallery and the National Palace Museum, Taibei.[3] These early Western Zhou *ding* are almost identical with the *Yin Guang fang ding* and illustrate continuity in bronze-casting at the time of the Zhou conquest.

The inscription on this *ding* describes a grant of cowries from the king to Yin, the casting of the *ding*, and notes that the king was attacking the Jing Fang, peoples known from oracle-bone inscriptions to have been in conflict with the Shang.[4] The small neat characters are paralleled on a few other late Shang vessels.[5]

1. *Kaogu* 1965.5, pp. 215–24, pl. 2.
2. *Kaogu* 1965.5, pp. 215–24, pl. 3:10.
3. Pope *et al.* 1967, no. 34; Taibei 1958, 2.2.63,64 (one of these has been deemed a fake).
4. Li Xueqin 1959.
5. Compare New York 1980, no. 54.

10▷

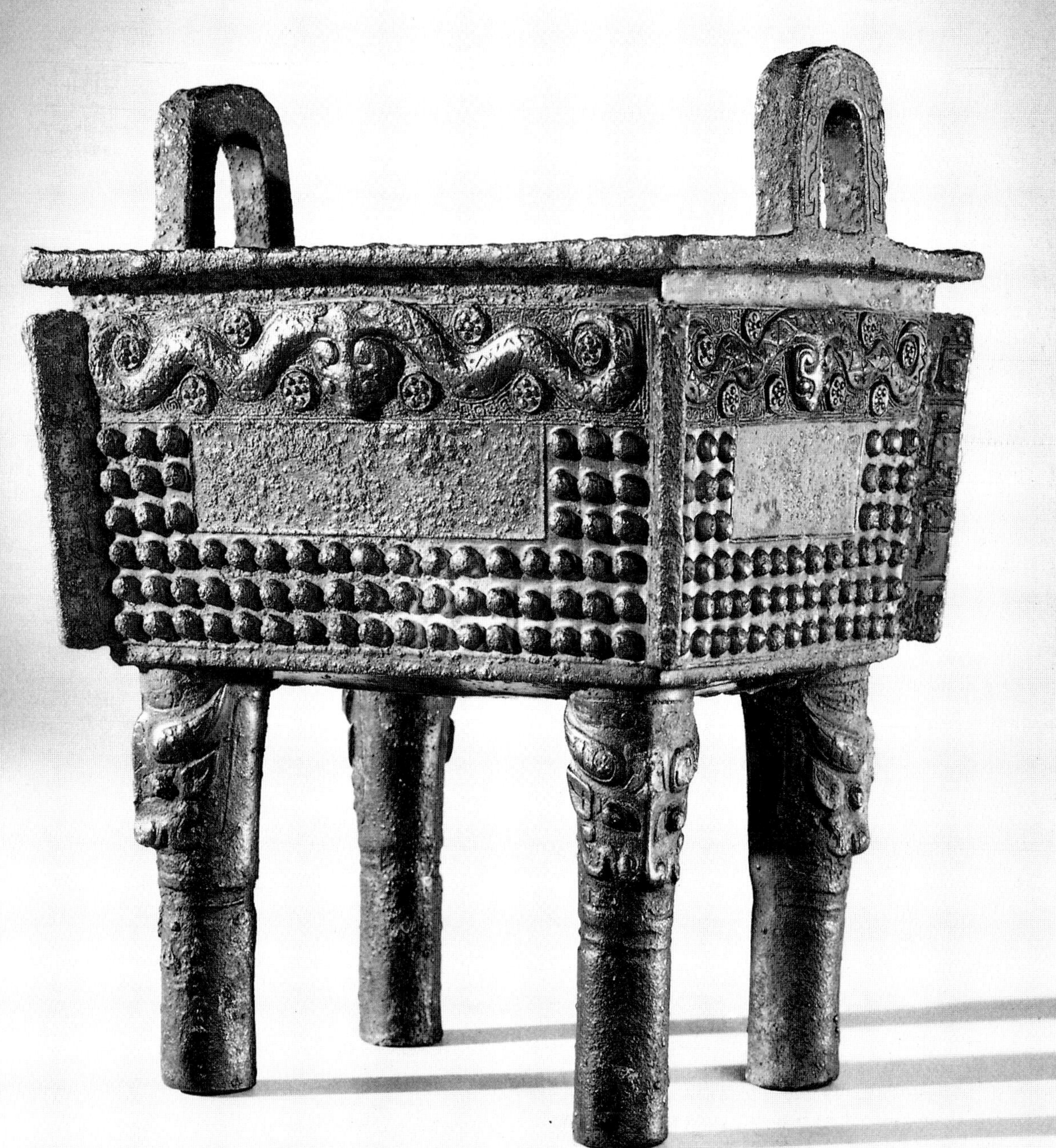

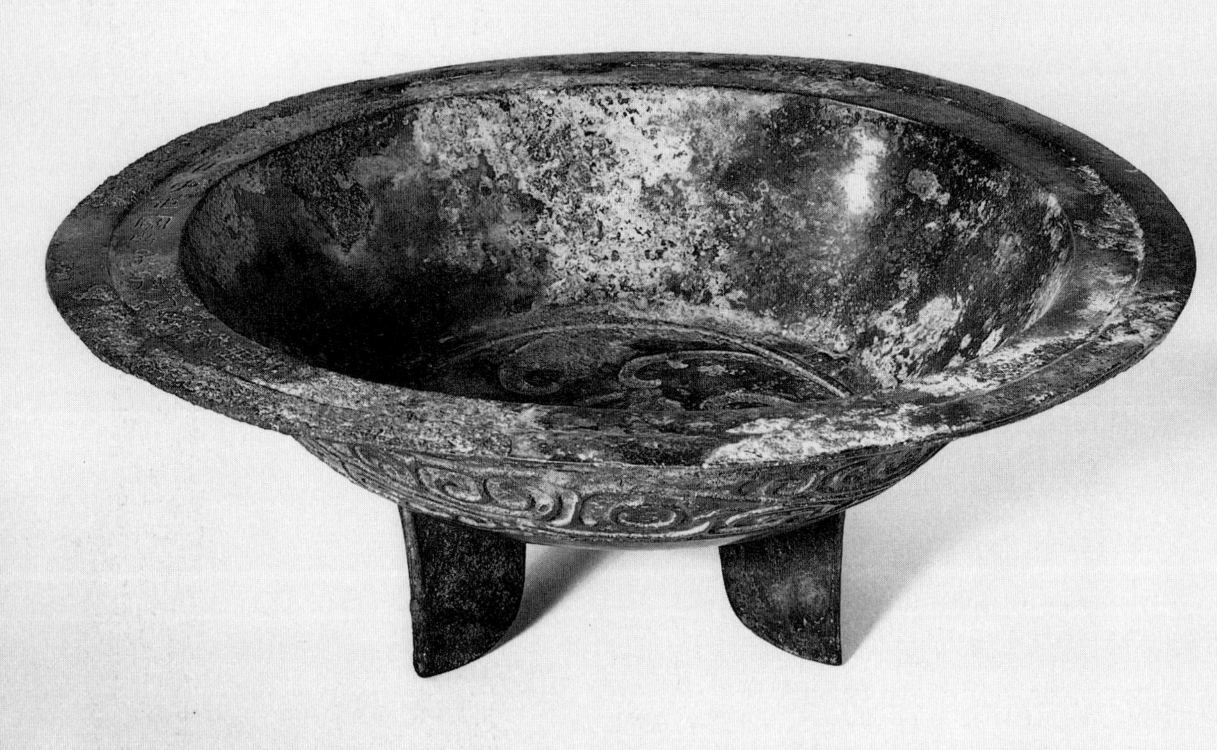

11

11 *Pan*

Shang or early Western Zhou.
H. 14.8 cm; DIAM. 38.6 cm.
Inscription; rubbing no. 12.
1983.7–29.1; Brooke Sewell Fund.

Extremely unusual and beautifully cast, this *pan* carries elegant scrolls around the outside. It has the rare feature of three blade-like legs, which support a steeply sloping bowl, flattened at the centre and filled with a deeply sunken roundel.[1] Relief roundels stand in a few early vessels, including a *yu* from a deposit at Zhengzhou illustrated in Figure 5. This sunken version is probably a later descendant. A distinctive ledge on the broad lip also has early antecedents, appearing on a *pan* from the Erligang-period site at Hubei Huangpi Panlongcheng.[2] Later *pan* from Qingjian Xian in northern Shaanxi retained this ledge. Like some other northern vessels the Qingjian *pan* are embellished with fish and a turtle in intaglio lines.[3]

Qingjian lies in northern Shaanxi to the west of the Yellow River (where it runs north-south). Other very unusual bronzes have come to light at Suide in the same part of Shaanxi and at Shilou in Shanxi.[4] It seems possible that the British Museum's *pan* was a product of this small enclave north of the main Shang area, which assimilated Erligang-period ceramic and bronze traditions but thereafter deviated from many Anyang practices.

The inscription on the *pan*, typical of the early Western Zhou, seems too late to be contemporary with the *pan*. However, the characters do not give the impression of being incised.

1. A *pan* with three dragon-shaped legs was excavated at Shanxi Shilou (*Wenwu* 1960.7, pp. 50–2, fig. 3).
2. *Wenwu* 1976.2, pp. 26–41, pl. 5:3.
3. Beijing 1979, no. 63. A *pan* from Fu Hao's tomb seems to be related to these northern vessels by its intaglio decoration and stepped rim (Beijing 1981a, no. 171).
4. New York 1980, nos 21, 22.

12 *Two ibex-headed knives*

Shang dynasty.
L. (from left to right) 24.8 cm, 25.1 cm.
1955.5–19.1, given by P. T. Brooke Sewell; 1973.7–26.30, Seligman Bequest
Literature: Hansford 1957, A31.

Small curved knives with integral blades and handles were current among peoples living along the northern marches of Shang power. Knives decorated with ibex heads, as here, were only one of several major types used in the area.[1] Curved knives were known in China from a very early date; a knife with a handle decorated by a row of oval depressions has been recovered from tomb M2 at Henan Yanshi Erlitou.[2] In subsequent centuries such knives were more popular with peoples of the northern zone than with the Shang and Zhou inhabitants of Shaanxi and Henan. It is, therefore, possible that even in the Erlitou period such knives illustrate contact with northern peoples. Alternatively, the spread of Erligang culture may have taken such knives from central Henan to the periphery.

Knives with ibex-head terminals are later. One has come from Fu Hao's tomb. Such Anyang knives resemble the knife on the left: they share its delicate casting and realistic detail.[3] The heavier casting of the second knife is reminiscent of that of knives from sites west and north of Henan.[4]

1. For discussion of the northern zone see Watson 1971 and Lin 1986; general articles on straight, as opposed to curved, knives are found in *Kaogu* 1978.5, pp. 324–33, 360; *Wenwu* 1984.2, pp. 37–49; *Kaogu xuebao* 1985.2, pp. 135–56. It has been suggested by Emma Bunker that some of these knives were cast by the lost-wax process (private communication).
2. *Kaogu* 1983.3, pp. 199–205, 219.
3. Beijing 1980f, pl. LXVI:1.
4. Beijing 1979, no. 90; Beijing 1980a, no. 83.

13 *Double-ram zun* *(illustrated in colour)*

Shang.
H. 43.2 cm; W. at lip 17 cm.
1936.11–18.1; ex-Eumorfopoulos Collection.
Literature: Yetts 1929, A11–A12; Umehara 1933a, 1.37–8; Watson 1963, pl. 3; Hayashi 1984, vol. 2, pl. 246, *niao shou xing zun* no. 12; Li Xueqin 1985b, no. 122.

This vessel is probably the British Museum's most famous ancient Chinese bronze. The container, presumably for wine, is flanked by the heads and forequarters of two rams. By convention the vessel is termed a *zun*. The rams are more lifelike and convincing than any of the other creatures de-

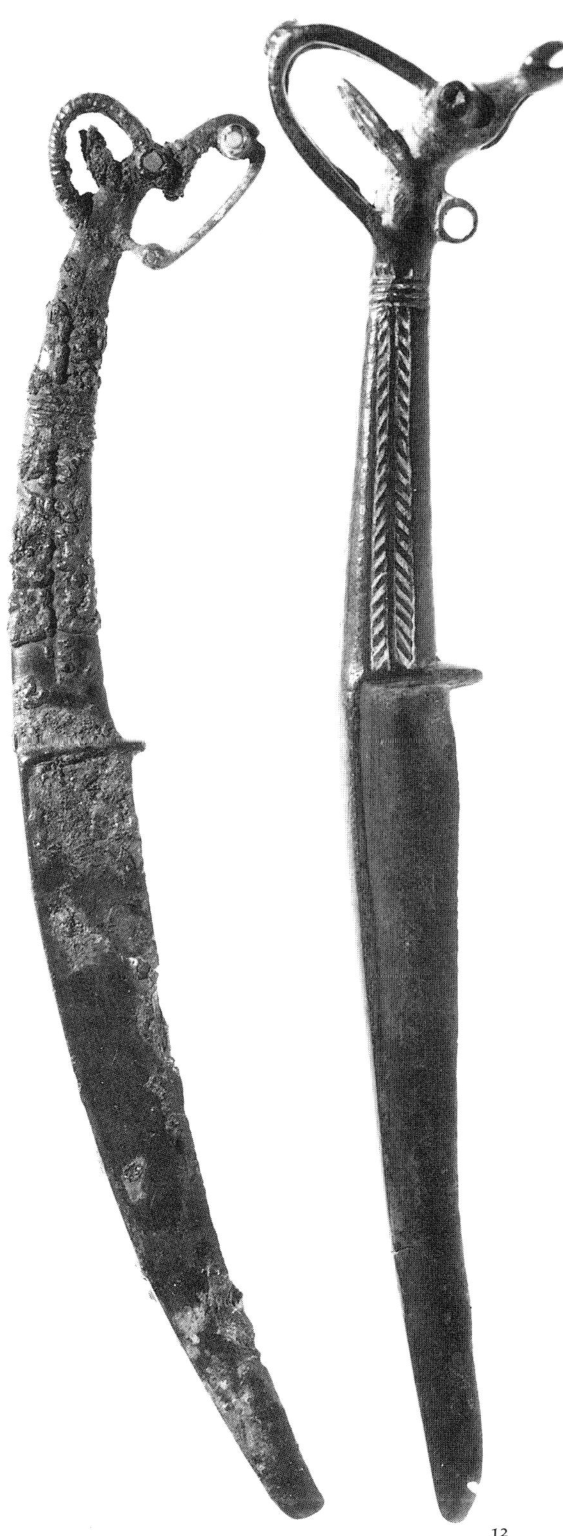

12

scribed so far. In part the freely curling horns are responsible for this effect. Unlike the rams' horns on no. 8, which were neatly confined to the panels of the vessel sides, here the horns are fully rounded and project away from the animals' heads. They were probably cast first and then inserted into the moulds used for casting the rest of the bronze.

The bodies of the rams are covered with small scales, very like the feathers of birds on no. 7. On each of the haunches standing out in slight relief a *long*-dragon is embedded among the scales, its head, crowned by two small bottle-horns, hanging down towards the hooves. Pairs of C-shaped projections fill the spaces between the legs. Directly above lies the oval opening of the *zun*. The rectangular panels below this opening on the two sides of the vessels are filled with somewhat unorthodox *taotie* faces which have large round pupils and bottle-horns in relief; the rest of the faces are executed in thick scrolling reminiscent of Style II. The obscured features of the *taotie* contrast with the very realistic rams' heads.

In almost every respect the *zun* differs from Anyang-style bronzes (nos 4–10). To date vessels of this shape have not been found at the main Shang centres. Two comparable vessels are known: a double-ram vessel in the Nezu Museum in Tokyo, said to have come from Changsha in Hunan province, and a four-ram vessel found at Hunan Ningxiang.[1] The British Museum's *zun* is also likely to have come from the south, possibly also from Hunan.

1. Hayashi 1984, vol. 2, pl. 246, *niao shou xing zun* no. 13; New York 1980, no. 20.

14 *Pou*

Shang.
H. 28.5 cm; DIAM. at lip 27.4 cm.
1980.1–28.1.

Although much less striking than the ram *zun*, this

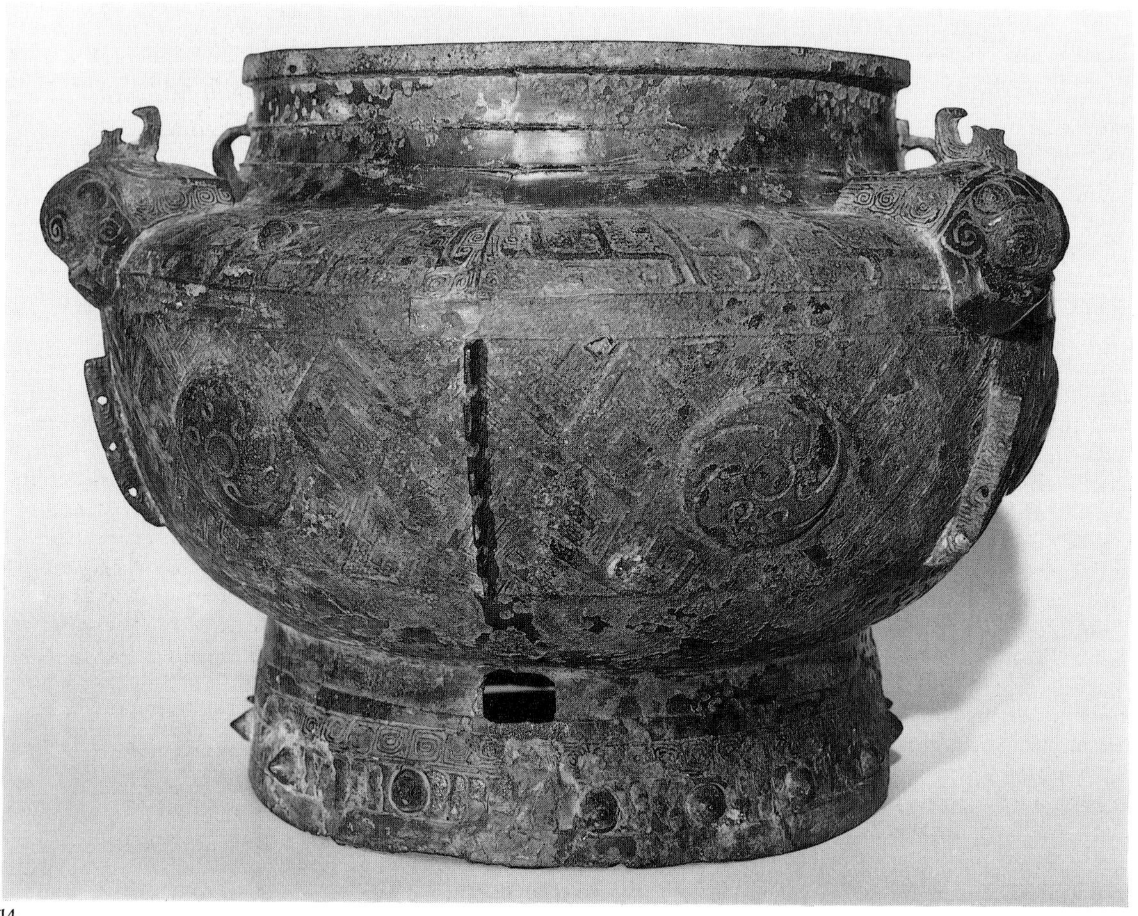

14

large container probably also comes from southern China. Its comparatively large size and summary casting are characteristic of some southern bronzes. In addition the slightly uneasy combination of relief roundels with a continuous pattern of interlocking TS is an unorthodox and therefore probably provincial rendering of metropolitan Shang motifs. Inside the body the relief roundels are reflected by deep recesses. This device is found on other provincial bronzes, including a *pou* in the Art Museum, Princeton University. Similar vessels are in the Shanghai Museum and in the Museum of Far Eastern Antiquities, Stockholm. These unprovenanced vessels are identified as southern castings because they are similar to *zun* found in Hunan province.[1] Like the *pou* many of these *zun* carry hooked flanges descended from Erligang-period examples.

1. These bronzes, which are sometimes called *lei*, are discussed in Kane 1974; see also Bagley 1987, no. 43; Hayashi 1984, vol. 2, pl. 31, *pou* nos 49–52.

15 *Finial*

Shang.
H. 11 cm.
1968.4–22.6; Sedgwick Bequest.

This exquisite tiny bronze is made as a tier of creatures. At the base is a small rectangular slot to attach it to a wooden staff. Crouched above the slot is a monkey-like figure with trailing feathers and, perched on his head, a human-looking figure clutching a bird in his hands; a tiger clambers up the back of this second figure and grasps his head in its jaws. The black surface of the bronze is embellished with intaglio lines. Like the ram *zun* this casting lies outside the mainstream of Shang bronze art; however, unlike the ram it is difficult to place. The neat sculptural figures may indicate that the finial too comes from the south.

There are a number of bronzes and jades that provided a context, however little understood, for the theme of a man, or man-like figure, grasped by a tiger. At Anyang a simplified version was employed, with a head alone flanked by a pair of tigers, as on an axe from Fu Hao's tomb and on the handles of a large rectangular *ding*, known as the *Si Mu Wu fang ding*.[1] On other apparently provincial vessels vivid examples are found. Earliest in date is a *zun* from Anhui Funan Xian, on which both the figure and a tiger with a divided double body are cast in relief.[2]

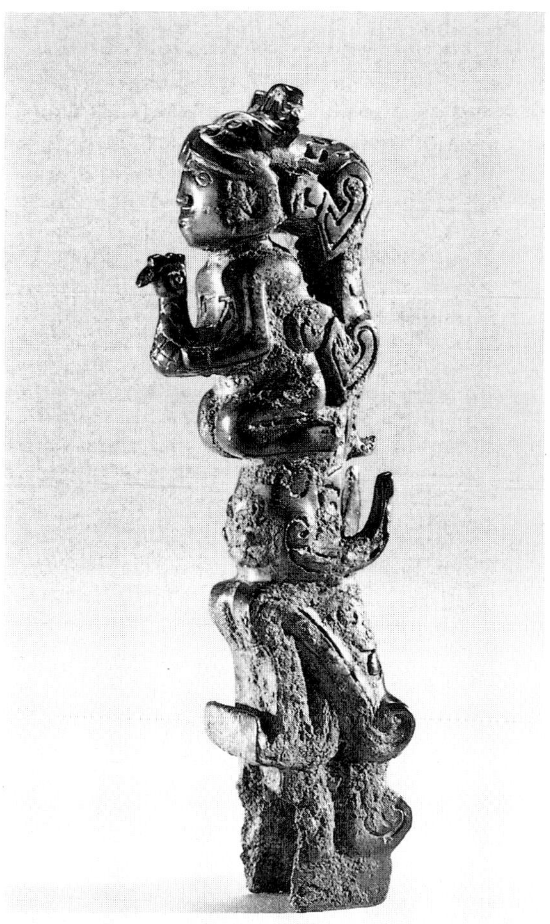

15

Two almost identical *you* in the shape of beasts clutching human figures just below their jaws are later in date, the profusion of creatures decorating their bodies being similar to the dense ornament of no. 7; one is in the Cernuschi Museum, Paris, and the other in the Sumitomo Collection, Kyoto.[3] A finial formerly in the collection of the King of Sweden and a ritual knife in the Freer Gallery, Washington, are early Western Zhou examples of similar subjects.[4] A few jades also illustrate figures grasped in the jaws of creatures (Fig. 11).[5]

1. Beijing 1980f, colour pl. 13; Akiyama *et al.* 1968, pl. 9.
2. Akiyama *et al.* 1968, pl. 43.
3. Elisseeff 1977, no. 46; Hayashi 1984, vol. 2, pl. 288, *niao shou xing you* no. 15.
4. Lion-Goldschmidt and Moreau-Gobbard 1980, no. 28; Ackerman 1945, pl. 1 (left).
5. Salmony 1938, pl. xx: 2,3.

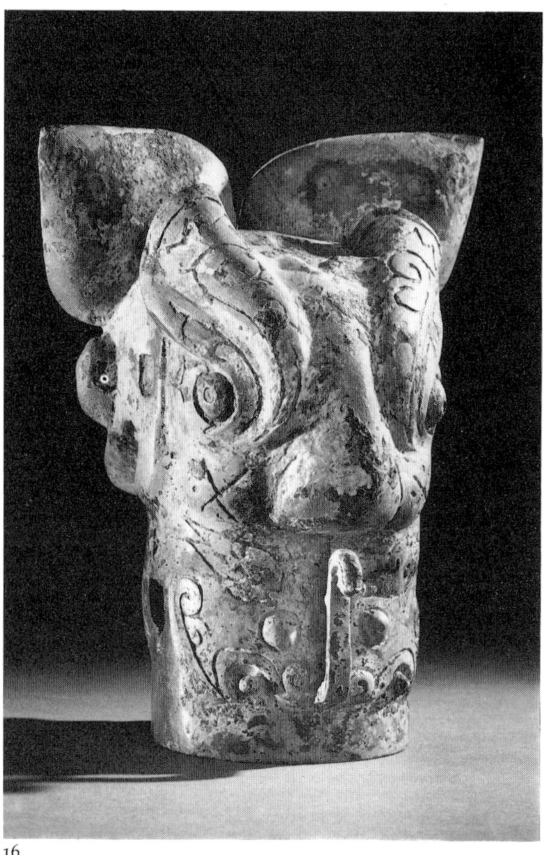

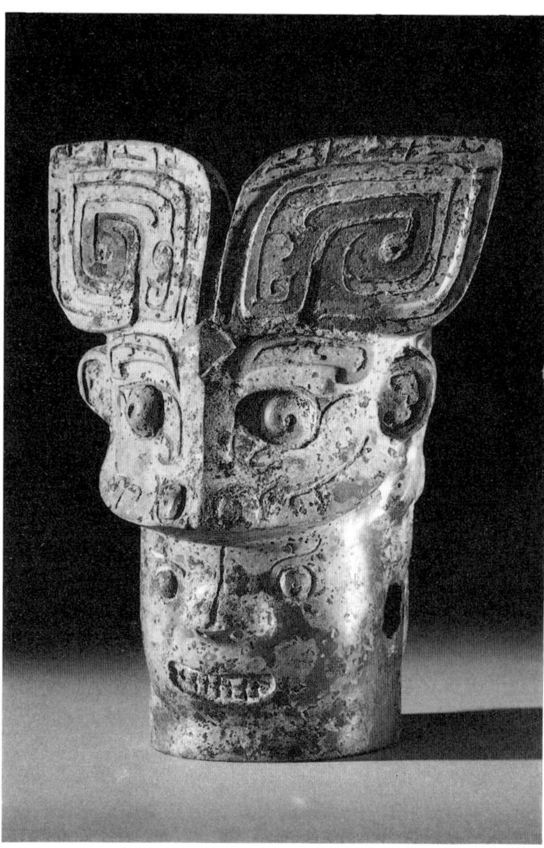

16

16 *Finial*

Early Western Zhou.
H. 15.2 cm.
1953.11–18.1; given by P.T. Brooke Sewell.
Literature: Watson 1963, pl. 12.

This second finial is larger than no. 10; it is also later in date. The casting is hollow, being square in cross-section with rounded corners. There are four rectangular holes, two on each side, for securing the bronze to a shaft, presumably in wood.

Four heads or faces decorate the bronze: a large *taotie* with angular horns overhangs a second head, that of a man with parted lips showing his two rows of teeth. On the other side the upper head has short blunt horns embellished with sunken star-like points. This creature seems to be related to animal heads with spiky horns that decorate handles on several early Zhou bronzes; both are descended from bottle-horned dragons with stars centred on the tops of their horns.[1] An intaglio cross punctuated with dots appears on the creature's cheeks. Like the human face the second lower face is flattened against the tube's sides. A small projecting trunk suggests that it represents an elephant. Ears with two sharp points resemble those of the elephants on the *Xing Hou gui* (no. 25).

It is difficult to identify the piece. However, a bronze of very similar shape, and presumably for an identical purpose, was excavated from a chariot pit at Shaanxi Baoji Rujiazhuang, and is dated to the end of the early or beginning of the middle Western Zhou. The fitting was almost certainly part of the chariot or charioteer's equipment.[2] The Baoji finial is decorated with a monster face rather like a *taotie*, grasped from behind by a figure of a man.[2] Two deer on the back of the figure's coat hint at connections with the nomadic tribes of the north-west. A number of other unprovenanced finials are known.[3]

1. Rawson (forthcoming), no. 118.
2. Beijing 1984b, no. 94; Beijing 1986, vol. 1, pp. 139–62, fig. 6:5.
3. *Wenwu* 1966.5, p. 69; Ackerman 1945, pl. 64; Karlgren 1952, no. 64; van Heusden 1952, p. 180, pl. LV; d'Argencé 1966, pl. XXIV; Lion-Goldschmidt and Moreau-Gobard 1980, no. 30.

17 *Axe*

Shang dynasty.
H. 24.8 cm; W. 19.6 cm.
1947.7–12.413; Oppenheim Bequest.
Literature: Watson 1963, pl. 11a.

A monstrous face fills both sides of the axe. Eyes, eyebrows, nose and ears are almost human; the mouth with serrated teeth and two fangs is much more sinister. A rectangular tang decorated with a coiled dragon would have projected beyond the wooden shaft mounted at right angles to the blade.

Two similar axes found in a small pit in the outer trench of a large burial at Sufutun in Shandong province may have been used to slaughter the sacrificial victims interred in the access ramp to the tomb. The tomb dates to the end of the Shang or early Zhou period.[1] All such wide axes descend from neolithic stone axes drilled with small holes near the top to attach them to wooden hafts.[2] By the Erlitou period ceremonial axes were carved in jade in which these functional holes had been enlarged to occupy much of the centre of the axe. Almost central holes also dominate several early bronze axes, including two from Panlongcheng in Hubei province.[3] On later bronze axes, such as the present example, the central hole was adapted to make the gaping mouth of a demon or monster.[4]

1. *Wenwu* 1972.8, pp. 17–30, fig. 10.
2. *Kaogu* 1985.9, pp. 820–9; Beijing 1986, vol. 1, pp. 128–38.
3. *Wenwu* 1976.2, pp. 26–41, figs 9,34.
4. Beijing 1977, fig. 18; *Kaogu xuebao* 1986.2, pp. 153–97, fig. 19.

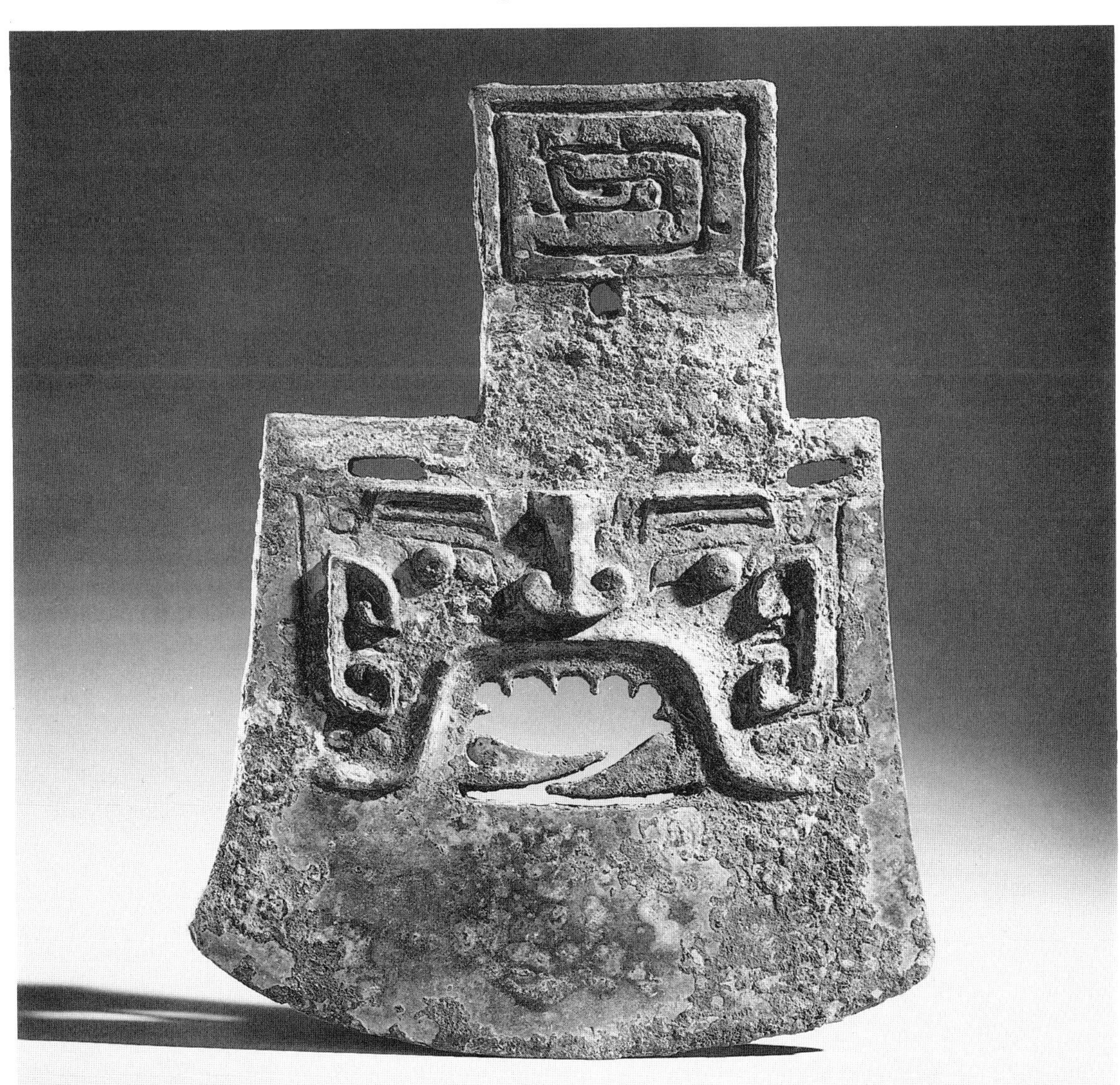
17

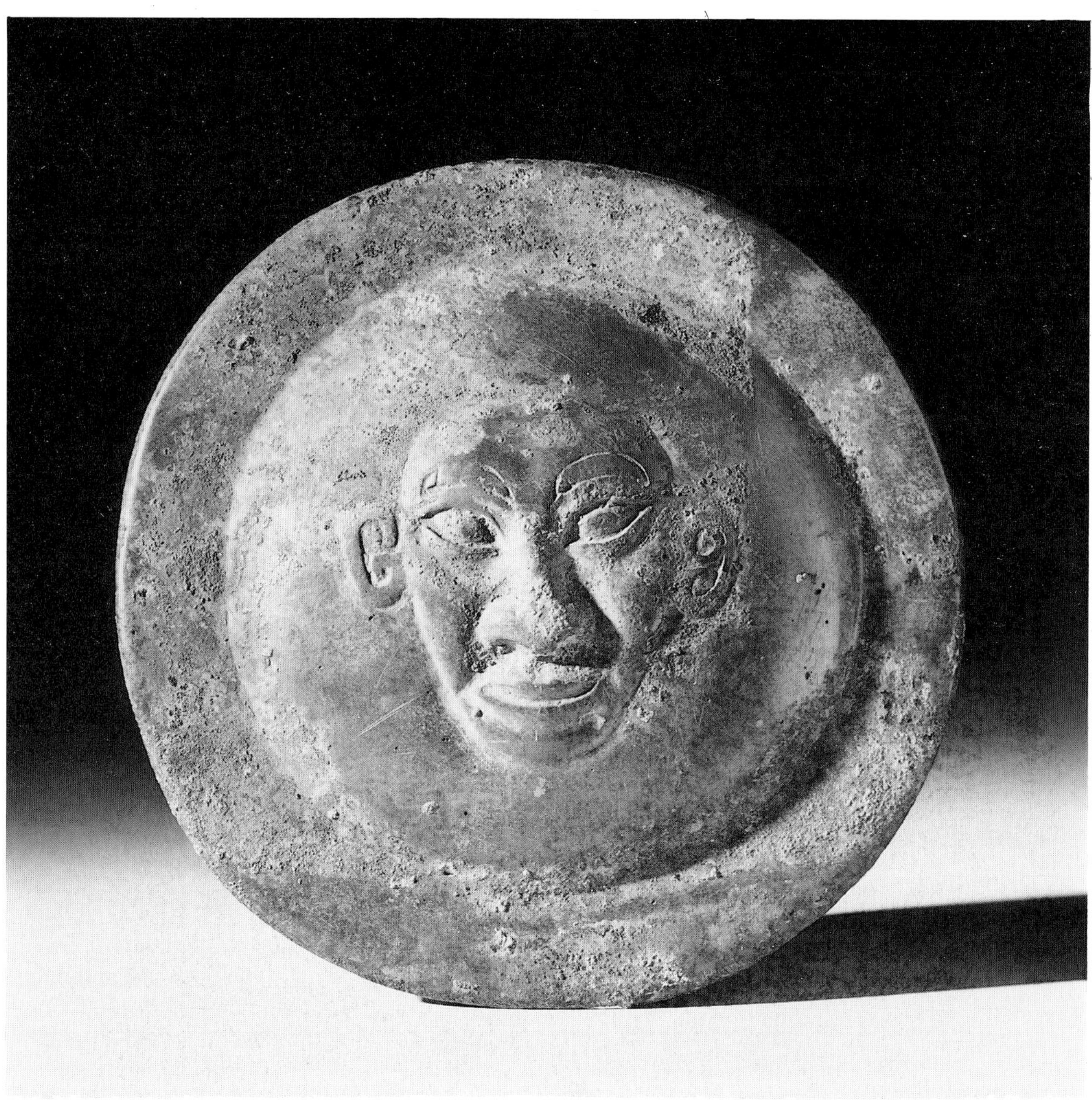

18

18 *Harness plaque*

Shang.
DIAM. 10 cm.
1947.7–21.3; Raphael Bequest.

This small disc-shaped plaque has two loops on the back through which thongs, part of a harness, may have passed. Although animals and monsters predominated in Shang art, a few human representations have been found, mainly in jade. Slanting eyes, arched brows, a broad nose, full lips and projecting ears, depicted here, are evident on small carvings from Fu Hao's tomb.[1] A few human heads in ceramic are also known, but bronze representations are much less common.[2] Apart from a famous, but unusual, provincial Shang *fang ding* from Hunan province, most of the bronzes are chariot or harness fittings.[3]

1. Beijing 1980f, colour pls 22–5.
2. Beijing 1980a, no. 54; *Wenwu* 1984.7, pp. 1–29, fig. 43:8; for a ceramic mould see Qian Hao *et al*. 1981, fig. 28.
3. The *fang ding* was exhibited in London 1973–4 (Watson 1973a, no. 79); for harness fittings see Li 1977, pl. 20; *Kaogu* 1976.1, pp. 31–8, pl. 3:2; *Kaogu* 1980.3, pp. 211–18, pl. 5:4; Beijing 1986, vol. 1, pp. 139–62, fig. 4:8.

19 *Openwork harness frontlet*

Western Zhou.
H. 23 cm; W. 25.5 cm.
1961.12–18.1; Brooke Sewell Bequest.

Openwork bronze masks adorned the heads of horses pulling chariots. From the second half of the Anyang period chariots, their horses and sometimes their charioteers were interred in pits beside tombs of kings, nobles and high officials.[1] It has been argued that the chariot was originally foreign to ancient China, being introduced from further west.[2] The bronze fittings developed seem to have been almost entirely Chinese.

Several different bronze masks have been found. Some consist of small detached features – eyes, nose, jaws and horns – which were probably attached to cloth or some other soft material; others are complete, as here.[3] The almost circular eye holes on the British Museum's mask are characteristic of the genre; in other respects the features of the face resemble typical early Western Zhou *taotie*. An openwork blade in two segments, which stands above the nose, and tiny holes at the outer edges of the face must have been part of the harness fixings.

1. von Dewall 1964; Beijing 1986, vol. 1, pp. 139–62.
2. Piggott 1978.
3. *Wenwu* 1985.8, pp. 25–40, fig. 18.

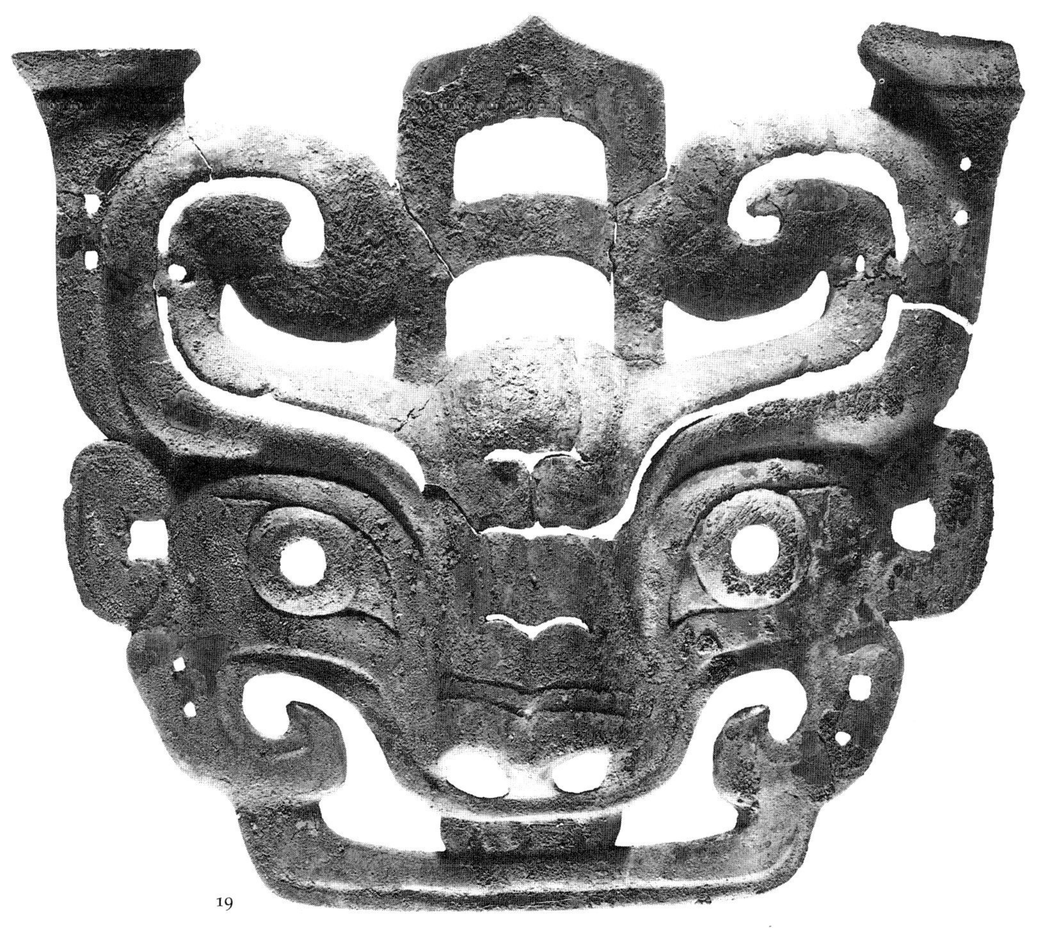

19

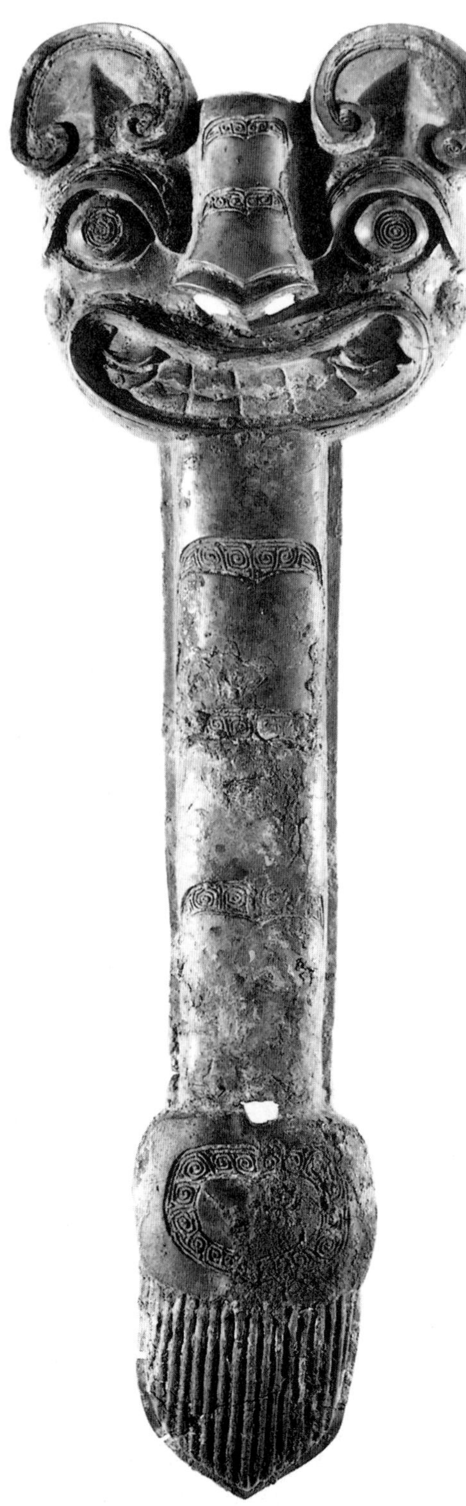
20

20 *Harness frontlet*

Western Zhou.
L. 33.4 cm.
1947.7–21.2; Raphael Bequest.

The bar of this harness frontlet presumably lay along the nose of a horse, with the monster face at the top sitting on the horse's forehead. Cords passing through slots in the back would have held the bronze in place. Heavy relief emphasises the staring eyes and a grinning jaw. Similar, almost circular eyes and teeth-filled jaws appear on two axes found in a tomb at Sufutun in Shandong province, mentioned in connection with a Shang-period axe (no. 17). The faces on the axes have grotesque human features, whereas the creature displayed here seems to be a tiger-like monster. The pointed arrow-shaped relief within the ears is very unusual. Areas of *leiwen* within some features of the face and arranged in scalloped horizontal registers across the vertical bar contrast with the relief of the face. A similar frontlet without the horizontal registers was found in a burial near Beijing.[1]

1. *Kaogu* 1976.4, pp. 246–58, 228, fig. 18.

21 *Pan*

Early Western Zhou.
H. 13.1 cm; DIAM. 34 cm.
Inscription: rubbing no. 6.
1952.12–16.1; given by P.T. Brooke Sewell.
Literature: Hayashi 1984, vol. 2, pl. 362, *pan* no. 36.

A dragon is coiled on the interior of this water basin. The same beast also appears in profile with only one horn visible just below the rim. Bottle-shaped horns and a long snaky body are the defining characteristics of the *long*, or dragon, which is represented with precisely these features in oracle-bone graphs.[1] Although many *long*-dragon motifs differed slightly from the graph, being equipped with pointed horns and claws, it is still possible to discern the original snake-like features. They are quite different from the Erligang-period profile creatures composed of quills, or the very varied creatures made up from parts of Style IV and V *taotie* in the Anyang period, illustrated on no. 5.

From an early date water basins, *pan*, were decorated with creatures such as fish, turtles and birds that were at home with water. Some of these motifs appear on Erlitou-period ceramic *pan*.[2] Among them is the dragon, a creature associated in Chinese lore with water and plenty. Erligang *pan*

21▷

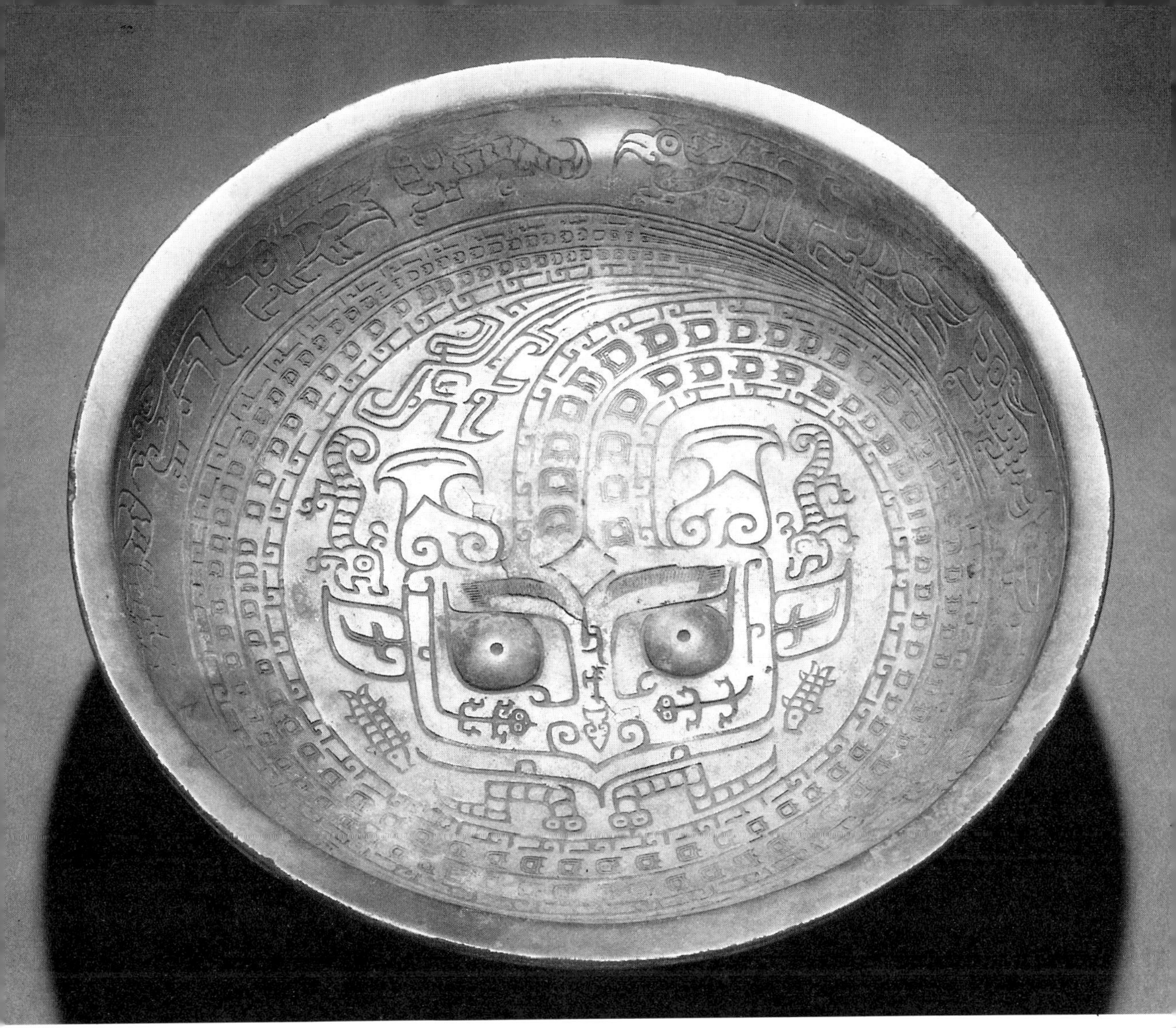

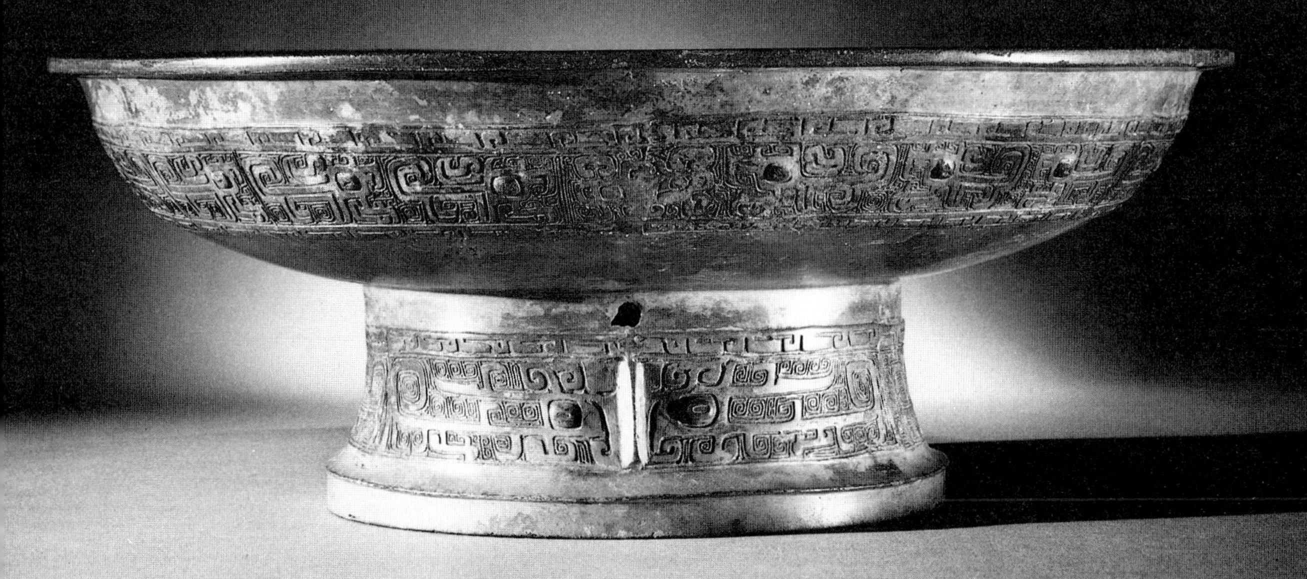

were not usually decorated in this way (Fig. 5), but on the northern borders of China's central plain more realistic creatures were used as on a *pan* from Beijing (see p. 29). *Pan* similarly decorated in Fu Hao's tomb suggest, as does the presence of an ibex-headed knife, that there was contact between Anyang and the north at this date.[3] The present *pan* is a later descendant of the Anyang *pan*. An inscription runs down the nose of the dragon and comprises the ancestor designation Fu Wu followed by a clan sign.

1. Rawson 1983; *Wenwu* 1984.1, pp. 75–83, 29.
2. *Kaogu* 1965.5, pp. 215–24, pl. 3:10.
3. Beijing 1980f, figs 21, 22.

22 *Kang Hou gui* *(illustrated in colour)*

Early Western Zhou.
H. 21.6 cm; DIAM. at lip 26.6 cm.
Inscription: rubbing no. 9.
1977.4–4.1; ex-Malcolm Collection.
Literature: Rong Geng 1941, 2.259; Chen Mengjia 1955, pt. 1, pp. 161–5; Yang Shuda 1959, pp. 244–5; Shirakawa 1962, 4.14.141; Hayashi 1984, vol. 2, pl. 95, *gui* no. 123.

This vessel is famous for its inscription, which describes an attack on the Shang by the Zhou king and the establishment of the Kang Hou (sometimes entitled the Marquis of Kang) in Wei, near present-day Hui Xian in Henan province, where the vessel is said to have been found. It was cast by a Mei Situ Yi, possibly in conjunction with the Kang Hou. The defeat of the Shang referred to in the inscription is not the initial Zhou conquest of the Shang but the suppression of rebellion by the remnants of the Shang. This rebellion occurred in the reign of Cheng Wang, the successor of the conqueror Wu Wang. A number of other vessels, including a cylindrical *zun* in the Burrell Collection in Glasgow, bear inscriptions that refer either to the Kang Hou or to the Mei Situ Yi.[1]

In addition to its great historical importance the *Kang Hou gui* is an imposing vessel. Its high foot-ring and large handles add dignity to decoration that on many other lesser vessels is almost routine. The handles consist of large tusked animal heads, crowned by openwork upright horns, swallowing birds whose beaks just emerge from their jaws; below, the handles are decorated with birds' wings, bodies and tails.

1. For a full list of references, including a note of the publication of the Burrell *zun*, see Chen Mengjia 1977, A329.

23 *Gui*

Early Western Zhou.
H. 14.8 cm; DIAM. at lip 18 cm.
1984.5–31.1; ex-Collection of Mr and Mrs Richard Bull.

Large profile dragons with coiled bodies are identified with Western Zhou bronze-casting. They appear, for example, on the *Da Feng gui* in the Historical Museum, Beijing, a vessel whose inscription refers to Wen Wang, father of the conqueror Wu Wang.[1] Such dragons embellish other vessels, especially *gui*, with inscriptions that can be dated to the early Western Zhou period.[2] The motif also appears on bronzes excavated in western China, in Shaanxi and Sichuan provinces, including *lei* with extravagant flanges discussed in the Introduction (Fig. 13).

Coiled dragons seem to have been invented at the very beginning of the Western Zhou period, or just before the conquest, taking advantage of a Shang design. The large coiled body is based upon a dragon such as that shown in no. 21. To create a profile version of the creature the head seems to have been cut off the body and a new profile head attached.[3] Other early Western Zhou bronzes display similarly naïve inventions.

1. Shirakawa 1962, 1.1.1.
2. Hayashi 1984, vol. 2, pls 92, 96, *gui* nos 90–3, 125–9.
3. Rawson 1983.

24 *Ding* *(illustrated in colour)*

Early Western Zhou.
H. to handles 32.2 cm; DIAM. at lip 26.8 cm.
1945.10–17.219; Raphael Bequest.

This smooth rounded *ding* bears highly idiosyncratic bird motifs. Three pairs are compressed into a narrow border, each pair lying between the mould seams whose traces are aligned with the centres of the legs. The birds have small heads, prominently large eyes, curved open beaks, round compressed wings and long horizontal tails with intriguingly hooked feathers. Their equally long crests carry similar hooks.

This sort of bird motif never appears on Shang bronzes. It is indeed extremely rare, being found on only six other published bronzes. These are a *gui* on an integral square base in the Sackler Collections; a *gui* on a high moulded foot-ring in the Shanghai Museum; two almost identical *gong* of rectangular cross-section – one in the Brundage Collection in the Asian Art Museum, San Francisco, and the other in the Art Museum, Princeton University; a *you* known

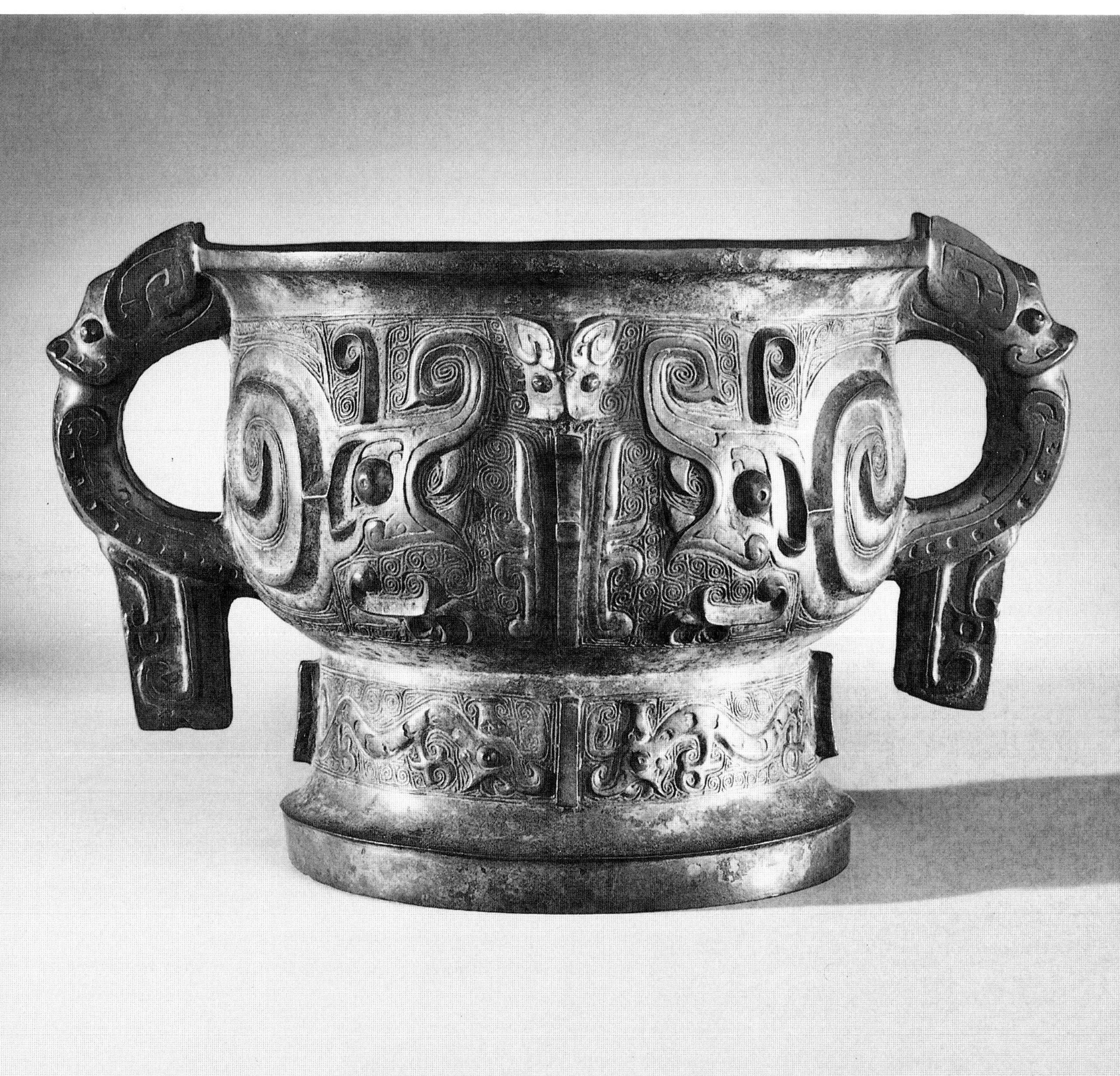

23

only from a reproduction in the catalogue of the Qing dynasty Imperial Collection – *Xi Qing gu jian*; and a *fang ding* in the museum at Baoji Xian, Shaanxi province.[1]

Of these vessels the *gui* on a square base is the best known. It was published by Umehara Sueji as one of a set of vessels thought to come from a tomb at Shaanxi Baoji Xian. The group was known only from a photograph, obtained by Umehara in Taiwan, in which a number of vessels, the *gui* included, were shown standing on and around a rectangular altar or *jin*.[2] Most of the vessels have subsequently been identified in Western collections; the altar was rediscovered in Tianjin. Holes in the altar designed to take three vessels have proved to be the wrong shape and size to hold any of the

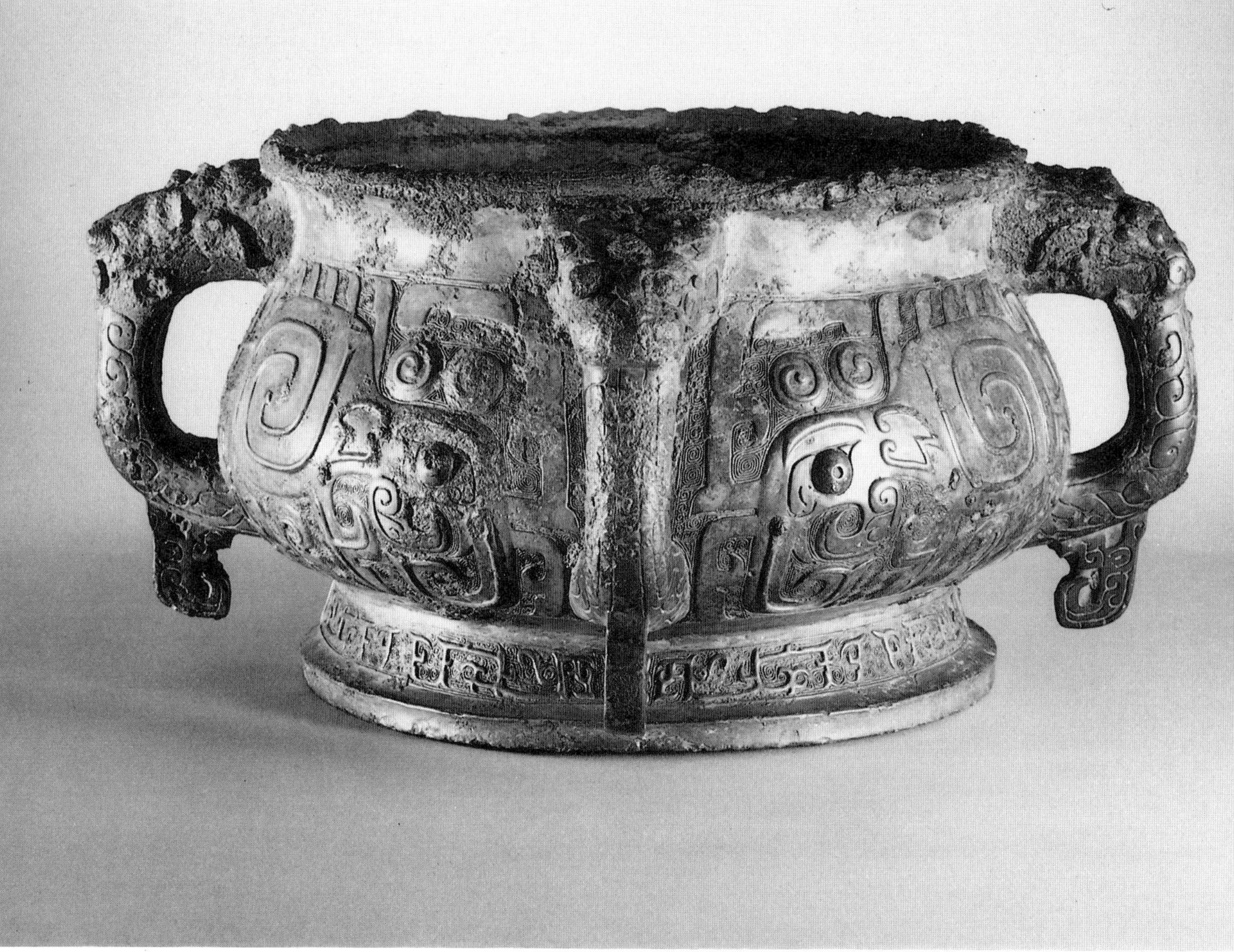

25

vessels illustrated in the photograph.[3] Nor are the vessel types consistent with what are now known to have been the typical vessel sets of the early Zhou period. Suggestions that the vessels in the photograph, including the *gui*, are part of the contents of a single pre-conquest or early Western Zhou tomb are therefore without foundation. On the other hand, the discovery of the *fang ding* at Baoji does suggest that vessels with this idiosyncratic bird decoration probably come from Shaanxi province.

1. The six vessels are published as follows: Watson 1962, pl. 32; Hong Kong 1983, no. 25; von Erdberg 1978, no. 42; d'Argencé 1977, pl. xxv; *Xi Qing gu jian* 17.11; Li Xueqin 1985b, no. 137.
2. Umehara 1959b; Rawson (forthcoming), Appendix 3.
3. New York 1980, no. 48.

25 *Xing Hou gui*

Early to middle Western Zhou.
H. 18.5 cm; DIAM. at lip 27.8 cm.
Inscription: rubbing no. 10.
1936.11–18.2; ex-Eumorfopoulos Collection.
Literature: Yetts 1929, A16–A18; Umehara 1933a, 2.103; Guo Moruo 1935, *kao* 39–40; Luo Zhenyu 1937, 6.54.2; Rong Geng 1941, 2.282; Chen Mengjia 1955, pt. 3, pp. 73–7, pl. 3; Yang Shuda, 1959, pp. 108–9; Shirakawa 1962, 11.59.591; Watson 1963, pl. 13; Zhou Fagao 1977, no. 1531; Hayashi 1984, vol. 2, pl. 107, *gui* no. 229.

Like the *Kang Hou gui* this vessel is famous first and foremost for its inscription, which records the grant of three groups of men to a Xing Hou (Marquis of Xing) and dedication of the *gui* to the illustrious Zhou Gong. Descendants of Zhou Gong (the Duke

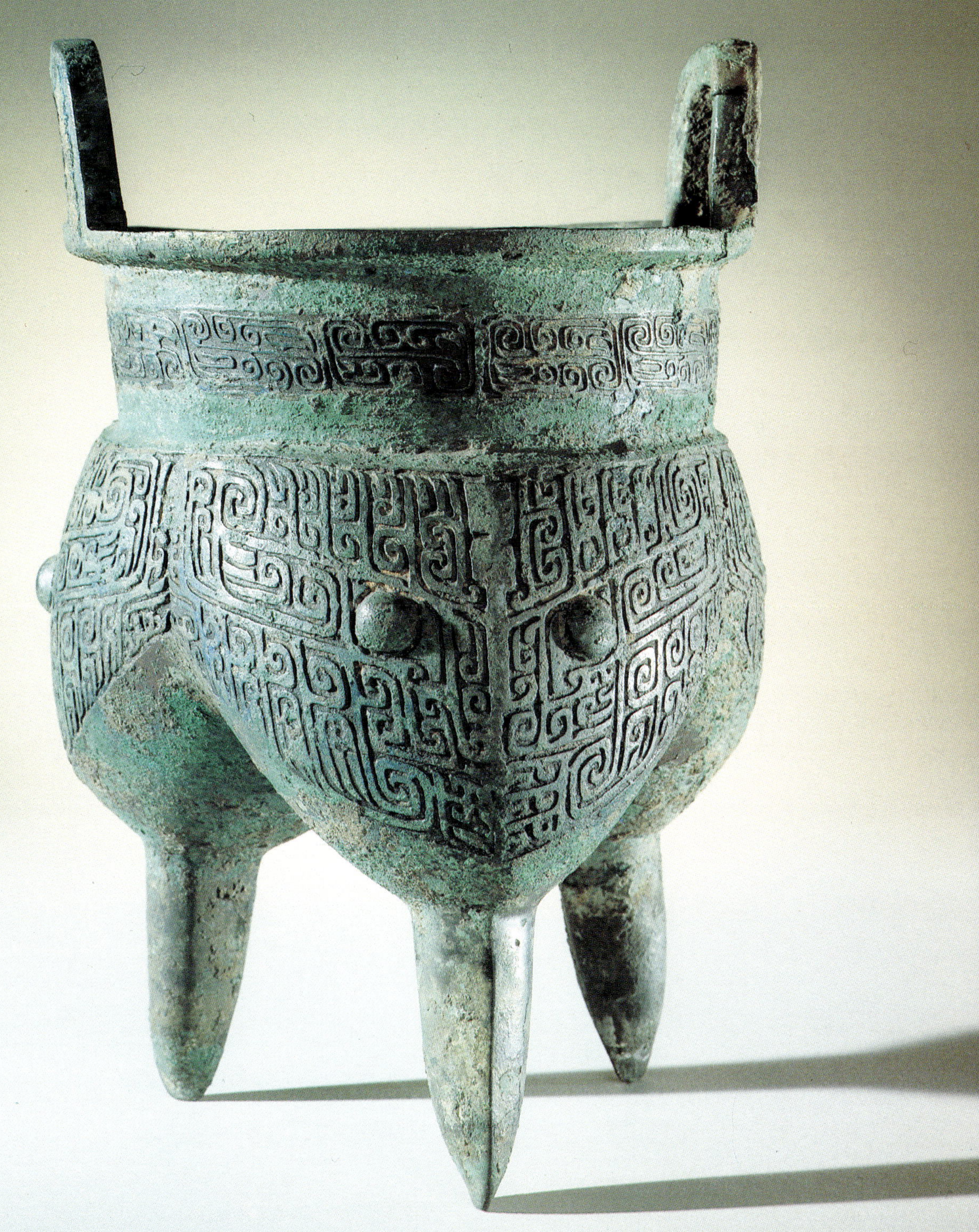

2

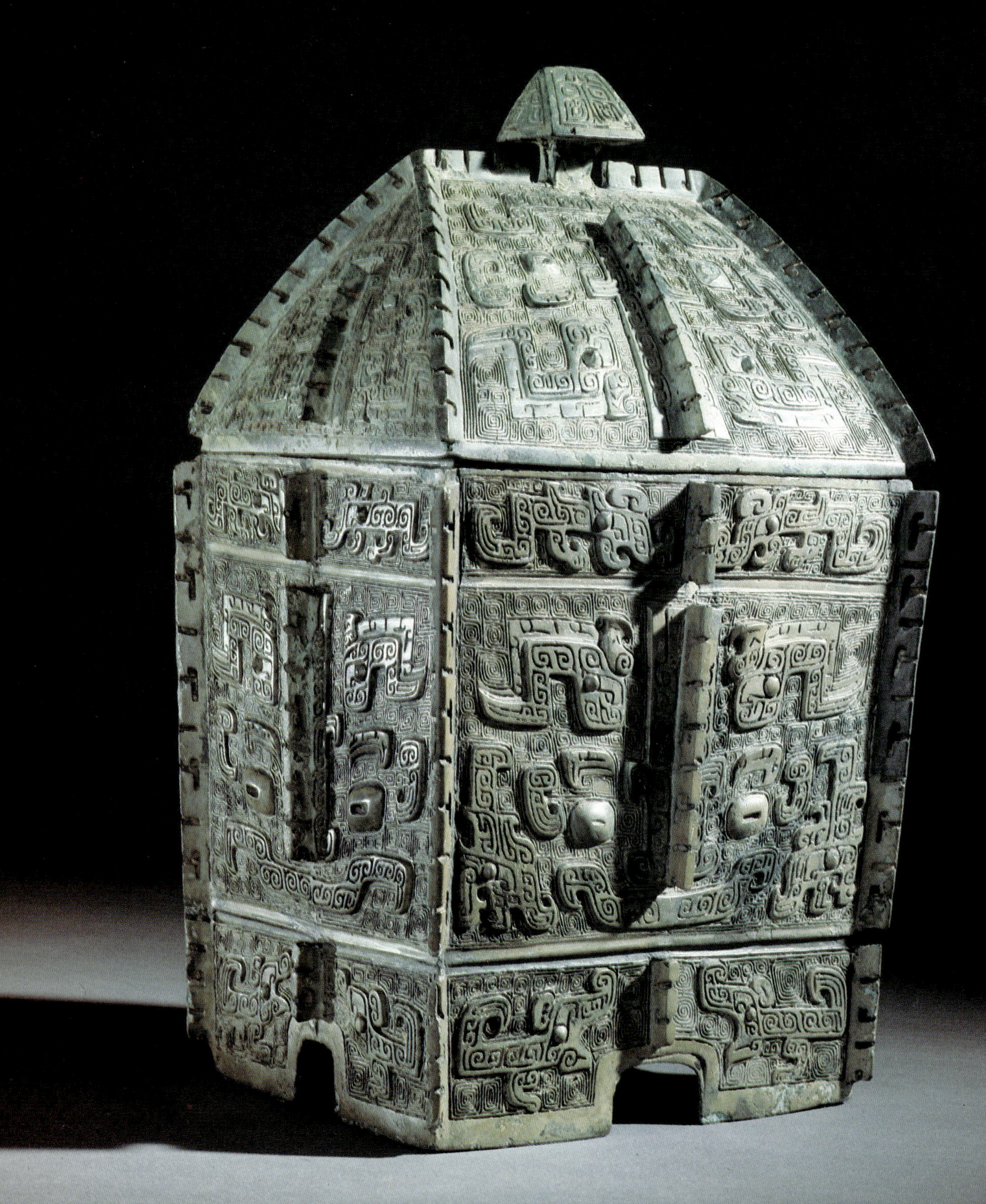

5

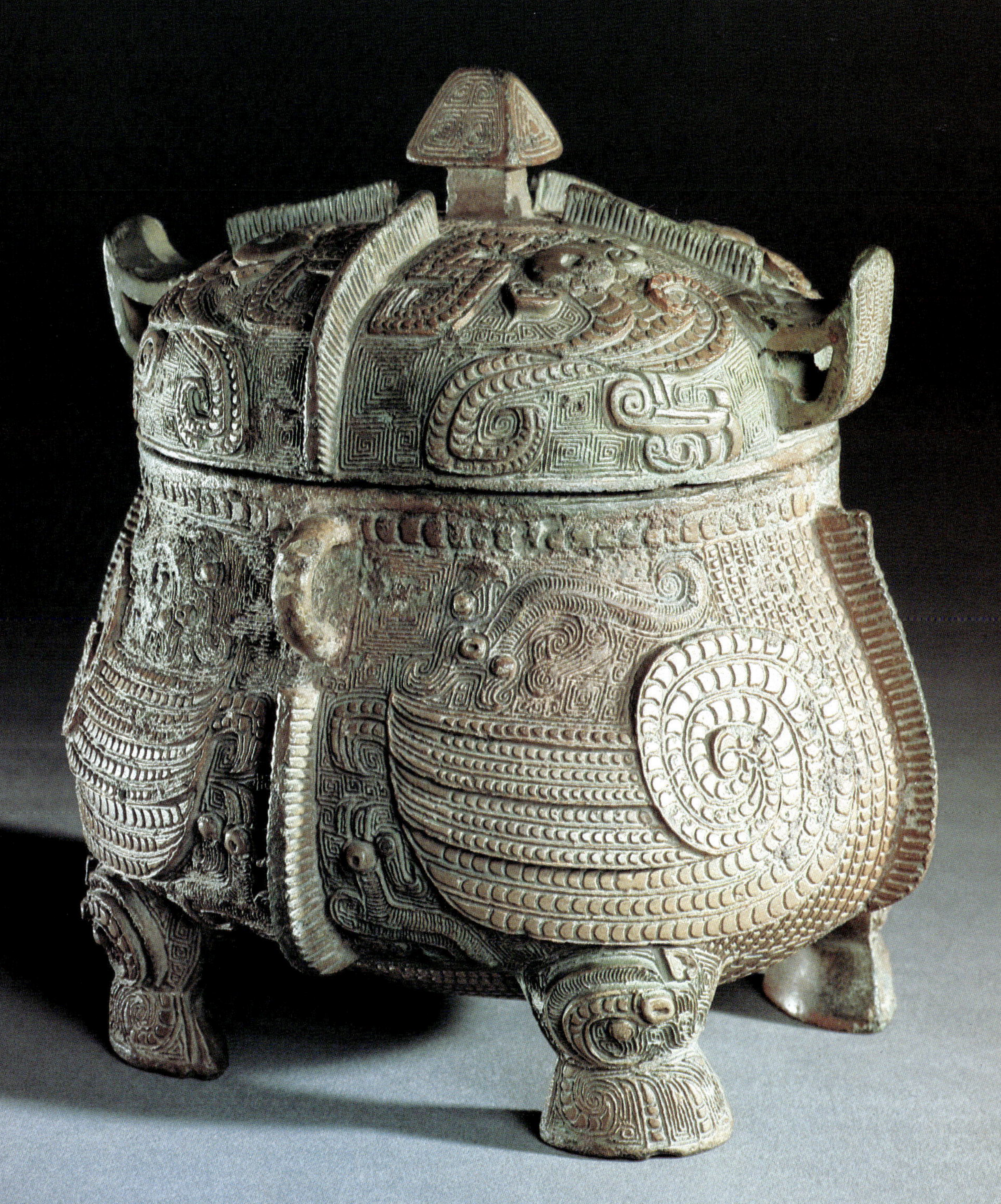

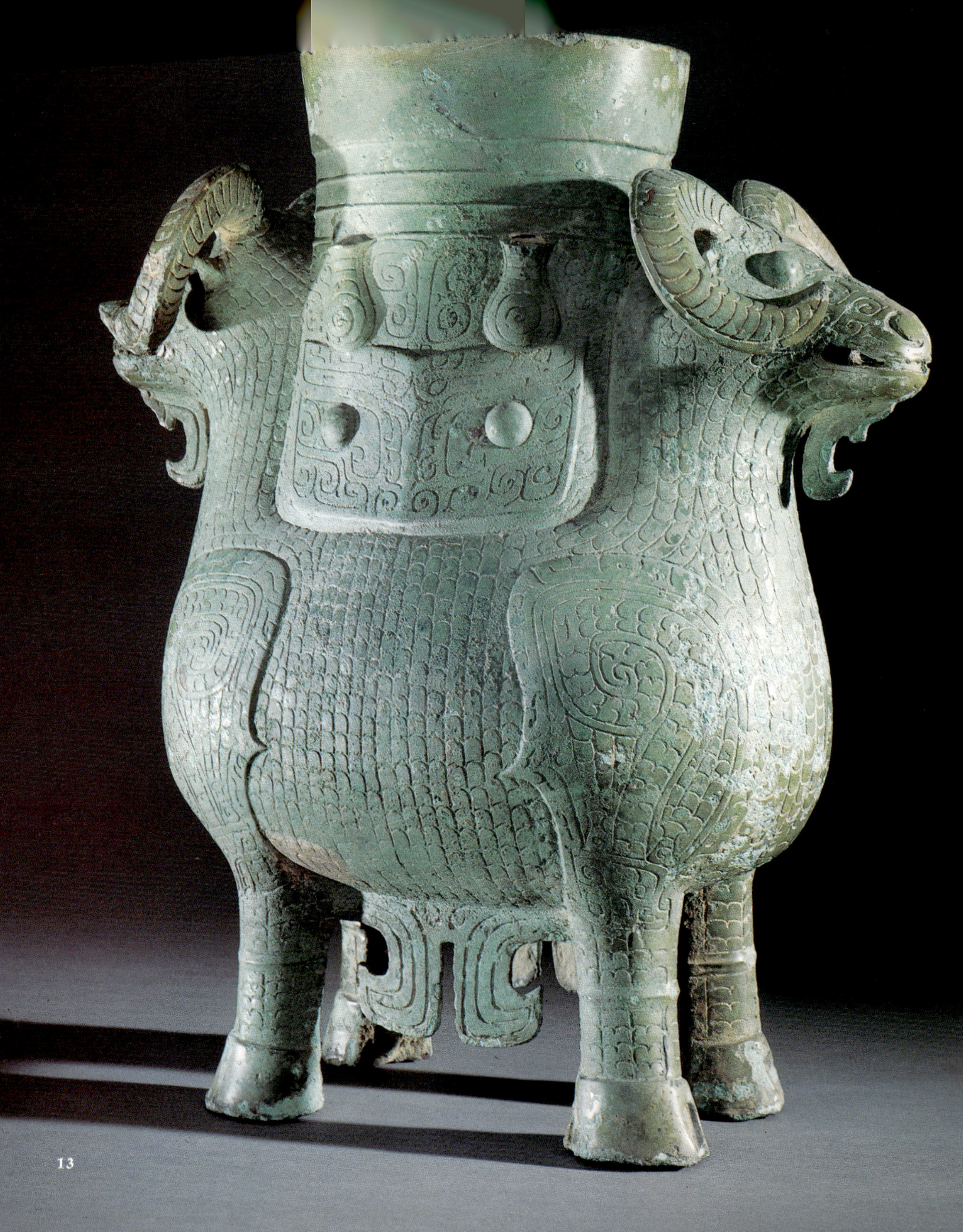

13

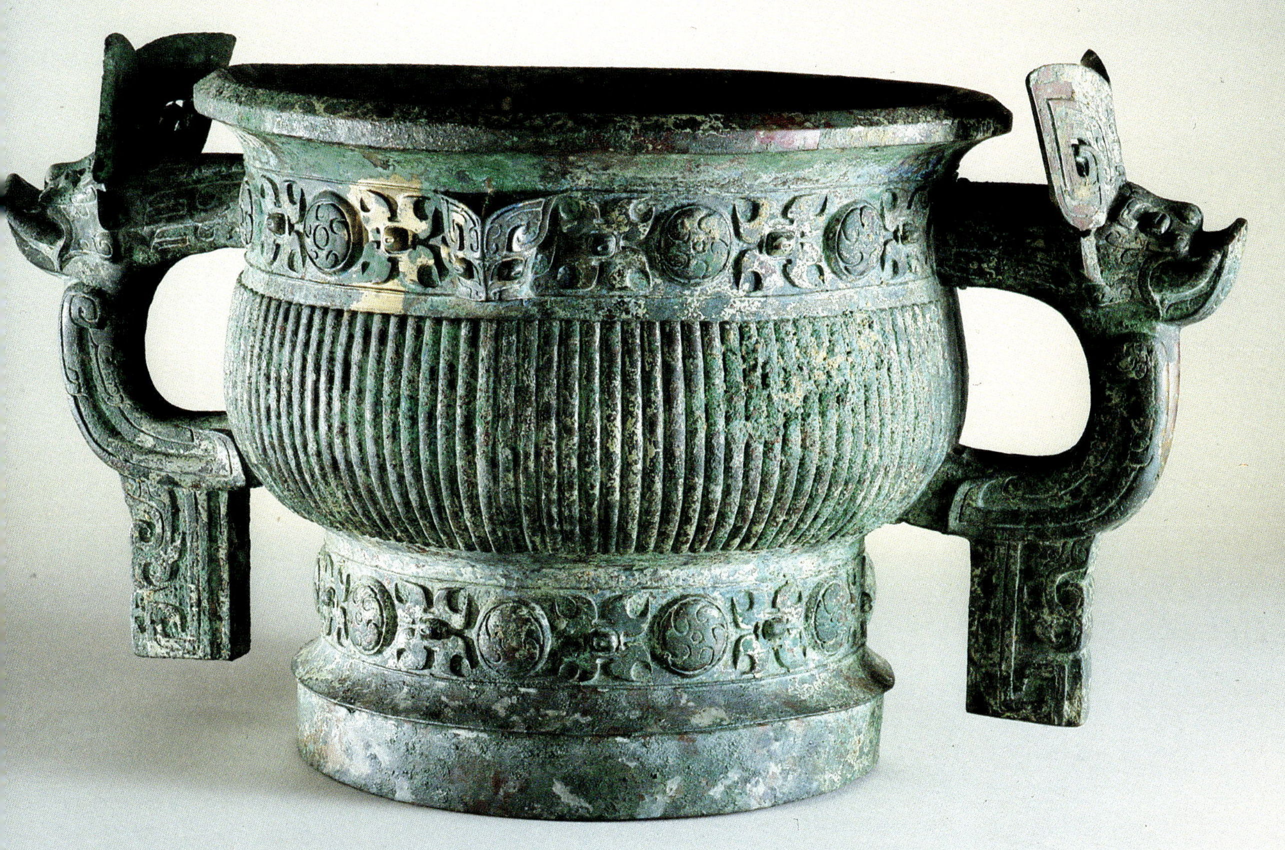

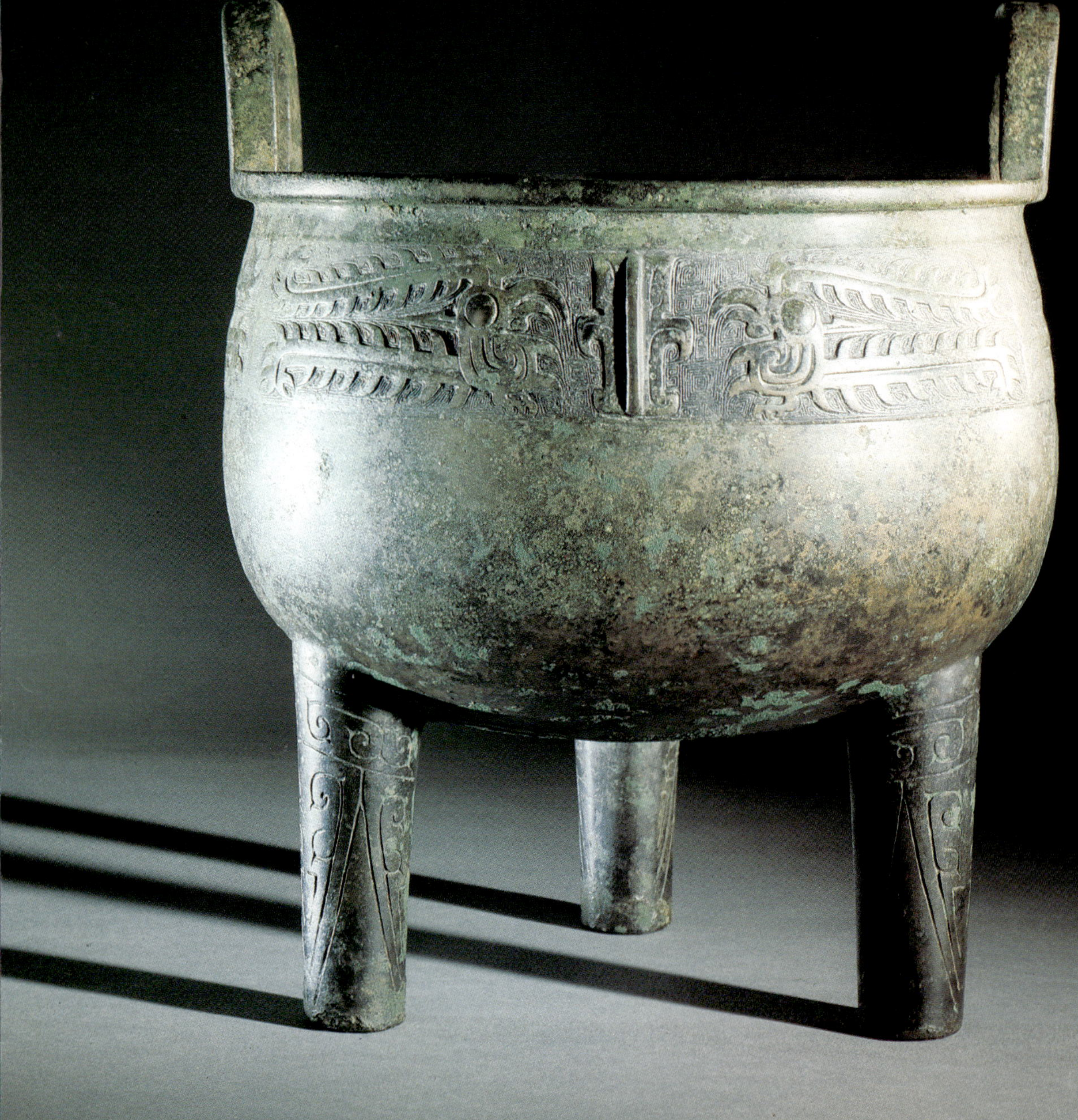

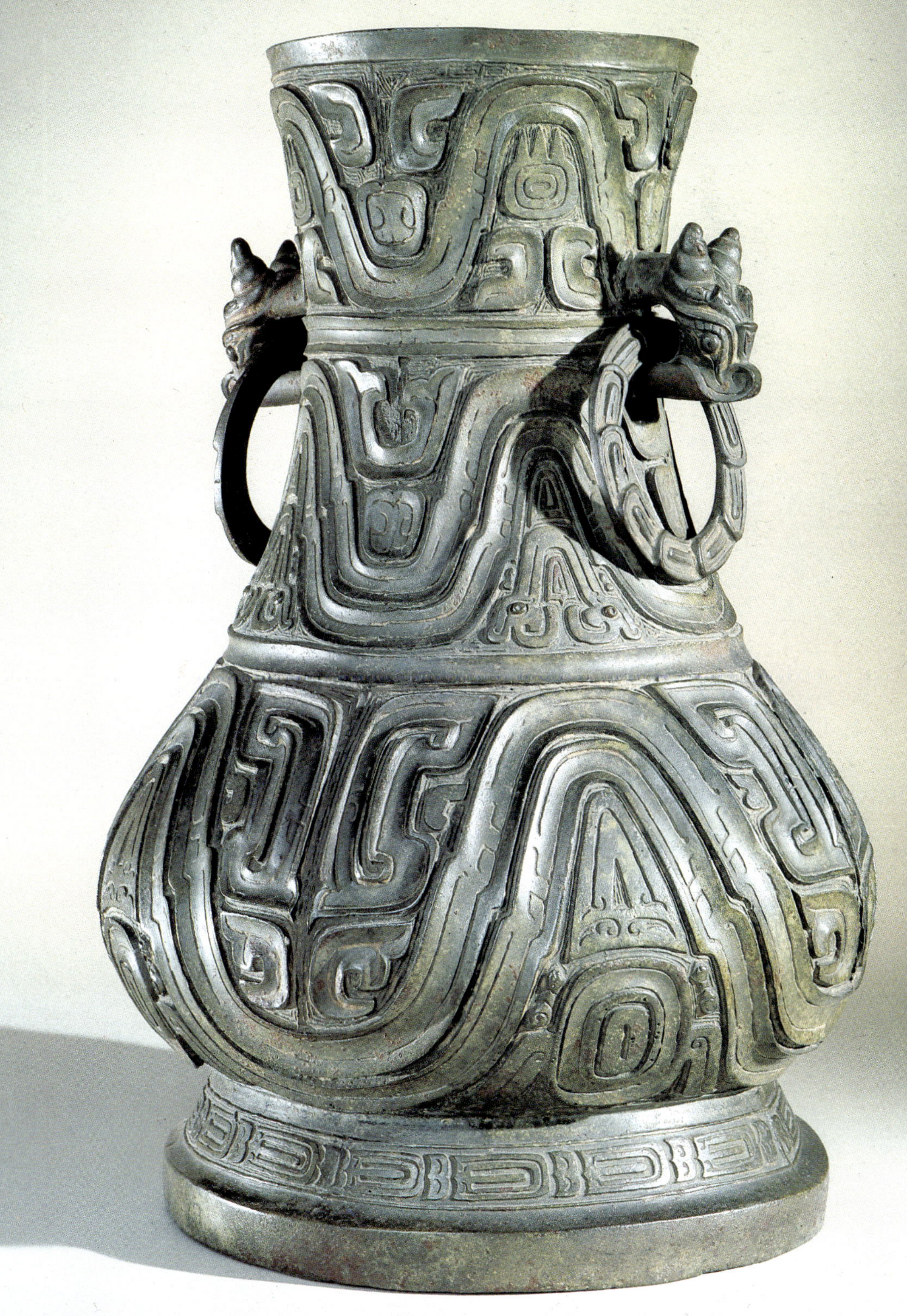

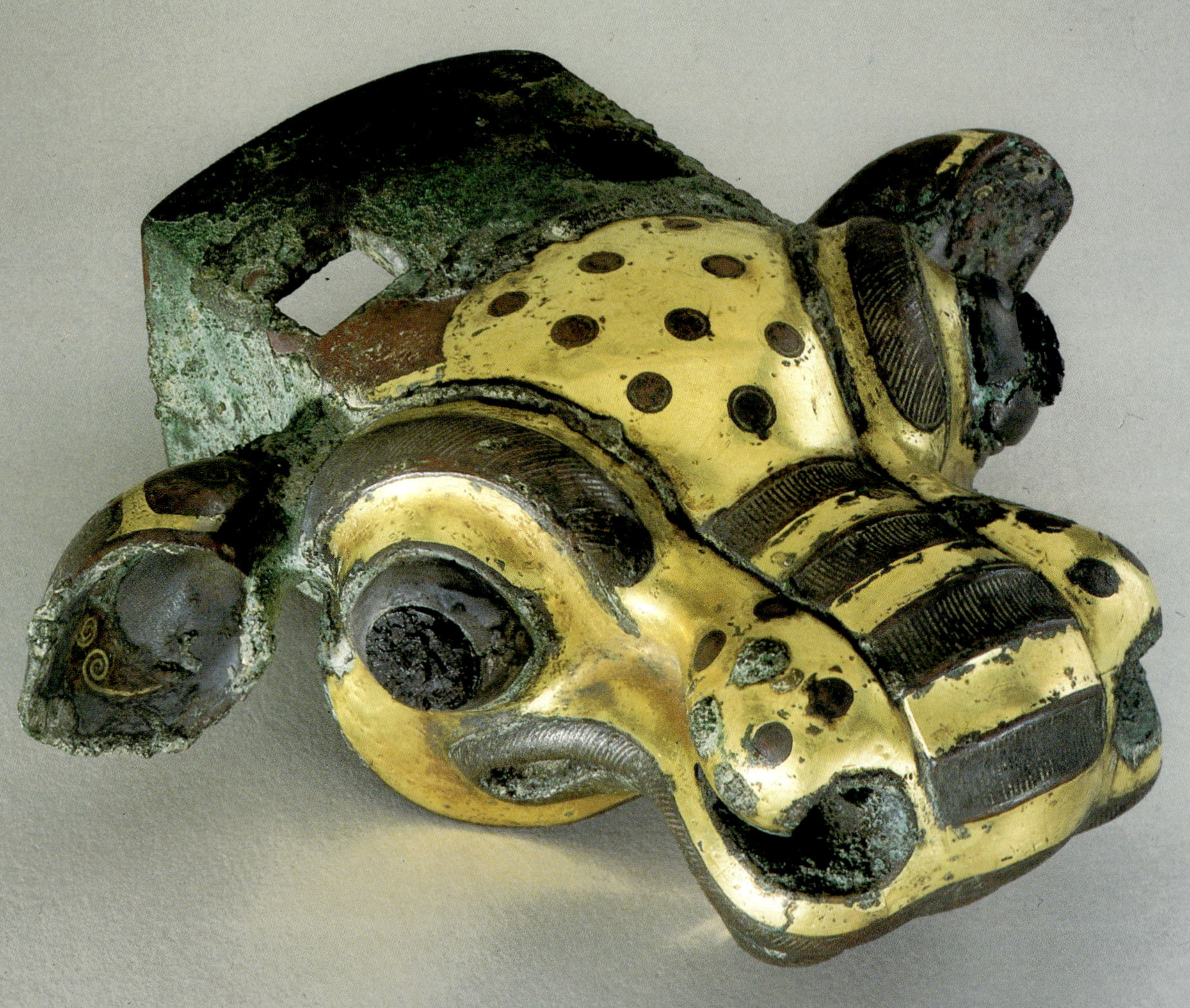

of Zhou) held the Xing fief in what is now southern Hebei. A very similar example, the *Chen Jian gui*, has come from the same area. Its inscription also mentions the Xing Hou.[1]

Like the *Xing Hou gui* the *Chen Jian gui* has a rounded body constricted at the neck; deeply curving sides are complemented by four handles on both vessels. Four-handled *gui* seem to have been a peculiarity of Zhou casting.[2] On the *Xing Hou gui* an intaglio cicada is located opposite each handle. Each of the four compartments of the vessels' surfaces is filled with a fabulous creature that seems to have been based upon an elephant; it has a long trunk and two roundels above its head, suggesting the bumps on an elephant's forehead. Other features are taken from traditional bronze motifs, including quills used for its limbs and a spiralling ridge on its body derived perhaps from the earlier coiled dragon (no. 23).

This elephant motif is found on a number of well-known inscribed bronzes, including the *Shi Shang you* and *zun* in the Harvard University Art Museums and Hakutsuru Museum, Kobe.[3] The *Shi Shang zun* resembles the *Zhe zun* (Fig. 12a) and probably also dates to the latter part of the early Western Zhou. The *Xing Hou gui*, the *Chen Jian gui* and a further elephant-decorated *gui* – the *Yi Gong gui* – may be slightly later in date.[4] Their steeply inward-sloping profiles match those of the *Ban gui* and a bird-decorated example from Beijing Fangshan Liulihe, vessels that are generally assigned to the first stages of the middle Western Zhou.[5]

1. *Kaogu* 1979.1, pp. 23–6, 56–9, 88.
2. Four-handled *gui* were used from the very beginning of the Western Zhou period; cf. the *Da Feng gui* (Shirakawa 1962, 1.1.1).
3. Also known as the *Chen Chen you* and *zun*; Hayashi 1984, vol. 1, pp. 236 ff., pl. 32, no. 51.
4. New York 1980, no. 57.
5. Hayashi 1984, vol. 2, pl. 108, *gui* nos 233, 234.

26 *Zhi*

Middle Western Zhou.
H. 19.7 cm; W. at lip 14.2 cm.
Inscription: rubbing nos 7, 8.
1957.11–18.1; given by P.T. Brooke Sewell.
Literature: Watson 1963, pl. 15a; Hayashi 1984, vol. 2, pl. 350, *zhi* no. 142.

Zhi wine vessels were inherited by the Zhou from the Shang. In Zhou tomb groups they appear singly with pairs of other wine vessels, such as *jue* or *gu*. Handles are found on only a few. Four large birds with long semi-detached tails cover the body of the *zhi*, and another four occupy the lid. In the border below the lip are pairs of small s-shaped dragons.

Plumed birds are typical of the first part of middle Western Zhou. Almost identical birds decorate inscribed bronzes of this period, including the *gui*

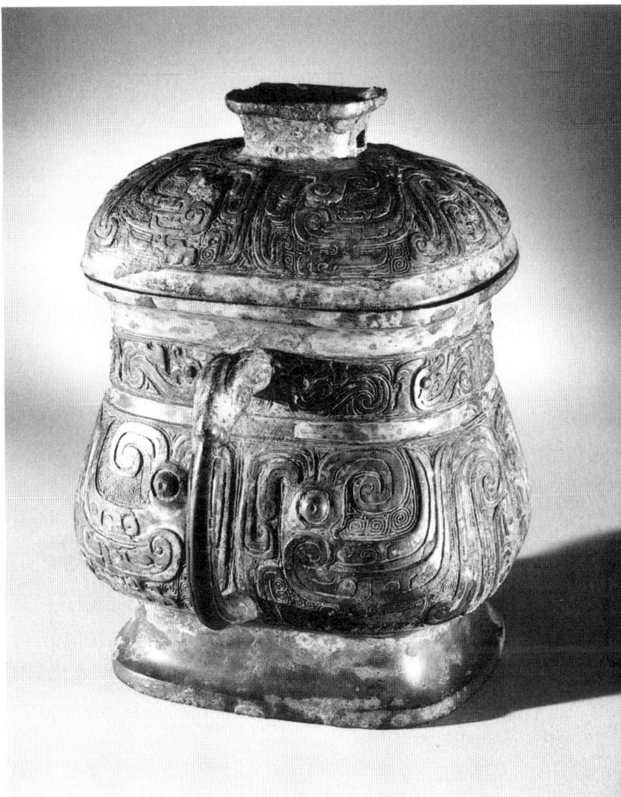

26

from Chang'an Xian discussed in the Introduction (Fig. 16).[1] These generously curving motifs were employed on vessels with rounded profiles, creating a new and highly influential bronze style.

1. Compare the *Meng gui* from Shaanxi Chang'an Zhangjiapo, the *Zhong gui* from Shaanxi Fufeng Famen and the *Jing gui* in the Sackler Collections (Hayashi 1984, vol. 2, pls 117, 118, *gui* nos 298, 300, 309).

27 *You*

Middle to late Western Zhou.
H. to handle 62 cm; to lip 35.8 cm.
1983.2–2.1

This large, unusual vessel is a southern provincial bronze. It copies the profile of a metropolitan *you* of

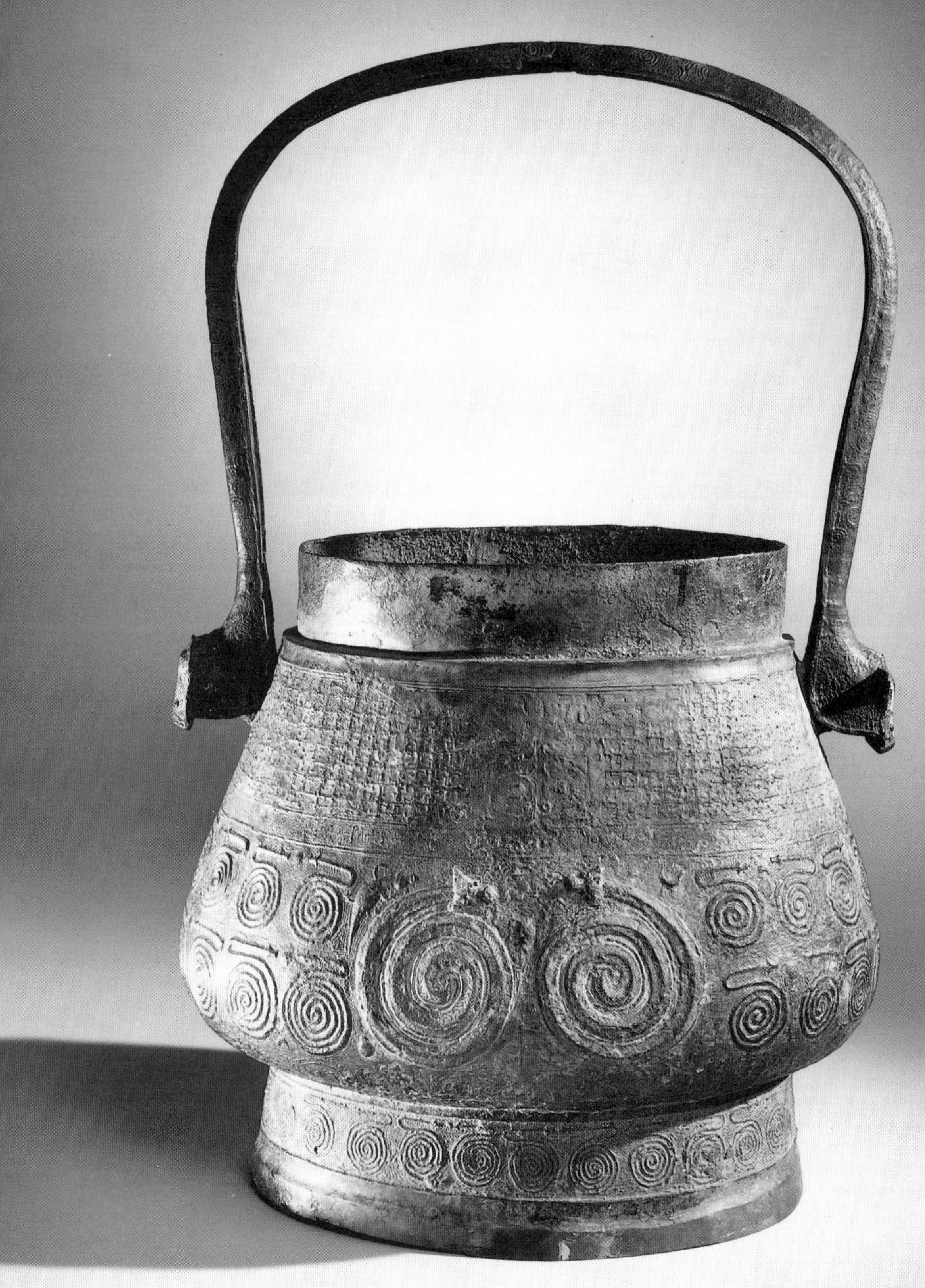

the latter part of the early Western Zhou; the vessel's enormous size, unconventional motifs and slightly rough finish betray its provincial origins.

As discussed in the Introduction, metropolitan bronzes were introduced to south-eastern China in the middle Western Zhou, when bird-decorated vessels were in vogue. A *you* from Tunxi in Anhui province is a product of this contact (Fig. 21). However, few south-eastern bronzes follow the metropolitan model as closely. Like the British Museum's *you* many are large, thinly cast and bizarrely decorated.[1]

Pairs of coiled snakes on the belly of the *you* are probably a local motif two stages removed from the coiled dragons of no. 23. In between stand vessels such as a *zhi* in the Shanghai Museum decorated with deeply sunken spirals.[2] On one side of the British Museum's *you* a small reptile is tucked in above the snakes.[3] A dense background of hatching is based upon impressed patterns employed on ceramics of the area.

1. *Wenwu* 1980.8, pp. 3–9; *Wenwu* 1984.5, pp. 1–10; *Kaogu yu wenwu* 1985.5, pp. 90–101; *Wenwu ziliao congkan* 2, 1978, pp. 66–9, fig. 8.
2. *Wenwu* 1984.6, pp. 21–3, pl. 1.
3. During the Eastern Zhou middle Western Zhou vessel shapes preserved in the south-east were transmitted to both central and southern China. Pear-shaped *zun* from Hengshan in Hunan province and from Gongcheng in Guangxi province are products of this development (New York 1980, no. 66, fig. 87); they follow the shape of *zun* such as a vessel found at Danyang in Jiangsu province (Li Xueqin 1985b, no. 191).

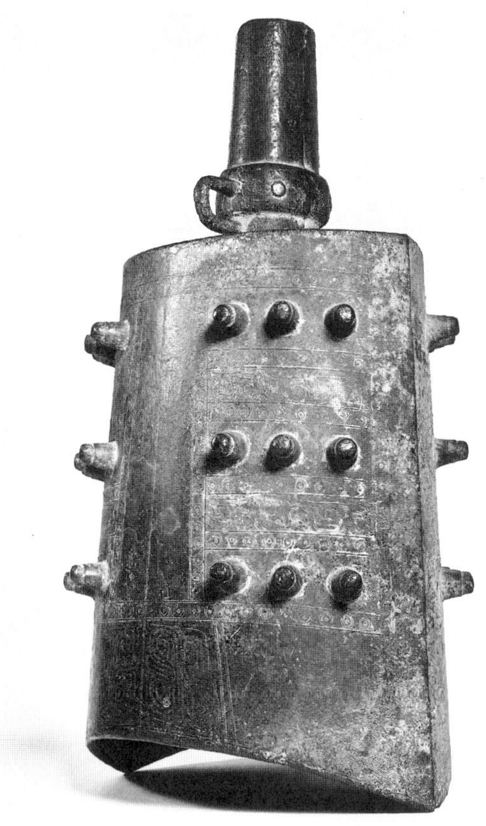

28

28 *Zhong*

Western Zhou.
H. 45 cm; W. (max.) 27.3 cm.
1984.5–28.1.

Bells suspended from a small loop attached to a tubular handle are known as *zhong*; this bell is an early example of the type. *Zhong* were derived from a much earlier bell type, the *nao*, which were mounted the other way up. Both types were struck from the outside, giving two notes, one at the centre of the lip, the other at the corner.[1]

Nao were employed at Anyang in sets of graded size. They went out of use at metropolitan Shang and early Zhou centres but were greatly elaborated in the south. Many examples have been found in Hunan and Anhui provinces. On early *nao* large eyes derived from the *taotie* were surrounded by almost abstract meander patterns, either in intaglio lines or in relief ridges. A further type was decorated with pairs of eyes embedded in fine relief lines and dotted circles. These *nao* were the ancestors of the present bell. On all bell types the *taotie* eyes were multiplied to make rows of projecting bosses.[2]

◁27

During the Western Zhou period the sides of southern *nao* were lengthened, and the bells hung the other way up from small loops, as here.[3] At this stage the bells were reintroduced to the north, appearing first in the far west, as in the tomb of a Yu Bo buried at Shaanxi Baoji Rujiazhuang (Fig. 17). Such bells were embellished with small studs, enlarged from the small dots at the centres of circles on southern bells. In due course provincial decorative schemes were replaced by metropolitan decoration. The Xing bells display both types of ornament (Fig. 12d).

1. *Kaogu xuebao* 1981.1, pp. 131–46; New York 1980, no. 19.
2. Full discussion of southern bells is found in Kao 1986.
3. *Wenwu* 1983.10, pp. 72–4, fig. 4; *Wenwu* 1985.4, p. 90.

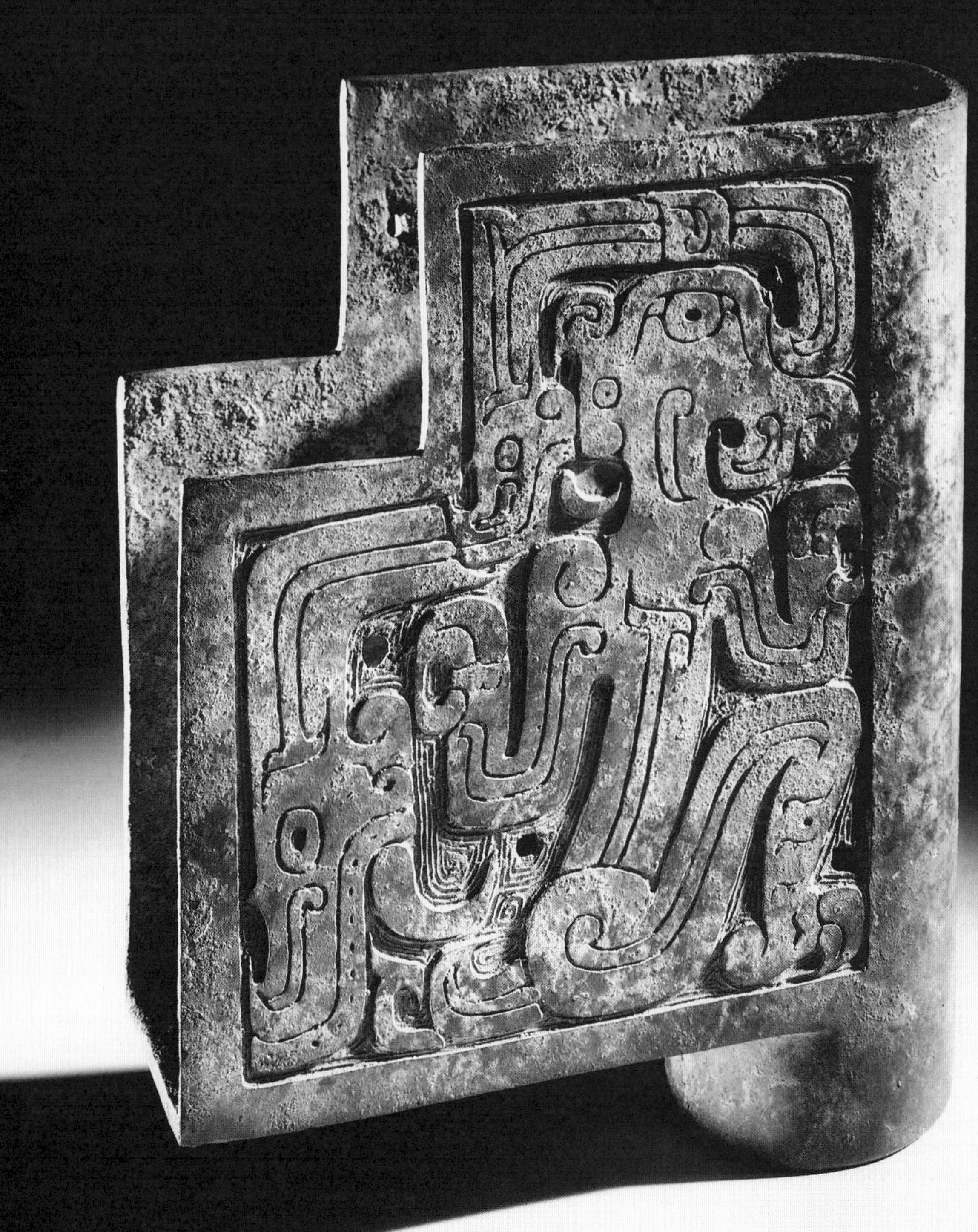

29 *Shi Wang hu* *(illustrated in colour)*

Late Western Zhou.
H. 45.5 cm; DIAM. at lip 16.8 cm.
Inscription: rubbing no. 11.
1970.11–4.1; Brooke Sewell Bequest, ex-Cohen Collection.
Literature: Luo Zhenyu 1937, 12.17.4; Shirakawa 1962, 22.130.79; Zhou Fagao 1977, no. 2506; Hayashi 1984, vol. 2, pl. 306, *hu* no. 94.

This *hu* was dedicated by one Shi Wang. A *ding* also dedicated by Shi Wang is known; a *gui* inscription mentioning the same individual is recorded by Shirakawa.[1] Li Xueqin has argued that Shi Wang belonged to the same clan as one Shi Zai who cast a large *ding* excavated at Shaanxi Fufeng Qiangjiacun. The inscription on this austerely decorated *ding* also mentions the deceased Mu Wang and is therefore thought to date to the succeeding Gong Wang reign.[2] The Shi Wang vessels are likely to be somewhat later.

In the middle Western Zhou tall *you* were enlarged to make slender *hu*. These vessels were employed singly; examples have come from middle Western Zhou tombs, such as that of the Yu Bo at Shaanxi Baoji Rujiazhuang.[3] In the second half of middle western Zhou the *hu* shape was altered to make *hu* of the present type, used in pairs. The deep wave pattern seen on the *Shi Wang hu* was one of the motifs invented concurrently with the marked changes in ritual vessel shape.

1. Chen Rentao 1952, no. 6; Shirakawa 1962, 22.129.67.
2. *Wenwu* 1975.8, pp. 57–62, pl. 9:1; Li Xueqin 1979.
3. *Wenwu* 1976.4, pp. 34–56, pl. 8:1.

30 *Door pivot*

Early Eastern Zhou, 8th century BC.
H. 28.6 cm; W. 22.6 cm; D. 7.9 cm.
1946.11–11.1.

Effectively a hinge, this bronze fitted over one of the lower corners of a door, the projecting circular stub turning in a socket. It may have been part of a piece of furniture or of a building. Decoration of a half-human figure surrounded by dragons can be paralleled on jades of the same period.[1]

Early Eastern Zhou bronze fittings from buildings and furniture have come from several parts of China. Many angular bronze architectural ornaments were excavated from pits at Fengxiang Xian in Shaanxi province.[2] Like other bronzes from this western area, at the time part of the state of Qin, the bronze sections carry large, slightly rough dragon
◁30 interlace. Very similar fittings are in the Art Institute of Chicago. Others have come from the southern provinces of Jiangsu and Hubei.[3]

1. Salmony 1938, pl. XXIX:6.
2. *Kaogu* 1976.2, pp. 121–8.
3. Li Xueqin 1985c, pp. 290–4.

31 *Ding*

Early Eastern Zhou, 7th century BC. Qin state.
H. to handles 18.2 cm; DIAM. at lip 22.3 cm.
1982.6–21.1.

Small shallow tripods were made in western China, the area controlled by Qin. With the fall of the Zhou capital near Xi'an bronze manufacture declined. Burial groups in ceramic and bronze illustrate the

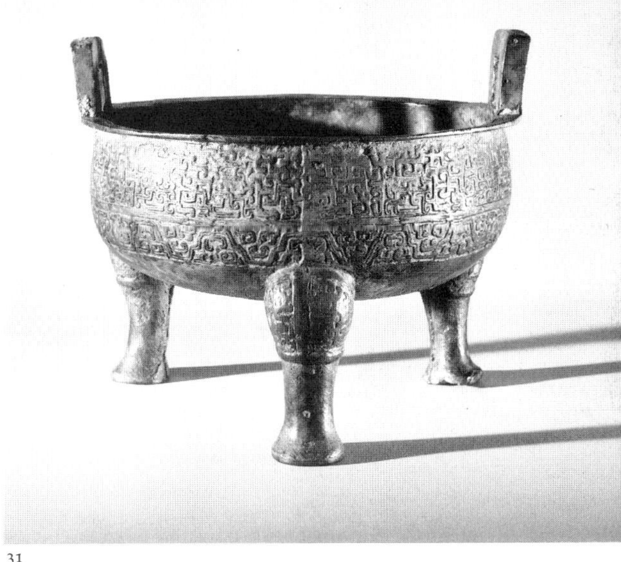

31

persistence of late Western Zhou vessel types. Tombs at Baoji and Hu Xian contain sets of *ding* and *gui*, pairs of *hu*, and single *yan*, *pan* and either a *ying* or a *yi*. *Ding* from these tombs are shallow with cabriole legs, like the present vessel. The Baoji bronzes are decorated with late Western Zhou scale patterns, while the vessels and chariot fittings from Hu Xian carry interlace.[1] Rather later and tighter interlace appears on a set of three *ding* from Qin state tombs at Fengxiang Xian.[2] These *ding* are very like the tripod illustrated here.

1. *Kaogu* 1979.6, pp. 564, 563; *Wenwu* 1975.10, pp. 55–67; see also Li Xueqin 1985c, p. 224.
2. *Wenwu ziliao congkan* 3, 1980, pp. 67–85, pl. 13:1; compare *Kaogu* 1963.10, pp. 536–43, pl. 3:3; *Wenwu* 1965.5, pp. 1–5, pl. 3:6.

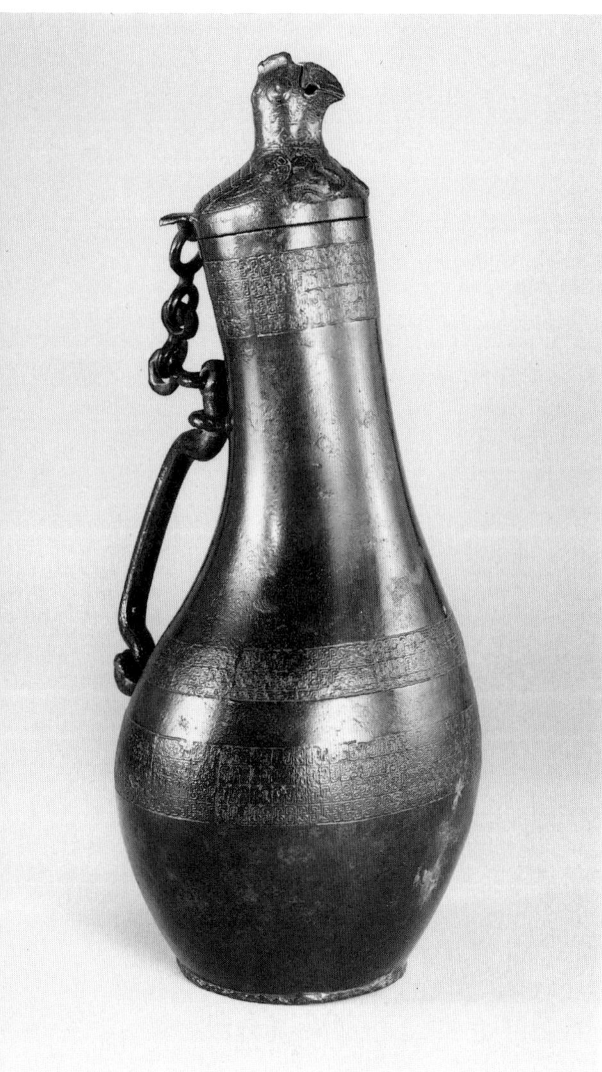

32

32 *Hu*

Eastern Zhou, 6th–5th centuries BC. Jin state.
H. 32 cm; DIAM. at lip 6 cm.
1973.7–26.26; Seligman Bequest.
Literature: Hansford 1957, A27.

A tall slender flask, circular in cross-section, this *hu* is sharply bent to one side, seemingly in imitation of a leather bottle. Three narrow registers are packed with tiny s-shaped dragons; such decoration is typical of the sixth century but probably persisted into the fifth century BC. A bird-shaped lid, with an articulated beak, is attached by a chain to a bowed handle.

An earlier *hu*, much more like a leather bottle, with a full body and tightly angled neck, was discovered in a tomb at Hubei Sui Xian Bajiaolou. It carried deeply curved chevrons.[1] Later examples are decorated with a wide variety of motifs in several different techniques.[2] During the Eastern Zhou ceramic, leather and lacquer shapes were rendered in bronze as bronze-casting spread geographically and as the use of bronze was extended from ritual to secular items.

1. *Wenwu* 1980.1, pp. 34–41, fig. 21; compare a vessel in the Museum of Far Eastern Antiquities, Stockholm (Hayashi 1984, vol. 2, pl. 308, *hu* no. 108).
2. *Wenwu* 1986.6, pp. 1–19, fig. 44; Weber 1968, fig. 37b.

33 *Lü zhong*

Eastern Zhou, 6th–5th centuries BC. Jin state.
H. 31 cm; W. (max.) 15 cm.
Inscription: rubbing no. 14.
1936.11–18.5; ex-Eumorfopoulos Collection.
Literature: Yetts 1930, B1–B2; Guo Moruo 1935, *kao* 232–4; Liu Tizhi 1935, 1.75; Luo Zhenyu 1937, 1.56.2; Yang Shuda 1959, p. 170; Shirakawa 1962, 35.203.125; Zhou Fagao 1977, no. 100; Beijing 1984d, 1.233.

The inscription on the bell, which is one of twelve or thirteen known examples from a single set, records the manufacture of the bells by Lü Qi, a minister of the state of Jin, to perform sacrifices to his ancestors. The inscriptions on the bells describe the set as comprising eight sub-sets. We have a better knowledge of what such a complex of bells involved from the magnificent set of sixty-five found in the tomb of the Zeng Hou Yi (Marquis Yi of Zeng) at Sui Xian in Hubei province.[1] By analogy with that find the Lü Qi bells probably numbered sixty-three.[2] The inscriptions say that the bells were accompanied by sets of musical chimes. The bells are said to have been found at Ronghe in Shanxi province.

The present bell bears three different types of decoration. On the flat top are tightly packed interlaced dragons, current in the mid-seventh to mid-sixth centuries (Fig. 22c). Compressed spirals, apparently stamped into the moulds, fill the registers between the bosses. At the mouth of the bell a *taotie* face lies upside down. It has blank eyes and therefore appears not so much a creature as a filling device. Rubbing no. 14 illustrates its construction from snakes similar to those seen on some sixth-century bronzes (Fig. 22a).

1. Beijing 1980d; McClain 1985.
2. Ma Chengyuan 1982, pp. 118–19.

33▷

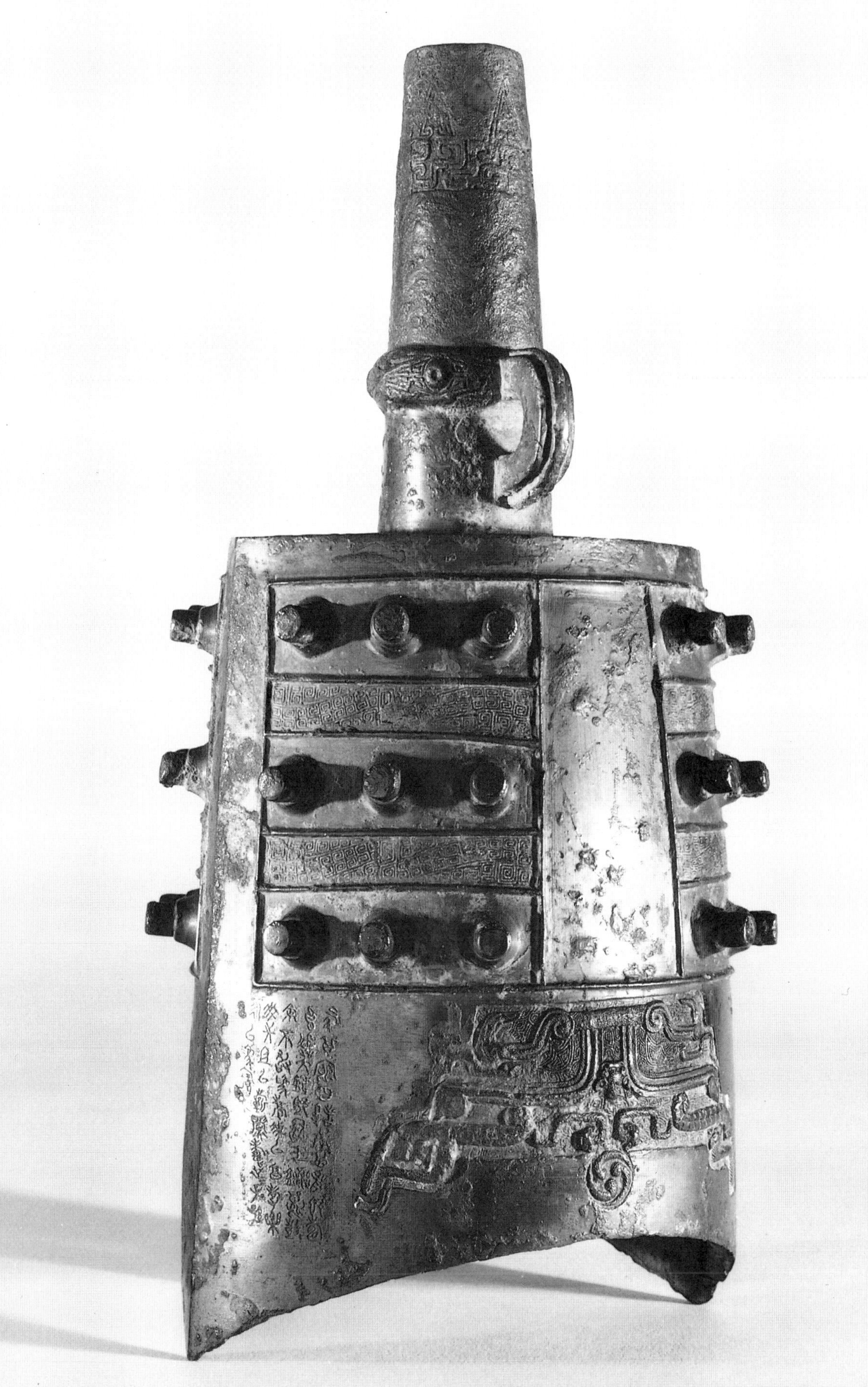

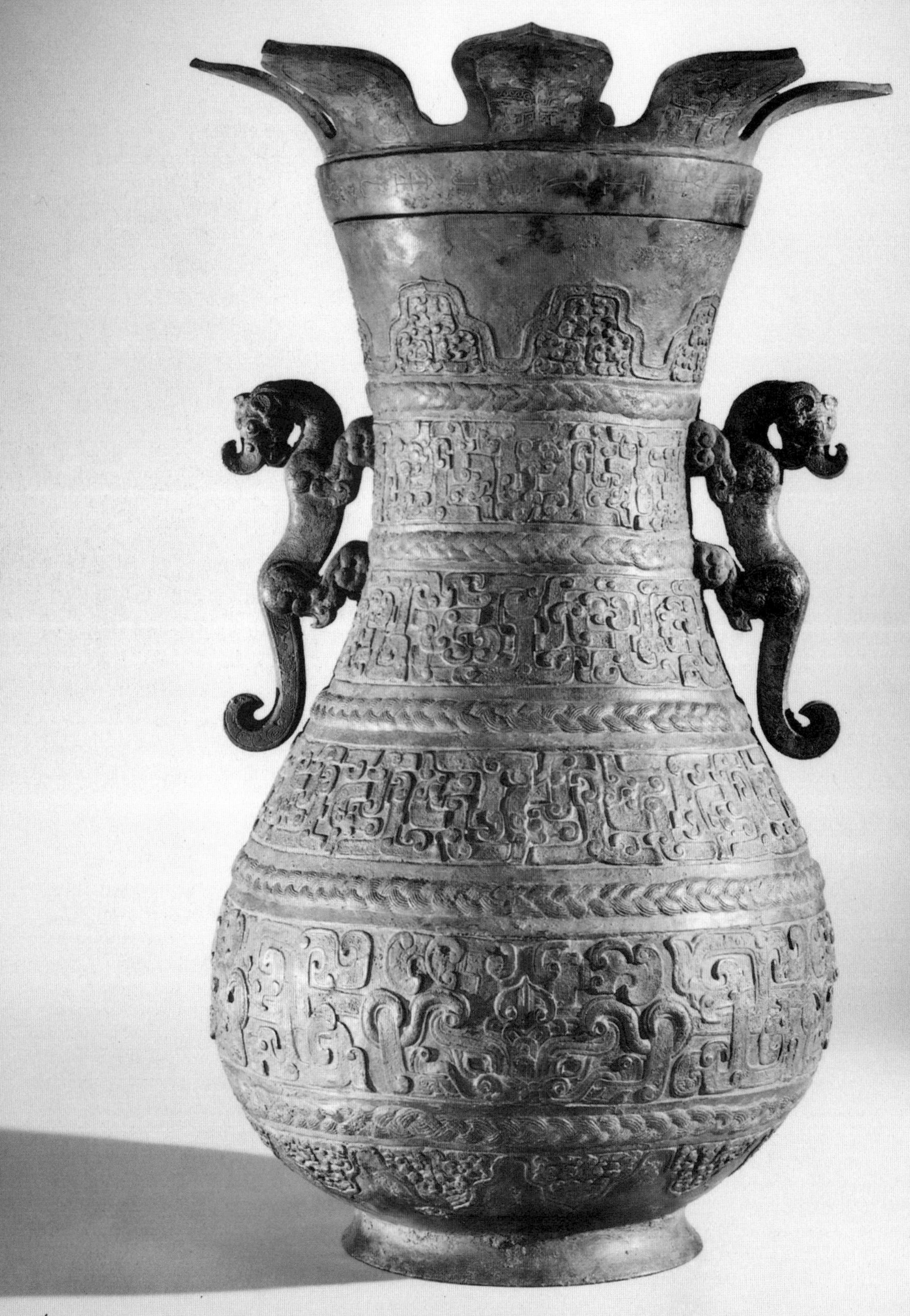

34 *Zhao Meng jie hu* (*see cover*)

Eastern Zhou, early 5th century BC. Jin state.
H. 48.3 cm; DIAM. at lip 17 cm.
Inscription: rubbing no. 13.
1972.2–29.1a; given by Mrs U. E. K. Cull.
Literature: Sun Haibo 1939, *tu* 20; Yetts 1939, no. 12; Rong Geng 1941, 2.743; Yang Shuda 1959, p. 192; Shirakawa 1962, 36.204.195.

The inscription around the outer rim of the lid of this delicately cast *hu*, which is one of a pair, records a meeting with the King of Wu at Huangchi in the year 482 BC. There are considerable differences of opinion about the interpretation of the inscription.[1] However, it is accepted that the reference to the meeting, at which an alliance between the states of Jin and Wu was renewed, is correct. Zhao Meng, an individual named in the inscription, was a minister in Jin, and the vessels are characteristic of Jin casting.[2] The vessels are said to have been found at Hui Xian in Henan province.

The precise date of the events described helps to establish the chronology of Jin state bronzes, especially of the type called Liyu, now known to have been made at a foundry at Houma in Shanxi province. The *hu* belong to a fairly advanced stage, in which engaging *taotie* faces composed of snakes, such as the one seen on the Lü bell (no. 33), were added to layered interlace developed in several parts of China, including the territories along the east coast (Fig. 23) and the central southern area dominated by Chu (Fig. 26). Openwork crowns and tiger or dragon handles with reverted heads descended from Western Zhou models and were employed on Eastern Zhou *hu* in many parts of China. The vessels are damaged, particularly in the lower half, and have lost the bottom sections of their foot-rings.

1. Loehr 1948.
2. Li Xueqin 1985c, pp. 46–7.

35 *Bo*

Eastern Zhou, 5th century BC. Jin state.
H. 54 cm; W. (max) 40.3 cm.
1965.6–12.1; Brooke Sewell Fund, ex-Adolphe Stoclet Collection.
Literature: Watson 1965.

Like the *Zhao Meng jie hu* this imposing bell was probably a product of the Houma foundries of the Jin state. Large *taotie* faces above the mouth of the bell amplify features already seen on the *hu*. In

◁34

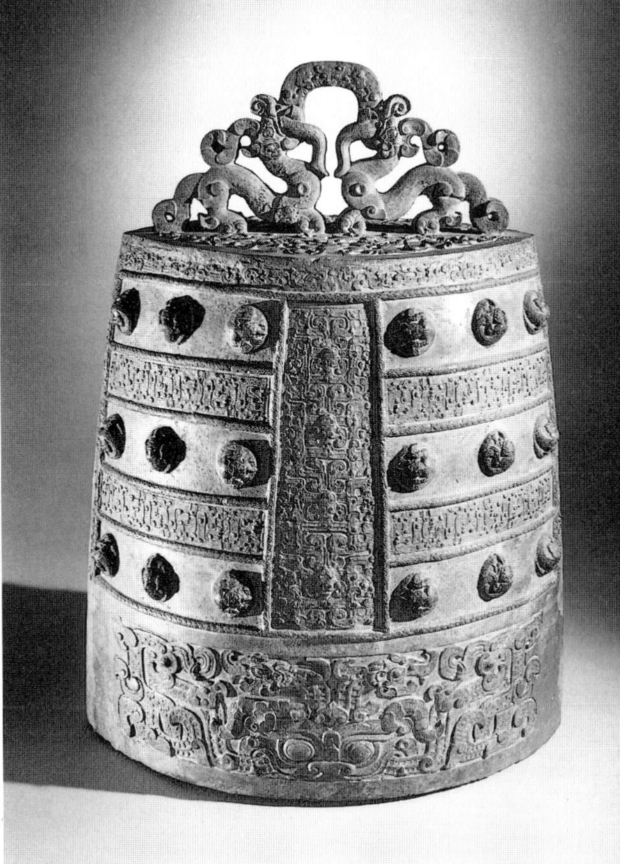

35

addition to the snake-like horns of the creature two large scaly dragons sprout from the centres of the faces. The rest of the lower border is filled with invented beasts. Eighteen bosses on each side of the bell are made as small coiled creatures, with unassuming interlace between the rows. Two exquisitely cast dragons make a loop handle, and large relief faces, like those at the lip, lie across the top of the bell.

As the bell hangs from a loop set on the top flat surface rather than from one attached to a tubular handle, it is known as a *bo* or as a *niu zhong*, to distinguish it from the other type, known as *yong zhong*. In large sets of bells, such as that from the tomb of the Marquis Yi of Zeng, *bo* were included with sets of *yong zhong*. Watson has suggested that five bells known from Western collections belonged to the same set as this bell.[1] However, these five can only be a small portion of the original assemblage.

1. Watson 1965.

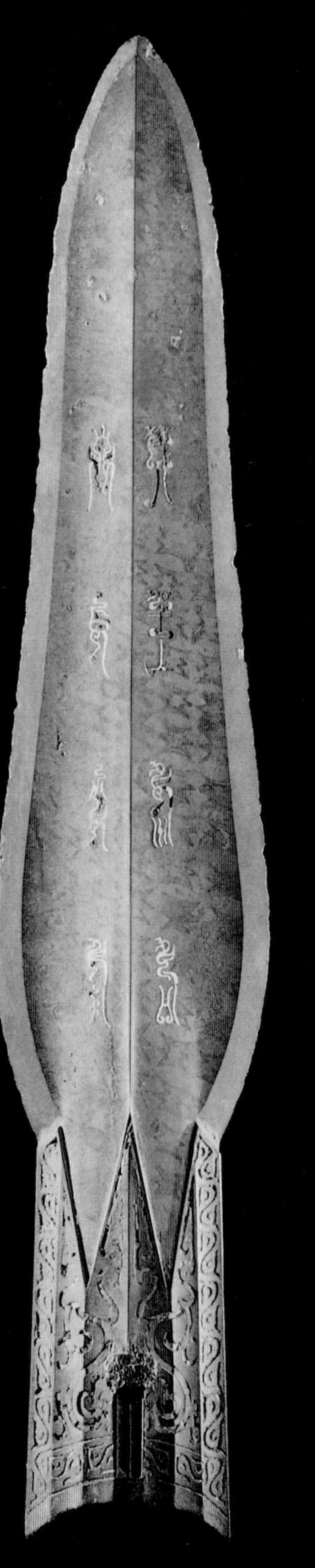

36 *Spearhead*

Eastern Zhou, 5th century. Yue state.
L. 28.6 cm.
1947.7–12.426; Oppenheim Bequest.
Literature: Watson 1963, pl. 29a; Hayashi 1972, p. 515, fig. 59.

Eight elegant bird-script characters on this spearhead proclaim this fine weapon as belonging to King Zhu Ju of Yue (r. 448–412 BC). Yue state weapons famous for their elegance and keen edges were prized in many areas. Swords and spearheads have come from sites outside the Yue state in southeast China, particularly from Jin and Chu state tombs. Jin was often in alliance with Yue against Chu, and this probably lead to the exchange of gifts. Chu no doubt seized such weapons in combat. Like the present spearhead many of the blade surfaces are decorated in geometric patterns executed in a technique as yet not understood.[1] The spearhead combines gold-inlaid characters and a variegated surface with turquoise inlay around the socket.

1. Hayashi 1972, pp. 496–536; Li Xueqin 1985c, pp. 189–203, 277–280.

37 *Chariot fitting* *(illustrated in colour)*

Eastern Zhou, 4th–3rd centuries BC. Zhou kingdom.
L. 17.5 cm; W. 21.5 cm.
1934.2–16.3.
Literature: White 1934, pls I, II.

The animal's head is cast fully in the round with projecting ears, large eyes set beneath striated brows, and modelled nostrils and jaw. Gold and silver inlays enhance the features and add a geometric patterned surface on the underside. The eyes were formerly set with glass which has now decayed. A rectangular socket at the back, pierced top and bottom by square holes, fitted the head to a wooden shaft.

The bull's head and a dragon-like head, now in the Freer Gallery of Art in Washington, were recovered from horse pits, perhaps chariot burials, next to tombs at Jincun north of Luoyang.[1] Li Xueqin has identified these tombs and their accompanying deposits as those of the Zhou kings, thus accounting for the very high quality of the bronzes discovered there.[2] The two animals' heads probably ornamented chariot shafts. Very similar animal ornaments have been recovered from chariot burials in Henan province at Guweicun in Hui Xian and at

Ma'anzhong in Huaiyang Xian, the latter in a chariot pit next to a Chu state tomb.[3]

1. White 1934, pl. III; Lawton 1982, no. 25.
2. Li Xueqin 1985c, pp. 31–4.
3. Beijing 1956a, colour frontispiece, pl. 50, p. 78; *Wenwu* 1984.10, pp. 1–17, colour pl. 1.

38 *Pair of cross-bow fittings*

Eastern Zhou, 4th century BC. Zhou kingdom.
L. 26.7 cm.
1934.2–16.1,2.
Literature: White 1934, pl. XXIV.

Like the bull's head, these fittings are thought to have come from a tomb at Jincun at Luoyang. They are similarly inlaid with gold and silver geometric patterns. Each fitting is a rounded socket terminating in a relief animal's head, its legs and claws dragged out behind, and a long s-shaped bar emerging in front from its lower jaw. This s-shaped bar is flat, undecorated and lined with tiny holes, as though something had been pinned to it.

Similar fittings have been found at several sites. It is thought that they were attached to the ends of a cross-bow shaft.[1] Modelled examples, as here, are rather rare and seem to reflect carved wood painted with lacquer, popular in the Chu state.[2] Rectangular sockets covered with geometrically arranged inlay seem to have been favoured. The fittings survived as late as the Han dynasty; examples of both the simple rectangular and animal-decorated types have been found in the Han tombs at Mancheng.[3]

1. *Kaogu* 1974.3, pp. 171–8, fig. 7.
2. *Kaogu xuebao* 1982.1, pp. 71–116, fig. 16.
3. Beijing 1980g, p. 198.

39 *Three garment hooks*

Garment hooks, or belt-hooks, as they are often called, originated in the early Eastern Zhou. Examples from the middle Yellow River basin are thought to be the earliest in date. They remained current throughout the Eastern Zhou and Han

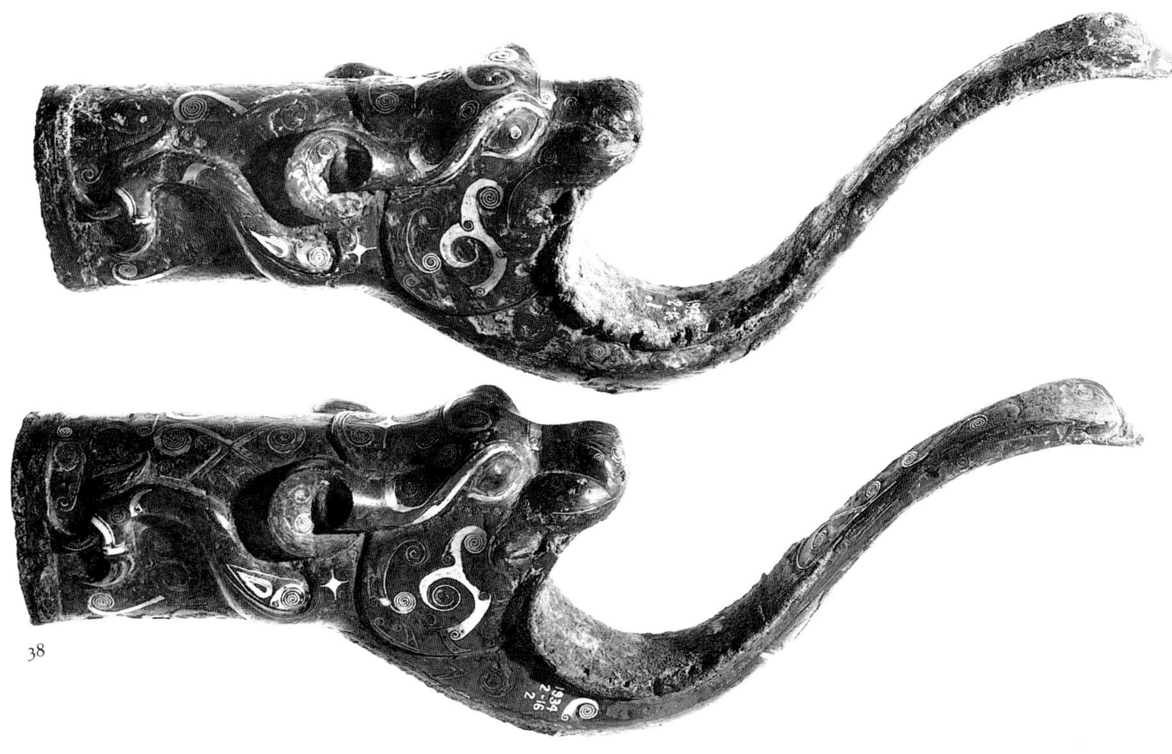

38

periods, at the end of which they were replaced by belt buckles. They were made in a wide variety of styles.[1]

a) *in the shape of a dragon*
Eastern Zhou, 4th–3rd centuries BC.
L. 21.3 cm.
1947.7–12.430; Oppenheim Bequest.

Hooks with flat gilded surfaces are generally described as chip-carved and were possibly made in imitation of wood. Similar hooks have come from tombs in Shanxi and Henan.[2]

b) *in the shape of three intertwined dragons*
Western Han, 2nd–1st centuries BC.
L. 20.5 cm.
1945.10–17.201; Raphael Bequest.
Literature: Watson 1963, pl. 26a.

Elaborately gilded ornaments set with semi-precious stones, as here, are paralleled in the tombs of Western Han princelings.[3]

c) *in the shape of a tiger*
Han dynasty, 1st century BC–1st century AD.
L. 16.3 cm.
1945.10–17.198; Raphael Bequest.
Literature: Watson 1963, pl. 26d.

The incised textures of the tiger's fur are typical of bronze-work of the first years AD, at which time bronzes with chased ornament replaced richly inlaid and gilded bronzes of the Western Han.[4]

1. *Kaogu xuebao* 1985.3, pp. 267–312; Lawton 1982, pp. 89–126.
2. Lawton 1982, nos 59, 60.
3. Beijing 1980g, p. 267.
4. Wang 1982, figs 134, 135.

39

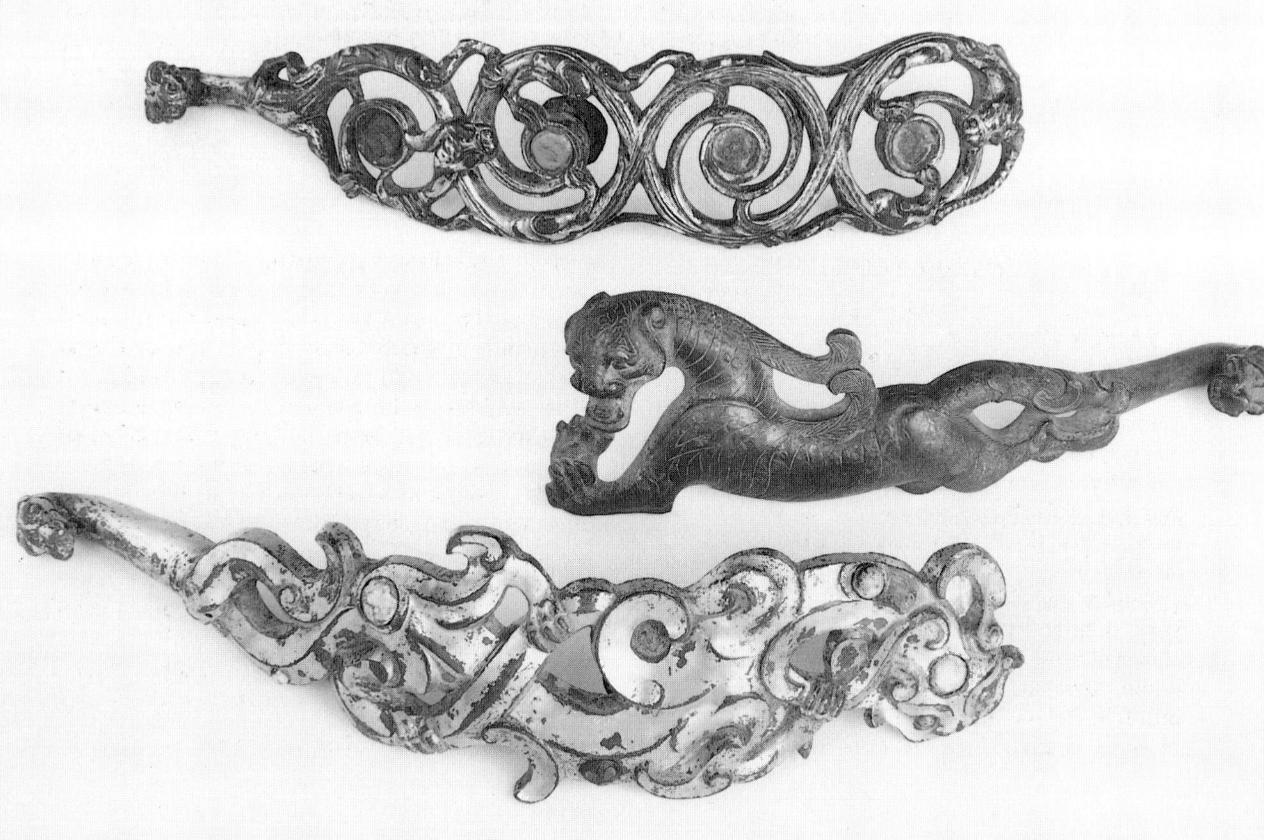

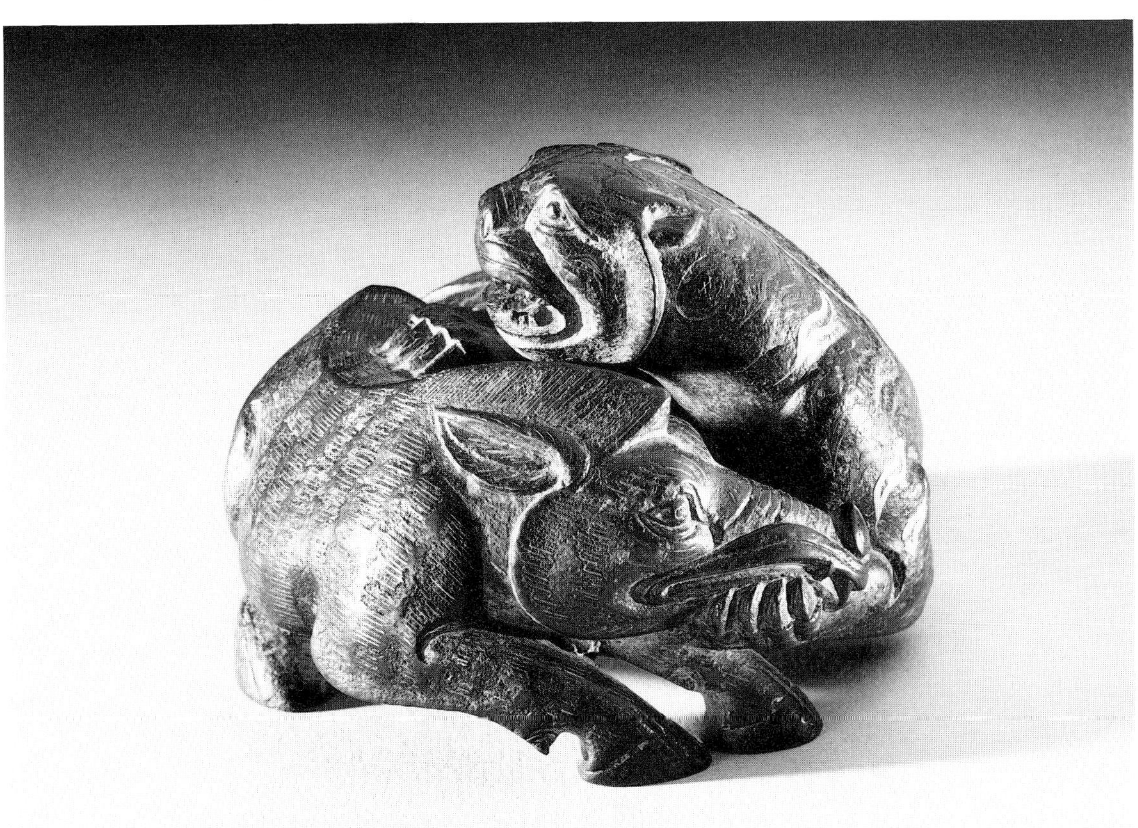

40

40 *Tiger attacking a boar*

Late Eastern Zhou or Western Han, 3rd–2nd centuries BC.
H. 6.8 cm; W. 7 cm.
1984.4–2.1; ex-Luff Collection. Purchased with funds bequeathed by Mrs Katherine Kitchingham.

Two creatures, a tiger and a boar, are locked in combat, chasing each other in a circle. Their different pelts are cunningly suggested with inlaid silver and gold.[1] Broken areas on the soles of the feet indicate that this bronze may have decorated some larger object.

The life and death struggle of the two animals is very different from the static, almost timeless, stance of creatures depicted on early bronzes: a tiger on no. 15 grasps a man's head not in anger but with indifference; the image is static, outside time. Animals in combat were favourite subjects in the ancient Near East and among China's nomadic neighbours, such as the peoples whose lords were buried in the frozen tombs of Pazyryk in the Altai Mountains of south Siberia.[2] It is probable that nomadic woodwork, textiles or bronze were known to the Chinese, who adapted similar scenes from them for the inlaid bronzes. A tiger devouring an ibex, vividly portrayed in a cast-bronze support inlaid in gold and silver, was found in a tomb at Pingshan near Beijing.[3] These tombs belonged to the Di rulers of the state of Zhongshan, who had entered China from the steppe lands to the north and who shared perhaps the tastes and practices of their northern neighbours.

1. Compare small leopard-shaped weights from the tomb of Dou Wan at Mancheng (Watson 1973a, nos 150, 151).
2. Rudenko 1970, figs 169, 170.
3. New York 1980, fig. 101; Paris 1984, no. 17.

RUBBINGS OF INSCRIPTIONS

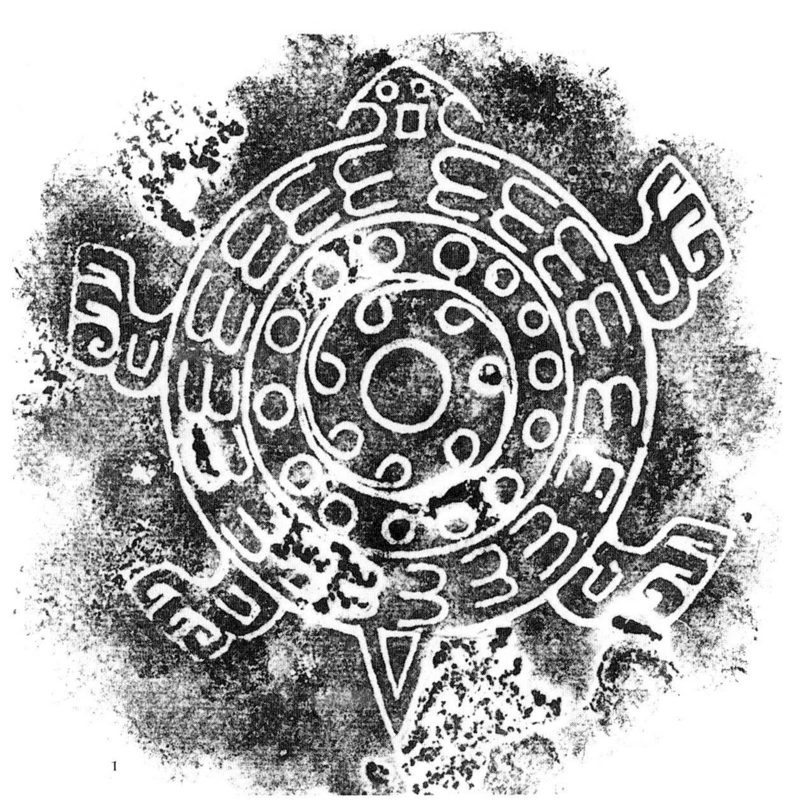
1

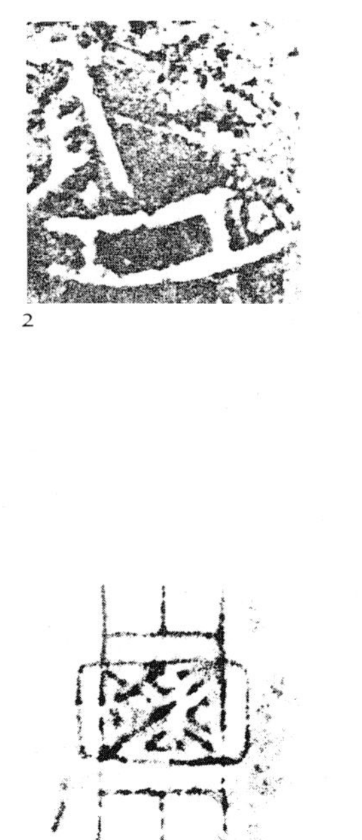
2

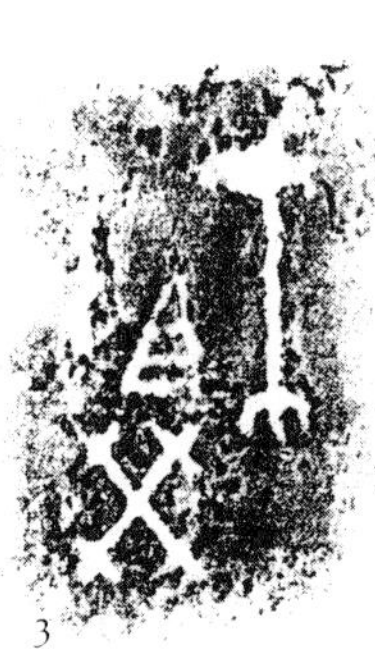
3

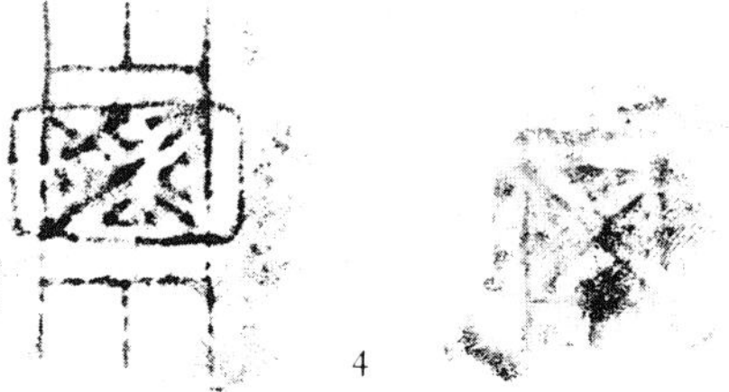
4

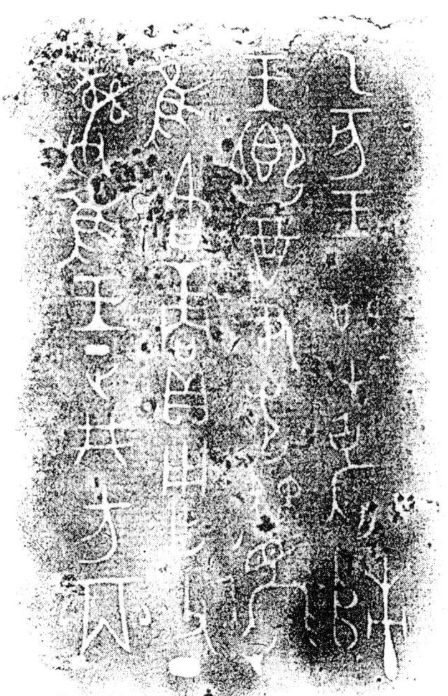
5

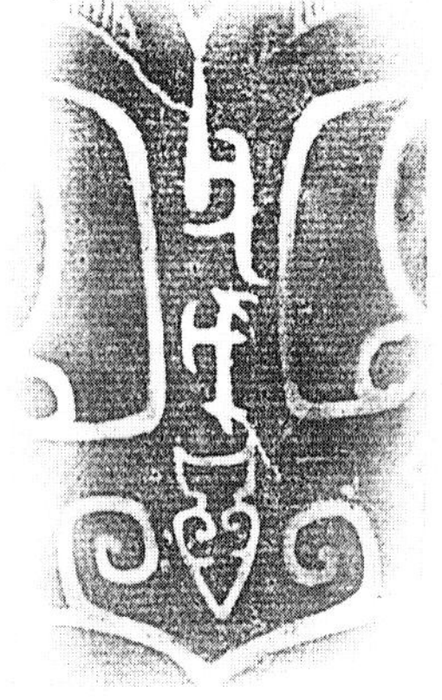

6

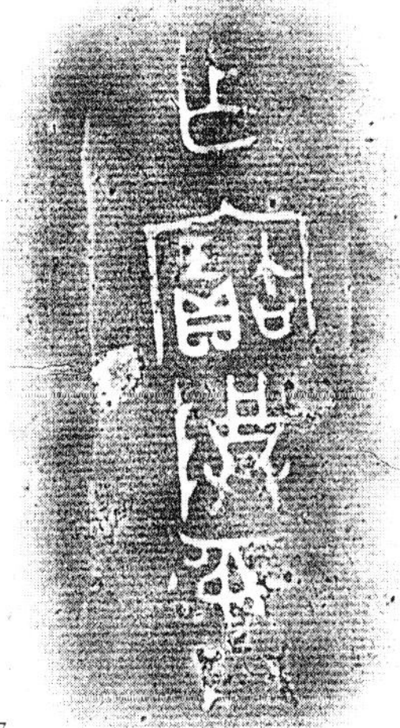

7

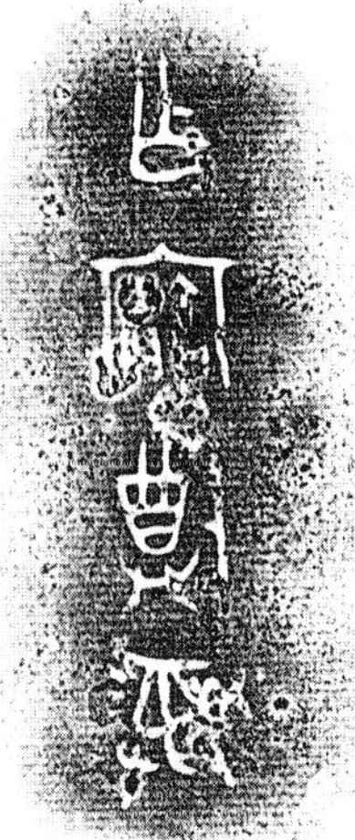

8

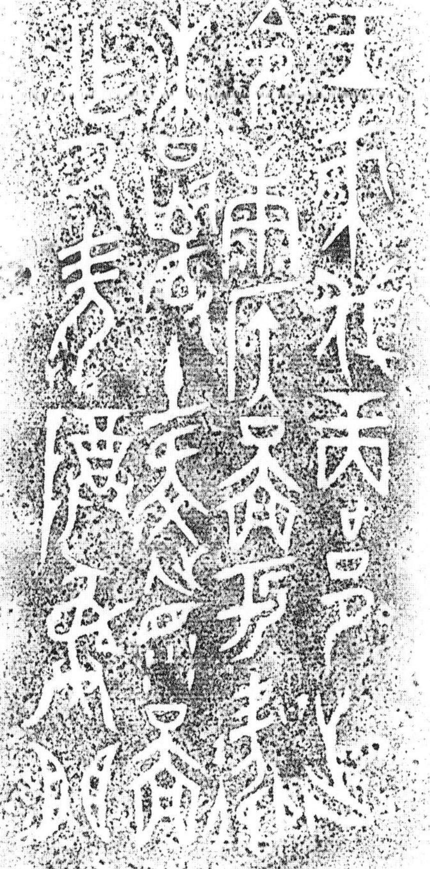

9

10

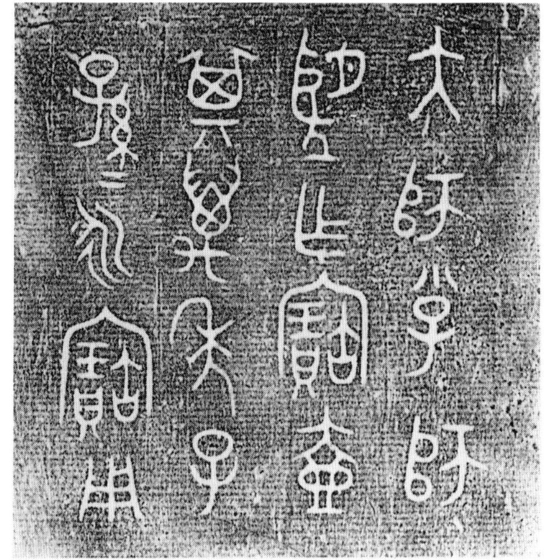
11

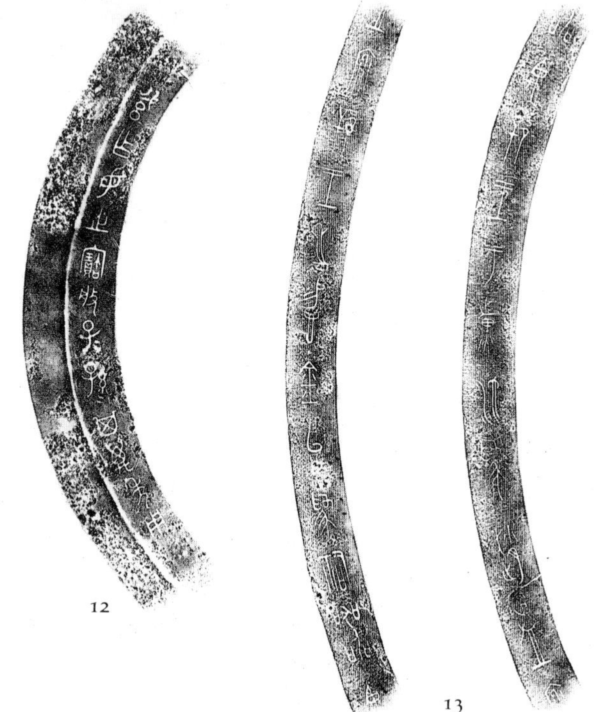
12

13

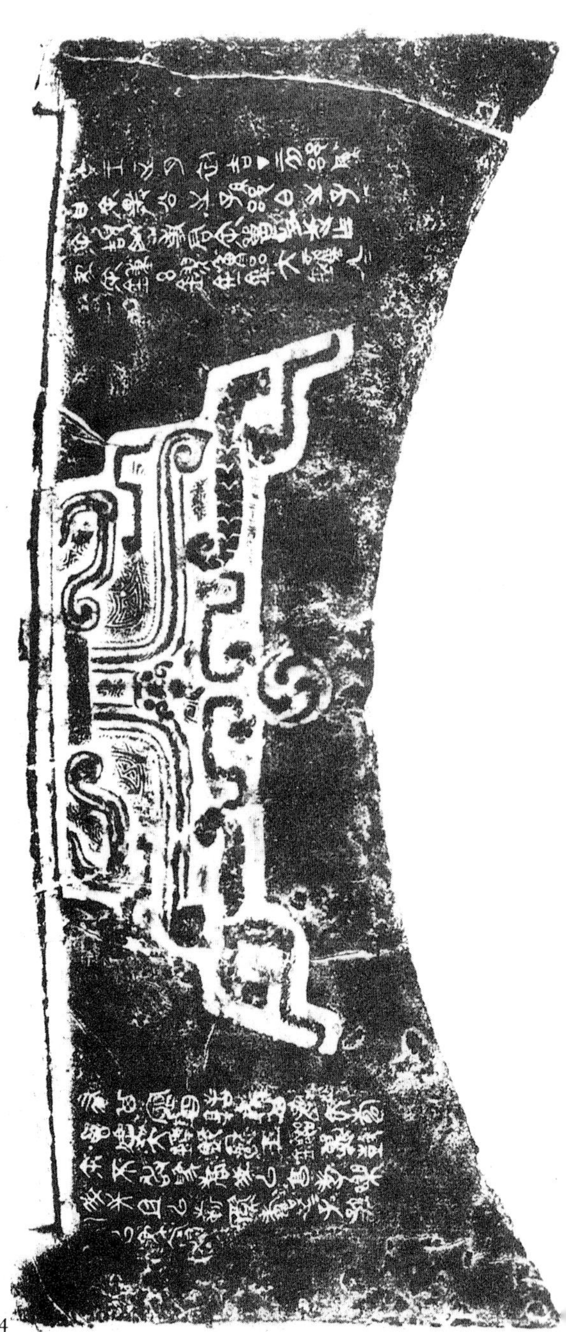
14

NOTES ON THE FIGURES

1. After *Kaogu* 1986.4, pp. 318–23, figs 4, 7.
3. *Top*, after *Kaogu* 1984.2, pp. 109–29, fig. 8:11; *left*, after *Kaogu* 1976.4, pp. 259–63, fig. 6:1; *right*, after *Kaogu* 1986.4, pp. 318–23, fig. 6.
4. After *Kaogu* 1965.10, pp. 500–6, fig. 2.
5. After *Wenwu* 1983.3, pp. 49–55, figs 14, 17, 18, 19.
7. After Beijing 1985a, figs 5, 12, 14:1, 15:2, 26.
8. After *Kaogu* 1986.8, pp. 703–12, 725, fig. 5.
10. After *Kaogu xuebao* 1977.2, p. 84, fig. 15.
11. *Left*, after Sotheby's auction catalogue 12 December 1981, lot 8; *centre*, after Salmony 1938, pl. XVI:6; *right*, after Salmony 1938, pl. XXIX:5.
12. (a) the Zhe vessels – *fang yi*, *zun*, *gong*, *jia*; (b) the Feng vessels – *you*, *zun*, *jue*; (c) the Shi Qiang vessels – *pan*, *jue*; (d) the Wei Bo Xing vessels – *gui*, three *jue*, *pen*, *xu*, *li*, *dou*, bells, two *hu* (with the exception of the three *Wei Bo xing jue* only one of each type is shown). After Beijing 1980b, nos 14, 15, 16, 17, 18, 19, 20, 24, 25, 27, 29, 31, 33, 41, 42, 43, 44, 49, 51, 54, 55.
13. After *Kaogu* 1981.6, pp. 496–9, 555, pl. 5:3.
14. After *Kaogu* 1986.1, pp. 22–7, 11.
15a. After Beijing 1984b, nos 136–45.
15b. After Beijing 1980c, nos 15–26.
16. After *Wenwu* 1986.1, pp. 1–31, figs 23, 24.
17. After Beijing 1984b, nos 61, 63, 65, 68, 73, 74.
18. After Beijing 1980c, nos 113–29.
19. *Left*, after Rawson (forthcoming), nos 27, 57, 116; *right*, after *Kaogu xuebao* 8, 1954, pp. 109–26, fig. 8; after *Kaogu* 1974.5, pp. 309–21, fig. 15:7; after*Kaogu xuebao* 1957.1, pp. 75–85, pl. 5:4.
20. After Beijing 1980c, no 138.
21. *Left*, after Beijing 1972a, no. 53.
22. (a) After Sun Haibo 1937, pp. 88b–9a; (b) after *Kaogu* 1963.5, pp. 229–45, fig. 12; (c) after *Kaogu* 1984.4, pp. 302–32, fig. 22; (d) after *Kaogu xuebao* 1974.2, pp. 63–85, fig. 7.
23. After *Wenwu* 1984.9, pp. 1–10, fig. 5
24. After New York 1980, no. 71.
25. After Beijing 1972b, p. 72.
26. After Tokyo 1983, no. 38.
27. After Li Xueqin 1986, no. 64.
28. (a) After Tokyo 1983, no. 41; (b) after *Kaogu* 1981.4, pp. 304–8, fig. 6; (c) after Weber 1968, fig. 65a; (d) after Weber 1968, fig. 34d; (e) after Nanjing 1985b, no. 20.
30. After Li Xueqin 1986, no. 108.

GLOSSARY

bo — A bell with a flat (as opposed to arched) lip suspended from a loop (see no. 34) The *bo* may have been invented in southern China, enlarging a smaller harness bell called a *ling*. *Bo* were introduced to northern metropolitan centres in the second half of the Western Zhou.

ding — A ritual vessel for cooked food with a round body and three legs (see no. 24). Used throughout the Shang and Zhou periods.

dou — A ritual vessel for offering food, shaped as a shallow cup on a high foot. Very common in ceramic and lacquer, *dou* were made regularly in bronze from the late Western Zhou (see Figs 12, 17). Some forms of *dou* are termed *fu*.

dui — A ritual vessel for offering food, a *dui* consists of two matching halves of equal size that make a rounded box when together and two bowls on legs when separated. *Dui* were not used before the Eastern Zhou.

fang ding — A rectangular form of *ding* used for cooked food (see no. 10)

fang yi — A rectangular ritual vessel for wine, shaped like a box (see no. 5). *Fang yi* were current from about the time of the construction of Fu Hao's tomb in the first half of the Anyang period (Fig. 7) until the end of middle Western Zhou.

fou — A lidded jar-shaped ritual vessel used from the Eastern Zhou for holding wine.

fu — A rectangular ritual vessel for holding food. The lid and body are usually identical in shape. The type was made in bronze from the late Western Zhou, but it seems that earlier bamboo examples had been used. An early

Western Zhou bronze that imitates such bamboo items is in the Palace Museum, Beijing. These containers are today known as *hu* or *gu*.

ge A dagger-shapped blade mounted at right angles to a wooden shaft and used like a halberd.

gong A ritual vessel for wine shaped like a ewer or jug and covered by a lid decorated with animal heads (see no. 6). The type was current from the time of the construction of Fu Hao's tomb in the first half of the Anyang period until the middle Western Zhou.

gu A ritual vessel for wine with a curved profile constricted at the waist (see no. 9). One of the most ancient forms of ritual vessel, ceramic *gu* were used from the Erlitou period.

guan A jar more common in ceramic than bronze; occasionally made in bronze in the Western Zhou, it was used more regularly from the Eastern Zhou when it was presumably part of the ritual assemblage.

gui A ritual vessel for offering food. For much of the Shang, *gui* seem to have been made without handles (these are sometimes termed *yu*); from late Shang and throughout the Zhou most *gui* had two handles (see no. 22).

he A ritual vessel for holding water. In Shang and early Western Zhou times the *he* was used to dilute wine and was therefore classed with wine vessels. During the Western Zhou its function was changed to hold water for ablutions in conjunction with the *pan* (see no. 8).

hu A ritual vessel for holding wine. Such vessels were used singly from the Shang period (see no. 4). From the late Western Zhou much larger *hu* were used in pairs (see no. 29).

jia A ritual vessel for wine drinking, with a cup-shaped body supported on three blade-like legs. Some have three lobes. *Jia* also have curved handles and small vertical posts at the lip. Their mouths are circular, not spouted or pointed like those of *jue*. The *jia* employed from the Erlitou period was abandoned during the middle Western Zhou.

jian A ritual vessel used from the Eastern Zhou for holding water (see Fig. 24).

jiao A ritual vessel for wine drinking, with a small cup-shaped body similar to that of a *jue*, which opens to a lip in two symmetrical points, without posts. The *jiao* was invented during the Shang and abandoned during the Western Zhou.

jin A rectangular altar-like table used to support ritual wine vessels. Few examples survive in bronze, and the majority were probably made in wood.

jue A ritual wine vessel used for drinking, shaped like a cup supported on three blade-like legs. The mouth has a spout at one end and a point at the other. It can be held by a small curved handle (see no. 1). Invented in the Erlitou period, *jue* went out of use at the end of the middle Western Zhou.

kui The name applied in the *Shuo wen* dictionary (compiled *c*. AD 100) to dragon motifs in profile. This term is not relevant to dragon motifs as analysed today and described in Chapter 4.

lei A ritual vessel shaped like a tall jar with a constricted neck for holding wine (see Fig. 5).

leiwen Angular intaglio spirals employed as a background to zoomorphic motifs on bronzes cast in the Shang and early Western Zhou periods (see nos 4–8, 21–6).

li A trilobed ritual vessel for cooking food (see no. 2).

ling A small bell with a clapper; the shape was much enlarged to make the *bo*.

long The Chinese term for a dragon. In the

oracle-bone graph the creature is shown with a long snaky body and a large head with a bottle horn. Such creatures appear among Shang bronze ornament (see no. 21).

nao A bell supported mouth upwards on a tubular handle and struck at two points on the outside. Such bells occur at Anyang but after the fall of the Shang were no longer used in metropolitan centres. Larger examples were, however, employed in southern China. During the Western Zhou *nao* were turned the other way up to make the *zhong*.

niu zhong An alternative name for *bo*.

pan A shallow basin used as a ritual vessel for holding water (see no. 21).

pou A ritual vessel of depressed jar shape for holding wine. The *pou* was particularly popular in the period transitional between Erligang and the main Anyang period (see Fig. 6).

Shi ji An historical text written by the court archivist Sima Qian (*c.* 145–86 BC) recording events of his own day and of all previous dynasties, including those of the Shang and Zhou.

Shi jing The 'Book of Poetry' compiled in the latter half of the Western Zhou period.

Shu jing The 'Book of Documents', a compilation of speeches and accounts of historical events purporting to describe the Shang and early Zhou periods. The genuine sections were probably written during the middle or latter half of the Western Zhou.

Shuo wen A dictionary compiled about AD 100.

taotie A term first used in a text of the Eastern Zhou to describe the varieties of monster face illustrated in Figure 9. We do not know how such designs were described in the periods in which they were current.

xu A rectangular ritual vessel for food based upon the *gui*. Used from the latter part of the Western Zhou (see Fig. 12).

yan A ritual vessel in the shape of a steamer consisting of the trilobed lower half, resembling a *li*, with a basin above, the two portions being divided by a perforated plate through which steam could rise.

yi A late Western Zhou vessel, also current in the Eastern Zhou, employed with *pan*, and in place of *he*, for ablutions (see Fig. 18).

yu A ritual basin-shaped vessel used for water (see Fig. 5). The name is also used for a food vessel not unlike a *gui*.

yue A large axe with a crescent-shaped blade (see no. 17).

yong zhong See *zhong*.

you A ritual wine vessel with an s-shaped profile, a lid and a long U-shaped handle (see Fig. 15). In use from the late Shang period until the middle Western Zhou.

zhi A ritual wine vessel used from the late Anyang period up until the middle Western Zhou (see no. 26).

zhong A modified form of *nao* bell suspended by a small loop on its tubular handle. Invented in southern China (see no. 27), such bells were imitated in the north from the middle Western Zhou (see Fig. 17).

zun A ritual wine vessel consisting of a jar with a widely flared lip supported on a tall foot ring (see no. 3). In the second half of the Shang the shouldered *zun* was replaced by a taller columnar vessel based on the *gu* and often designated as a cylindrical *zun*.

BIBLIOGRAPHY

Periodicals published in the People's Republic of China are referred to by their titles as follows: *Jianghan Kaogu, Kaogu, Kaoguxue jikan, Kaogu tongxun, Kaogu xuebao, Kaogu yu wenwu, Wenbo, Wenwu, Wenwu ziliao congkan.*

ACASA — *Archives of the Chinese Art Society of America*

Ackerman 1945 — Ackerman, Phyllis, *Ritual Bronzes of Ancient China*, New York, Dryden Press, 1945

Akiyama *et al.* 1968 — Akiyama Terukazu *et al.*, *Arts of China, Neolithic Cultures to the T'ang Dynasty: Recent Discoveries*, Tokyo and Palo Alto, Kodansha International, 1968

Allan 1979 — Allan, Sarah, 'Shang Foundations of Modern Chinese Folk Religion', Allan and Cohen 1979, pp. 1–21

Allan and Cohen 1979 — Allan, Sarah, and Alvin P. Cohen, *Legend, Love and Religion in China. Essays in Honor of Wolfram Eberhard on His Seventieth Birthday*, San Francisco, Chinese Materials Center Inc., 1979

An 1982 — An Zhimin, 'Some Problems Concerning China's Early Copper and Bronze Artifacts', *Early China*, 8 (1982–3), pp. 53–75, transl. by Julia K. Murray from an article publ. in *Kaogu xuebao* 1981.3, pp. 265–85

An 1986 — An Chin-huai, 'The Shang City at Cheng-chou and Related Problems', Chang 1986, pp. 15–48

d'Argencé 1966 — d'Argencé, René-Yvon Lefebvre, *Ancient Chinese Bronzes in the Avery Brundage Collection*, Berkeley, de Young Museum Society and Diablo Press, 1966

d'Argencé 1977 — d'Argencé, René-Yvon Lefebvre, *Bronze Vessels of Ancient China in the Avery Brundage Collection*, Asian Art Museum of San Francisco, 1977

Bagley 1977 — Bagley, Robert W., 'P'an-lung-ch'eng: A Shang City in Hupei', *Artibus Asiae*, 39 (1977), pp. 165–219

Bagley 1987 — Bagley, Robert W., *Shang Ritual Bronzes in the Arthur M. Sackler Collections*, Cambridge, Mass., and London, Harvard University Press, 1987

Barnard 1973 — Barnard, Noel, 'Records of Discoveries of Bronze Vessels in Literary Sources, and Some Pertinent Remarks on Aspects of Chinese Historiography'. *Journal of the Institute of Chinese Studies of The Chinese University of Hong Kong*, Vol. VI, no. 2 (1973), pp. 455–546

Barnard and Cheung 1978 — Barnard, Noel, and Cheung Kwong-yue, *Rubbings and Hand Copies of Bronze Inscriptions in Chinese, Japanese, European, American, and Australasian Collections*, Taibei, Yee Wen Publishing Co., 1978

Beijing 1956a — *Hui Xian fajue baogao*, Beijing, Kexue Chubanshe, 1956

Beijing 1956b — *Shou Xian Cai Hou mu chutu yiwu*, Beijing, Kexue Chubanshe, 1956

Beijing 1958 — *Wu sheng chutu zhongyao wenwu zhanlan tulu*, Beijing, Wenwu Chubanshe, 1958

Beijing 1959a — *Zhengzhou Erligang*, Beijing, Kexue Chubanshe, 1959

Beijing 1959b — *Shangcunling Guoguo mudi*, Beijing, Kexue Chubanshe, 1959

Beijing 1959c — *Luoyang Zhongzhoulu*, Beijing, Kexue Chubanshe, 1959

Beijing 1972a — *Xin Zhongguo chutu wenwu (Historical relics Unearthed in New China)*, Beijing, Waiwen Chubanshe, 1972

Beijing 1972b — *Wenhua da geming qijian chutu wenwu, di yi ji*, Beijing, Wenwu Chubanshe, 1972

Beijing 1977 — *Gaocheng Taixi Shang dai yizhi*, Beijing, Wenwu Chubanshe, 1977

Beijing 1979 — *Shaanxi chutu Shang Zhou qingtongqi*, vol. 1, Beijing, Wenwu Chubanshe, 1979

Beijing 1980a — *Hebei Sheng chutu wenwu xuanji*, Beijing, Wenwu Chubanshe, 1980

Beijing 1980b — *Shaanxi chutu Shang Zhou qingtongqi*, vol. 2, Beijing, Wenwu Chubanshe, 1980

Beijing 1980c — *Shaanxi chutu Shang Zhou qingtongqi*, vol. 3, Beijing, Wenwu Chubanshe, 1980

Beijing 1980d — *Sui Xian Zeng Hou Yi mu*, Beijing, Wenwu Chubanshe, 1980

Beijing 1980e — *Zhongguo Kaogu Xuehui di yi ci nianhui lunwen ji, 1979*, Beijing, Wenwu Chubanshe, 1980

Beijing 1980f — *Yinxu Fu Hao mu*, Beijing, Wenwu Chubanshe, 1980

Beijing 1980g — *Mancheng Han mu fajue baogao*, 2 vols, Beijing, Wenwu Chubanshe, 1980

Beijing 1981a — *Henan chutu Shang Zhou qingtongqi*, vol. 1, Beijing, Wenwu Chubanshe, 1981

Beijing 1981b — *Yunmeng Shuihudi Qin mu*, Beijing, Wenwu Chubanshe, 1981

Beijing 1984a — *Shang Zhou qingtongqi wenshi*, Beijing, Wenwu Chubanshe, 1984

Beijing 1984b — *Shaanxi chutu Shang Zhou qingtongqi*, vol. 4, Beijing, Wenwu Chubanshe, 1984

Beijing 1984c — *Jiangling Yutaishan Chu mu*, Beijing, Wenwu Chubanshe, 1984

Beijing 1984d — *Yin Zhou jinwen, jicheng*, vol. 1, Beijing, Zhonghua Shuju, 1984

Beijing 1985a — *Yinxu qingtongqi*, Beijing, Wenwu Chubanshe, 1985

Beijing 1986 — *Zhongguo kaoguxue yanjiu: Xia Nai xiansheng kaogu wu shi nian jinian lunwen ji*, 2 vols, Beijing, Wenwu Chubanshe, 1986

BMFEA — *Bulletin of the Museum of Far Eastern Antiquities, Stockholm*

Bunker 1983 — Bunker, Emma C. 'Sources of Foreign Elements in the Culture of Eastern Zhou', Kuwayama 1983, pp. 84–93

Bylin-Althin 1946 — Bylin-Althin, Margit, 'The Sites of Ch'i Chia P'ing and Lo Han T'ang in Kansu', *BMFEA*, 18 (1946), pp. 383–498

Chang 1964 — Chang Kwang-chih, 'Some Dualistic

Phenomena in Shang Society', *Journal of Asian Studies* (1964), pp. 45–61

Chang 1980 — Chang Kwang-chih, *Shang Civilization*, New Haven and London, Yale University Press, 1980

Chang 1983 — Chang Kwang-chih, *Art, Myth, and Ritual: The Path to Political Authority in Ancient China*, Cambridge, Mass., and London, Harvard University Press, 1983

Chang 1986 — Chang Kwang-chih, *Studies of Shang Archaeology. Selected Papers from The International Conference on Shang Civilization*, New Haven and London, Yale University Press, 1986

Cheng 1960 — Chêng Tê-k'un, *Archaeology in China, Volume II, Shang China*, Cambridge, W. Heffer and Sons, 1960

Cheng 1963a — Chêng Tê-k'un, *Archaeology in China, Volume III, Chou China*, Cambridge, W. Heffer and Sons, 1963

Cheng 1963b — Chêng Tê-k'un, 'Animal Styles in Prehistoric and Shang China' *BMFEA*, 35 (1963), pp. 129–40

Chen Mengjia 1955 — Chen Mengjia, *Xi Zhou tongqi duandai*, publ. in six parts: Part 1: *Kaogu xuebao* 9, 1955, pp. 137–75; Part 2: *Kaogu xuebao* 10, 1955, pp. 69–142; Part 3: *Kaogu xuebao* 1956.1, pp. 65–114; Part 4: *Kaogu xuebao* 1956.2, pp. 85–94; Part 5: *Kaogu xuebao* 1956.3, pp. 105–27; Part 6: *Kaogu xuebao* 1956.4, pp. 85–122.

Chen Mengjia 1977 — Chen Mengjia, *Yin Zhou qingtongqi fenlei tulu (In Shū seidōki bunrui zuroku: A Corpus of Chinese Bronzes in American Collections)*, edited from the original Chinese edn (1962) by Matsumaru Michio, 2 vols, Tokyo; Kyūko Shoin, 1977

Chen Rentao 1952 — Chen Rentao (ed.), *Jin Gui lun gu chu ji*, Hong Kong, 1952

Creel 1970 — Creel, Herrlee Glessner, *The Origins of Statecraft in China, Volume One, The Western Chou Empire*, Chicago and London, University of Chicago Press, 1970

Delbanco 1983 — Delbanco, Dawn Ho, *Art from Ritual: Ancient Chinese Bronze Vessels from the Arthur M. Sackler Collections*, Cambridge, Mass., and Washington, Fogg Art Museum and Arthur M. Sackler Foundation, 1983

Denwood 1978 — Denwood, Philip (ed.), *Arts of the Eurasian Steppelands. Colloquies on Art and Archaeology in Asia No. 7*, Percival David Foundation of Chinese Art, University of London, 1978

von Dewall 1964 — von Dewall, M., *Pferd und Wagen in Frühen China, Saarbrücker Beiträge zur Altertumskunde*, Bd. 1. Bonn, Rudolf Habelt Verlag, 1964

Elisseeff 1977 — Elisseeff, Vadime, *Bronzes archaïques Chinois au Musée Cernuschi*, Paris, L'Asiathèque, 1977

von Erdberg 1978 — von Erdberg, Eleanor, *Chinese Bronzes from the Collection of Chester Dale and Dolly Carter*, Ascona, Artibus Asiae Publishers, 1978

Franklin 1983 — Franklin, Ursula Martius, 'On Bronze and Other Metals in Early China', Keightley 1983, pp. 279–96

Gao Ming 1982 — Gao Ming, '*Gu, fu*, kaobian', *Wenwu* 1982.6, pp. 70–3, 85

Glum 1982 — Glum, Peter, 'Rain Magic at Anyang', *BMFEA*, 54 (1982), pp. 241–67

Gombrich 1960 — Gombrich, E. H, *Art and Illusion, A Study in the Psychology of Pictorial Representation*, Oxford, Phaidon Press Ltd, 1960

Griffin and McNamee 1972 — Griffin, Jane Tilley, and Harriet McNamee, *Chinese Art from the Ferris Luboshez Collection*, University of Maryland Department of Art, 1972

Guo Baojun 1959 — Guo Baojun, *Shanbiaozhen yu Liulige*, Beijing, Kexue Chubanshe, 1959

Guo Baojun 1981 — Guo Baojun, *Shang Zhou tongqiqun zonghe yanjiu*, Beijing, Wenwu Chubanshe, 1981

Guo Moruo 1935 — Guo Moruo, *Liang Zhou jinwenci daxi tulu kaoshi*, Tokyo, 1935

Hansford 1957 — Hansford, S. Howard, *The Seligman Collection of Oriental Art*, vol. 1, London, Lund Humphries, 1957

Hayashi 1972 — Hayashi Minao, *Chūgoku In Shū jidai no buki*, Research Institute for Humanistic Studies, Kyoto University, 1972

Hayashi 1980 — Hayashi Minao, 'Ōshū hakubutsukan shoken no Chūgoku kodai seidōki jakkan ni tsuite, *Kōkotsugaku*, 12, August 1980, pp. 149–99

Hayashi 1984 — Hayashi Minao, *In Shū jidai seidōki no kenkyū (In Shū seidōki sōran ichi)*, pt. 1, 2 vols, Tokyo, Yoshikawa Kōbunkan, 1984

Hayashi 1986 — Hayashi Minao, *In Shū jidai seidōki no kenkyū (In Shū seidōki sōran ichi)*, pt. 2, Tokyo, Yoshikawa Kōbunkan, 1986

van Heusden 1952 — van Heusden, Willem, *Ancient Chinese Bronzes of the Shang and Chou Dynasties, An Illustrated Catalogue of the van Heusden Collection with a Historical Introduction*, Tokyo, privately published, 1952

Higuchi and Enjōji 1984 — Higuchi Takayasu and Enjōji Jiro, *Chūgoku seidōki hyaku sen*, Tokyo, Nihon Keizai Shimbunsha, 1984

Hong Kong 1983 — *Ancient Chinese Bronzes in the Collection of the Shanghai Museum Exhibited at the Hong Kong Museum of Art*, Hong Kong, Urban Council, 1983

Huber 1983 — Huber, Louisa G., 'Some Anyang Royal Bronzes; Remarks on Shang Bronze Decor', Kuwayama 1983, pp. 16–43

Kane 1974 — Kane, Virginia C., 'The Independent Bronze Industries in the South of China Contemporary with the Shang and Western Chou Dynasties', *Archives of Asian Art*, 28 (1974–5), pp. 77–107

Kao 1986 — Kao Chih-hsi, 'An Introduction to Shang and Chou Bronze *Nao* Excavated in South China', Chang 1986, pp. 275–99

Karlgren 1937 — Karlgren, Bernhard, 'New Studies on Chinese Bronzes', *BMFEA*, 9 (1937), pp. 1–117

Karlgren 1952 — Karlgren, Bernhard, *A Catalogue of the Chinese Bronzes in the Alfred F. Pillsbury Collection*, Minneapolis, University of Minnesota Press, 1952

Keightley 1978 — Keightley, David N., *Sources of Shang History: The Oracle-Bone Inscriptions of Bronze Age China*, Berkeley, Los Angeles and London, University of California Press, 1978

Keightley 1983 — Keightley, David N. (ed.), *The Origins of Chinese Civilization*, Berkeley, Los Angeles and London, University of California Press, 1983

Kelley and Ch'en 1946 — Kelley, Charles Fabens, and Ch'en Meng-chia, *Chinese Bronzes from the Buckingham Collection*, Art Institute of Chicago, 1946

Keyser 1979 — Keyser, Barbara W., 'Décor Replication in Two Late Chou Bronze *Chien*', *Ars Orientalis* XI (1979), pp. 127–62

Kuwayama 1983 — Kuwayama, George (ed.), *The Great Bronze Age of China, A Symposium*, Los Angeles County Museum of Art, 1983

Lawton 1982 — Lawton, Thomas, *Chinese Art of the Warring States Period: Change and Continuity, 480–222 B.C.*, Washington, Freer Gallery of Art, 1982

Ledderose 1978 — Ledderose, Lothar, 'Some Observations on the Imperial Art Collection in China', *Transactions of the Oriental Ceramic Society*, 43 (1978–9), pp. 33–46

Ledderose 1983 — Ledderose, Lothar, 'The Earthly Paradise: Religious Elements in Chinese Landscape Art', in Bush, Susan, and Christian Murck, *Theories of the Arts in China*, Princeton University Press, 1983, pp. 163–83

Li 1977 — Li Chi, *Anyang*, Seattle, University of Washington Press, 1977

Lienert 1979 — Lienert, Ursula, *Typology of the Ting in the Shang Dynasty. A Tentative Chronology of the Yin-hsü Period*, Publikationen der Abteilung Asien Kunsthistorisches Institut der Universität Köln, Band 3, 2 vols, Wiesbaden, Franz Steiner Verlag, 1979

Li Ji and Wan Jiabao 1972 — Li Ji and Wan Jiabao, *Yinxu chutu wu shi san jian qingtong rongqi zhi yanjiu (Studies of Fifty-three Ritual Bronzes)*, Taiwan Nangang, Academia Sinica, 1972

Lin 1986 — Lin Yün, 'A Reexamination of the Relationship between Bronzes of the Shang Culture and of the Northern Zone', Chang 1986, pp. 237–74

Lion-Goldschmidt and Moreau-Gobard 1980 — Lion-Goldschmidt, Daisy, and Jean-Claude Moreau-Gobard, *Chinese Art: Bronzes, Jade, Sculpture, Ceramics*, English rev. edn, New York, Rizzoli International, 1980

Liu Tizhi 1935 — Liu Tizhi, *Xiaojiao jingge jinwen taben*, 1935

Li Xueqin 1959 — Li Xueqin, *Yin dai dili jian lun*, Beijing, Kexue Chubanshe, 1959

Li Xueqin 1977 — Li Xueqin, 'Lun "Fu Hao" mu de niandai ji youguan wenti', *Wenwu* 1977.11, pp. 32–7

Li Xueqin 1979 — Li Xueqin, 'Xi Zhou zhong qi qingtongqi de zhongyao biaochi-Zhouyuan Zhuangbai, Qiangjia liang chu qingtongqi jiaocang de zonghe yanjiu', *Zhongguo Lishi Bowuguan guankan*, 1979.1, pp. 29–36

Li Xueqin 1980 — Li Xueqin, *The Wonder of Chinese Bronzes*, Beijing, Waiwen Chubanshe, 1980

Li Xueqin 1981 — Li Xueqin, 'Xiaotun Nandi jiagu yu jiagu fenqi', *Wenwu* 1981.5, pp. 27–33

Li Xueqin 1985a — Li Xueqin, 'Yi Hou Ze gui yu Wu guo', *Wenwu* 1985.7, pp. 13–16, 25

Li Xueqin 1985b — Li Xueqin, *Zhongguo meishu quanji I: Gongyi meishu bian 4: Qingtongqi (1)*, Beijing, Wenwu Chubanshe, 1985

Li Xueqin 1985c — Li Xueqin, *Eastern Zhou and Qin Civilizations*, transl. by K. C. Chang, New Haven and London, Yale University Press, 1985

Li Xueqin 1986 — Li Xueqin, *Zhongguo meishu quanji I: Gongyi meishu bian 4: Qingtongqi (2)*, Beijing, Wenwu Chubanshe, 1986

Loehr 1948 — Loehr, Max, review of *The Cull Chinese Bronzes* by W. P. Yetts, *Monumenta Serica*, XIII, 1948, pp. 420–26

Loehr 1953 — Loehr, Max, 'The Bronze Styles of the Anyang Period', *ACASA*, 7 (1953), pp. 42–53

Loehr 1968 — Loehr, Max, *Ritual Vessels of Bronze Age China*, New York, Asia Society, 1968

Loehr 1980 — Loehr, Max, 'The Question of Content in the Decoration of Shang and Chou Bronzes', unpublished paper presented at the Symposium on the Great Bronze Age of China, Metropolitan Museum of Art, New York, 2–3 June 1980

London 1936 — *The Chinese Exhibition, A Commemorative Catalogue of the International Exhibition of Chinese Art, Royal Academy of Arts, November 1935–March 1936*, London, 1936

Luo Zhenyu 1937 — Luo Zhenyu, *Sandai jijin wen cun*, 1937

Ma Chengyuan 1982 — Ma Chengyuan, *Zhongguo gudai qingtongqi*, Shanghai, Renmin Chubanshe, 1982

Mackenzie 1982 — Mackenzie, Colin, 'The Evolution of the Zeng Hou Yi Bronze Styles', unpublished paper presented to the Early China Seminar at the School of Oriental and African Studies, London, 16 February 1982; summary publ. in *Early China*, 7 (1981–2), pp. 119–20

Mackenzie 1984 — Mackenzie, Colin, 'China or the West? The Origins of the Eastern Zhou Inlaid Bronze Style and Some Related Problems', unpublished paper presented to the Early China Seminar at the School of Oriental and African Studies, London, 1984

Malcolm 1947 — *Chinese Bronzes etc. belonging to Major Gen., Sir Neill Malcolm & Captain Dugald Malcolm*, London, privately produced, 1947

McClain 1985 — McClain, Ernest G., 'The Bronze Chinese Bells of the Marquis of Zeng: Babylonian Biophysics in Ancient China', *The Journal of Social and Biological Structures*, 1985.8, pp. 147–73

Meyers and Holmes 1983 — Meyers, Pieter, and Lore L. Holmes, 'Technical Studies of Ancient Chinese Bronzes: Some Observations', Kuwayama 1983, pp. 124–36

Mizuno 1959 — Mizuno Seiichi, *In Shū seidōki to gyoku*, Tokyo, Nihon Keizai Shimbunsha, 1959

Nanjing 1985 — *Zhongguo gudai tu'an xuan*, Nanjing, Jiangsu Meishu Chubanshe, 1985

New York 1980 — Fong, Wen (ed.), *The Great Bronze Age of China, An Exhibition from the People's Republic of China*, New York, Metropolitan Museum of Art, 1980

Nivison 1983 — Nivison, David S., 'Western Chou History Reconstructed from Bronze Inscriptions', Kuwayama 1983, pp. 44–55

Paris 1984 — *Zhongshan: Tombes des Rois oubliés, Exposition archéologique chinoise du Royaume de Zhongshan*, Paris, Galeries Nationales du Grand Palais, 1984

Piggott 1978 — Piggott, Stuart, 'Chinese Chariotry: An Outsider's View', Denwood 1978, pp. 32–51

Pope *et al.* 1967 — Pope, John Alexander, Rutherford John Gettens, James Cahill and Noel Barnard, *The Freer Chinese Bronzes, Volume 1, Catalogue*, Washington, Smithsonian Institution, 1967

Qian Hao *et al.* 1981 — Qian Hao, Chen Heyi and Ru Suichu, *Out of China's Earth, Archaeological Discoveries in the People's Republic of China*, New York and Beijing, Harry N. Abrams and China Pictorial, 1981

Rawson 1980 — Rawson, Jessica, *Ancient China, Art and Archaeology*, London, British Museum Publications, 1980

Rawson 1983 — Rawson, Jessica, 'Eccentric Bronzes of the Early Western Zhou', *Transactions of the Oriental Ceramic Society*, 47 (1982–3) pp. 11–32

Rawson (forthcoming) — Rawson, Jessica, *Western Zhou Ritual Bronzes in the Arthur M. Sackler Collections*, Cambridge, Mass., and London, Harvard University Press

Rong Geng 1941 — Rong Geng, *Shang Zhou yiqi tongkao*, 2 vols, Beijing, Harvard-Yenching Institute, 1941

Rong Geng and Zhang Weichi 1958 — Rong Geng and Zhang Weichi, *Yin Zhou qingtongqi tonglun*, Beijing, Kexue Chubanshe, 1958

Rudenko 1970 — Rudenko, Sergei I., *Frozen Tombs of Siberia, The Pazyryk Burials of Iron Age Horsemen*, London, J. M. Dent and Sons Ltd, 1970

Salmony 1938 — Salmony, Alfred, *Carved Jade of Ancient China*, Berkeley, Gillick Press, 1938

Shanghai 1964 — *Shanghai Bowuguan cang qingtongqi*, 2 vols, Shanghai, Renmin Meishu Chubanshe, 1964

Shaughnessy 1982 — Shaughnessy, Edward L., 'Recent Approaches to Oracle-Bone Periodization', *Early China*, 8 (1982–3), pp. 1–13

Shirakawa 1962 — Shirakawa Shizuka, *Kimbun tsūshaku*, Kobe, Hakutsuru Bijutsukan, 1962–

Shirakawa 1963 — Shirakawa Shizuka, *Kimbunshū*, 4 vols, Tokyo, Nigensha, 1963–4

So 1983 — So, Jenny F., '*Hu* Vessels from Xinzheng: Toward a Definition of Chu Style', Kuwayama 1983, pp. 64–71

Soper 1966 — Soper, Alexander C. 'Early, Middle, and Late Shang: A Note, *Artibus Asiae* 28 (1966), pp. 5–38

Sun Haibo 1937 — Sun Haibo, *Xinzheng yiqi*, Beijing, 1937

Sun Haibo 1939 — Sun Haibo, *Henan jijin tu zhi sheng gao*, Beijing, 1939

Sun Zhichu 1981 — Sun Zhichu, *Jinwen zhulu jian mu*, Beijing, Zhonghua Shuju, 1981

Taibei 1958 — *Gugong tongqi tulu*, 2 vols, Taibei, Zhonghua congshu Weiyuanhui, 1958

Thorp 1982 — Thorp, Robert L., 'The Date of Tomb 5 at Yinxu, Anyang', *Artibus Asiae*, 43 (1982), pp. 239–46

Thorp 1985 — Thorp, Robert L., 'The Growth of Early Shang Civilization: New Data from Ritual Vessels', *Harvard Journal of Asiatic Studies*, 45 (1985), pp. 5–75

Tokyo 1983 — *Kanan-shō Hakubutsukan (Chūgoku no hakubutsukan dai shichikan)*, Tokyo, Kōdansha, 1983

Tong Enzheng 1986 — Tong Enzheng, 'Discussion of shared cultural traits in north-eastern, north-western and western China', paper given in Chinese at the meeting of the British Association of Chinese Studies on 20 September 1986. Brief English summary pub. in the *Bulletin of the British Association of Chinese Studies*, 1986, p. 3. Full Chinese text pub. with the title 'Shi lun wo guo cong dongbei zhi xinan de biandi banyuexing wenhua zhuanbodai', in *Wenwu Chubanshe chengli sanshi zhounian jinian: wenwu yu kaogu lunji*, Beijing, Wenwu Chubanshe, 1987, pp. 17–43

Umehara 1933a — Umehara Sueji, *Ōbei shūcho Shina kodō seika*, 7 vols, Kyoto, Yamanaka and Co., 1933

Umehara 1933b — Umehara Sueji, *Henkin no kōkogaku-teki kōsatsu (Etude archéologique sur le Pien-chin, ou série de bronzes avec une table pour l'usage rituel dans le Chine antique)*, Kyoto, Tōhō Bunka Gakuin Kyōtō Kenkyūjo, 1933

Umehara 1959a — Umehara Sueji, *Nihon shūcho Shina kodō seika*, 6 vols, Osaka, Yamanaka and Co., 1959–64

Umehara 1959b — Umehara Sueji, 'Sensei-shō Hōkeiken shutsudo no dai ni no henkin (The Second Set of Ritual Vessels, *Pien-chin*, from Pao-chi-hsien, Shensi Province)', *Tōhōgaku kiyō*, 1, 1959, pp. iii–viii (English summary) and pp. 1–15

Wang 1982 — Wang Zhongshu, *Han Civilization*, New Haven and London, Yale University Press, 1982

Watson 1962 — Watson, William, *Ancient Chinese Bronzes*, London, Faber and Faber, 1962; see also Watson 1977

Watson 1963 — Watson, William, *Handbook to the Collections of Early Chinese Antiquities*, London, Trustees of the British Museum, 1963

Watson 1965 — Watson, William, 'A Chinese Bronze Bell of the Fifth Century B.C.', *British Museum Quarterly*, xxx (1965–6), pp. 50–6

Watson 1971 — Watson, William, *Cultural Frontiers in Ancient East Asia*, Edinburgh University Press, 1971

Watson 1973a — Watson, William, *The Genius of China, An Exhibition of Archaeological Finds of the People's Republic of China*, London, Times Newspapers Ltd, 1973

Watson 1973b — Watson, William, 'On Some Categories of Archaism in Chinese Bronze', *Ars Orientalis*, 9 (1973), pp. 1–13

Watson 1977 — Watson, William, *Ancient Chinese Bronzes*, London, Faber and Faber, 1977; reissue of Watson 1962 with new preface (pp. 15–22), bibliography, colour plates and new pagination

Watson 1979 — Watson, William, 'The City in Ancient China' in P.R.S. Moorey (ed.), *The Origins of Civilisation*, Wolfson College Lectures, 1978, Oxford, Clarendon Press, 1979

Watson 1981 — Watson, William, 'The Individuality of the Honan Tradition in the Shang Period', *Zhongyang Yanjiuyuan Guoji Hanxue Huiyi lunwen ji, yishu shi zu*, Taibei, Zhongyang Yanjiuyuan, 1981, pp. 171–90

Weber 1968 — Weber, Charles D., *Chinese Pictorial Bronze Vessels of the Late Chou Period*, Ascona, Artibus Asiae Publishers, 1968; originally published in *Artibus Asiae*, 28–30 (1966–8)

Weber 1973 — Weber, George W., jun., *The Ornaments of Late Chou Bronzes*, New Brunswick, New Jersey, Rutgers University Press, 1973

White 1934 — White, William Charles, *Tombs of Old Lo-yang*, Shanghai, Kelly and Walsh, 1934

Wu Dacheng 1885 — Wu Dacheng, *Heng Xuan suo jian suo cang jijin lu*, 1885

Wu 1984 — Wu Hung, 'A Sanpan Shan Chariot Ornament and the Xiangrui Design in Western Han Art', *Archives of Asian Art*, XXXVII (1984), pp. 38–59

Wu 1985 — Wu Hung, 'Bird Motifs in Eastern Yi Art', *Orientations*, 16, 10, October 1985, pp. 30–41

Xi Qing gu jian — Lian Shizeng *et al.*, *Xi Qing gu jian*, 1755

Xu Zhuoyun 1984 — Xu Zhuoyun, *Xi Zhou shi*, Taibei, Lianjing Chubanshe Shizong Gongsi, 1984

Yang Shuda 1959 — Yang Shuda, *Ji Wei Ju jinwen shuo*, rev. edn. Beijing, Kexue Chubanshe, 1959

Yetts 1929 — Yetts, W. Perceval, *The George Eumorfopoulos Collection, Catalogue of the Chinese and Corean Bronzes, Sculpture, Jades, Jewellery and Miscellaneous Objects. Volume 1, Bronzes: Ritual and Other Vessels, Weapons, Etc.*, London, Ernest Benn Ltd, 1929

Yetts 1930 — Yetts, W. Perceval, *The George Eumorfopoulos Collection, Catalogue of the Chinese and Corean Bronzes, Scultpure, Jades, Jewellery and Miscellaneous Objects. Volume 2, Bronzes: Bells, Drums, Mirrors, Etc.*, London, Ernest Benn Ltd, 1930

Yetts 1939 — Yetts, W. Perceval, *The Cull Chinese Bronzes*, University of London, Courtauld Institute of Art, 1939

Yin 1986 — Yin Wei-chang, *'A Reexamination of Erh-li-t'ou Culture*, Chang 1986, pp. 1–13

Yu Weichao and Gao Ming 1978 — Yu Weichao and Gao Ming, 'Zhou dai yong ding zhidu yanjiu', *Beijing Daxue xuebao (zhexue shehui kexue ban)*, 1978.1, pp. 84–98 (pt. 1); 1978.2, pp. 84–97 (pt. 2); 1979.1, pp. 83–96 (pt. 3)

Zhang Changshou 1979 — Zhang Changshou, 'Yin Shang shidai de qingtong rongqi', *Kaogu xuebao* 1979.3, pp. 271–300

Zhang Changshou 1980 — Zhang Changshou, 'Western Zhou Bronze Vessels Discovered at Baoji Rujiazhuang', unpublished paper presented at the Symposium on the Great Bronze Age of China, Metropolitan Museum of Art, New York, 2–3 June 1980

Zhou Fagao 1977 — Zhou Fagao, Zhang Risheng and Huang Qiuyue, *Sandai jijin wen cun zhulu biao*, Taibei, Xuesheng Shuju, 1977

Zou Heng 1980 — Zou Heng, *Xia Shang Zhou kaoguxue lunwen ji*, Beijing, Wenwu Chubanshe, 1980